AUTOBIOGRAPHIES

Heddiw'r wore cefais hyd i'r flwyddyn
newydd anedig ar gawreg fy niwes yn
crefu am gael croeso i'r tŷ. Petrusais
ennyd gan fod ofn arnaf weth a ddoi
i'w chanlyn. Ond dal i ymbil a wnaeth
hyd nes y'i codais, nid o dosturi ond
oherwydd y hen rhaid.

Neithiwr rhois ganwyll yn y
ffenestr i ddangos i ba ysbryd hynnaf
oedd ar goll yn y gwyll fod yma groeso
iddo yma. Ai hon a'i gwelodd? Roedd
y wore'n ddigon di-liw, ond chwaraeodd
y ddau walch glas uwchben coed Tŷ'n-
y Coed fel petaent â'u hwyd eisoes ar
gymharu. Fel y hen rhaid imi ddterlwyn y
flwyddyn newydd i'm tŷ, felly hwythau'n
gorfod ymateb i alwad hywyd trwy
ddangos eu bod yn gymwys i gymharu a
magu cywion er parhad eu rhywogaeth.

Pwy ydi Meri? Anfonodd gerdyn
Nadolig ataf heb roi ei chyfenw. A dyma
fi'n chwarae hefo'r syniad bod rhyw
hogan wedi fy ffansio? Ond sibrydda

R. S. Thomas

AUTOBIOGRAPHIES

Former Paths

The Creative Writer's Suicide

No-one

A Year in Llŷn

Translated from the Welsh, with an introduction and notes, by
JASON WALFORD DAVIES
Department of Welsh, University of Wales, Bangor

J. M. Dent   London

First published in Great Britain in 1997 by J. M. Dent,
a division of the Orion Publishing Group,
Orion House, 5 Upper St Martin's Lane,
London WC2H 9EA

A CIP catalogue record for this book is available
from the British Library.

ISBN 0 460 87639 2

Filmset by Selwood Systems, Midsomer Norton
Printed and bound in Great Britain by
Butler & Tanner Ltd, Frome and London

CONTENTS

NOTE ON THE AUTHOR
AND TRANSLATOR/EDITOR

R. S. THOMAS was born in Cardiff in 1913, but from the age of five was raised in Holyhead, Anglesey. After graduating in Classics at the University of Wales, Bangor, and following theological training at St Michael's College, Llandaff, he became from 1936 a priest in the Church in Wales in various parishes destined to become increasingly associated with his poetry, most notably the parishes of Manafon, Eglwys-fach and Aberdaron. In addition to the Heinemann Award in 1955, the Queen's Gold Medal for Poetry in 1964 and the Cholmondeley Award in 1978, he has received four Welsh Arts Council Literature Awards. In 1996 he was awarded the Lifetime Achievement Award for Poetry from the Lannon foundation, Los Angeles, and the Horst Bienek Prize for Poetry from the Bavarian Academy of Fine Art. His autobiography, *Neb*, was published in Welsh in 1985, and his *Collected Poems* in 1993. His most recent volume of poems is *No Truce with the Furies*, 1995. R. S. Thomas was nominated for the 1996 Nobel Prize for Literature.

JASON WALFORD DAVIES was born in Aberystwyth in 1971, and educated at the University of Oxford and the University of Wales. He is the author of a study of R. S. Thomas's poetic relationship to the Welsh literary tradition, and editor of *ABC Neb*, the poet's latest prose volume in Welsh. A Lecturer in the Department of Welsh at the University of Wales, Bangor, he is currently engaged in research in the field of medieval Welsh literature, and is completing an edition of the work of the fifteenth-century poet Dafydd ab Edmwnd.

NOTE ON TRANSLATION AND REFERENCES

The words of a poet, even in prose, are not to be treated lightly. The translation has therefore been kept reasonably close to the original. The main exceptions involve: phrases for which equivalent English idioms have been used, rather than a strict translation of the Welsh ones; avoidance of the repetition of a word that would cause stiffness in the English – the translation sometimes either substitutes a pronoun for a repeated noun or restores the noun instead of a repeated pronoun; occasional changes in punctuation, mainly involving a different use of the comma; silent correction of minor misquotations or obvious typesetting errors in the original.

The words of a poet are not to be treated lightly, but nor should they be lightly interrupted. It is nevertheless sometimes convenient for certain words or phrases in Welsh to be followed in the text by the English equivalent. A few others, whose translation in the text would hinder the flow of the syntax, are linked by asterisk to a translation at the bottom of the page. A phrase that requires an explanatory note as well as a translation is explained in the 'Notes and References' at the end of the volume.

INTRODUCTION

Knowing the Place for the First Time

We shall not cease from exploration
And the end of all our exploring
Will be to arrive where we started
And know the place for the first time.

T. S. Eliot, 'Little Gidding'

I

The psychology involved in writing one's own life is complex, balancing reticence and immodesty. The exercise is at base immodest, however natural the motive or admirable the outcome. We write autobiographies because we just don't agree with Philip Larkin's judgement that, 'Beneath it all, desire of oblivion runs'.[1] We want to survive. And yet an autobiography that gratifies only a personal desire for survival is unlikely itself to survive. Autobiographies survive when they are interesting. And they are interesting only when they are themselves interested – in places, periods and people, the things that give the author an identity in the first place, an identity as opposed to a mere ego. But to be interesting you can't afford any disabling modesty, either. You can't afford, for example, any reticence about speaking your mind, even as you wonder who or what you are to have opinions in the first place.

This relationship between self and audience modulates in particular ways when that 'self' is R. S. Thomas. Here is someone who is both a priest of the Anglican Church in Wales and a Welsh cultural nationalist in a mainly Nonconformist country. And here is a poet who, though clearly amongst the finest in English of the second half of the twentieth century, chooses to write his autobiography only in Welsh, a language he himself reclaimed after the age of thirty. These counterpoints are part of the irony of the negative title of the main autobiographical work here translated – *Neb*, meaning 'No-one'. So it will be useful to concentrate mostly on that oddly titled work, while considering also the other 'autobiographies' that are its satellites.

In *No-one* the poet puts down a title that is itself a put-down. To call yourself 'no-one' is to flirt with that modesty that, if justified, makes autobiographies themselves put-downable. But '*neb*' in Welsh actually means 'someone'; it is in colloquial speech – or titles – when the word is cut adrift from syntax, that it has, incorrectly, the negative force of 'no-one'. It is the same jack-knife ambiguity that one finds in that other basic Welsh word '*dim*', which can mean both 'nothing' and 'something'. A lax interpretation of a Welsh translation of King Lear's 'Nothing will come of nothing' would be volatile since it would allow that something might indeed come of nothing – or that the nothing came from something! In fact, in his latest volume of poems, *No Truce with the Furies* (1995), R. S. Thomas combines this convenient crease in the Welsh language with the actual line from *King Lear*:

> Promising myself before bedtime
> to contend more urgently
> with the problem. From nothing
> nothing comes. Behind everything –
> something, somebody?

> 'The Promise'

Ambiguity is something any poet worth his salt will relish. But the point is that '*neb*' and '*dim*' conflate meanings at once both seminal and terminal: a person is either *someone* or *no-one*, able to tell us *something* or *nothing*. So the words go deeper than, say, the secret-service tones of the title that Goronwy Rees's daughter gave her recent memoir of her father: *Looking for Mr Nobody*.[2] And deeper than the fact that R. S. Thomas's *No-one* is also written in the third person. Third-person narrative is often a matter of mere convenience; it can occur in what are otherwise totally egotistical autobiographies – those of Julius Caesar or of President de Gaulle, for example. But use of the third person at least gestures towards modesty and tact.[3] A relentless use of the first person is certainly not on. A biographer of the American president Theodore Roosevelt felt that the latter's 'love of the personal pronoun bordered on the erotic', and recorded that when Roosevelt's military memoir, *The Rough Riders*, went into print, 'a rumour circulated to the effect that halfway through typesetting, Scribner ran out of capital "I"s and had send to the foundry for an extra supply'.

Obviously, in an Anglican priest, modesty is to some degree theological ('What is man, that thou art mindful of him?'),[4] and simple Christian piety of that kind does indeed play its part:

> After years in such circumstances, R. S. would view with something less than enthusiasm the costly gravestones with their false words, or the unthinking rituals of the Church's conventional members; the monuments to the wretched youths killed in war; the pretentious, ugly gravestones that defaced so many graveyards in the heart of the countryside. All this only deepened the feeling within him that no memorial was necessary except for a plain wooden cross solely to indicate where your mortal remains were, for the sake of the family. (p. 83)

But to call yourself not only 'he' but 'no-one' does more than avoid the merely boorish or immodest. It emphasises the sheer Welsh *otherness* of this major English-language poet. It prompts us to wonder just how visible Wales *is* from centralising London or distant New York, to ask whether the culture of Wales is important, or just importable. After all, the Reverend R. S. Thomas's main earthly concern is for the survival of the Welsh language, the language of the oldest major European poetic tradition still living, and the one in which the poet has long since lived his daily life. A good deal flows, therefore, from the fact that Welsh is not the language in which his own poetry is written. The definitive treatment of this striking paradox is the essay translated here as 'The Creative Writer's Suicide', but the creative force of that decreating word '*neb*' – no-one – reaches into all the prose.

It is there, for example, in the description of the poet as a small boy in Holyhead, Anglesey, left alone one night:

> Slowly, he would realise that he was on his own. And yet, was he? A house is not a dead thing. It is given to sighing, squeaking and whispering. He would listen. Wasn't there someone upstairs? What was that noise, as of a man breathing? He would go to the bottom of the stairs and turn on the light. And yet the far end of the upstairs was in shadow. He would

shout. No answer. He would climb the stairs, step by step, and having
reached the top would listen again. Suddenly he would leap forward a
step or two, thundering with his feet and shouting: 'Boo!' Nothing. No-
one. (p. 31)

There we have it: '*Dim*', Nothing, next to '*Neb*', No-one. The words
are a leit-motif running right through until the poet asks, in the very
last sentence of *No-one*, 'What, any longer, is it fitting for man to do
but repeat, day after day, "*Miserere me, Domine*"?', where the Welsh
text returns to the immodest first person only in the modest formality
of Latin.

Along the way, more ordinary experiences feed this interest in the
useful ambiguity of such words. In the 1930s, the young, energetic
undergraduate at the University of Wales, Bangor, felt wounded by
the jealous taunt of his contemporaries, 'Who does he think he is?'
The insult is successfully parried with the reply that 'he didn't know
who he was. He was no-one' (p. 38) – but parried only in retrospect.
Repartee is what you think of on the way home. In *A Year in Llŷn*
the shy poet imagines himself delivering a withering reply to an
English bird-watcher who obviously considered himself 'someone'
and had sought to embarrass the poet on his own home ground of
Anglesey. But, turning to the reader, Thomas says, 'No, friend, that
was *not* what I said. I am not one of those people who have a ready
answer. Like many another person I will think of a humorous answer
about half an hour too late' (p. 150). Repartee is what you think of
on the way home, but it is also the beginning of autobiography.

In this way the agility of the word '*neb*' is a weapon for satire as
well as self-defence. When one of Thomas's parishioners in Eglwys-
fach in the Cardiganshire of the 1950s and 1960s boasted that he
was socially quite 'someone', the poet could genuinely sympathise:
after all, 'Can a man face life if he feels that he is no-one?' (p. 74).
But to be *really* someone has little to do with class-pretensions. The
Welsh pun in '*neb*' is therefore at its most telling when applied to a
person in the act of genuine creation. After the birth of his son
Gwydion in the hospital at Newtown in 1945, the poet asks, 'How
can anyone be a father to someone?' (p. 56). In English he is certainly
asking how 'anyone' can bear the heavy responsibilities of parent-
hood; but in Welsh he is also asking how a mere 'no-one' could
possibly be a father at all. And later, as vicar of Aberdaron between
1967 and 1978, seeing his shadow fall on the golden pre-Cambrian

rocks of the Llŷn Peninsula, the poet is forced to ask the age-old question 'Who am I?' Against the ageless rocks that created that magnificent north-west arm of Wales, the answer seems almost frighteningly literal – '*Neb*', No-one – until it is completed with 'But a no-one with a crown of light about his head' (p. 78).

That halo is saved from immodesty by its source in the verse from Pindar that Thomas is at that point quoting – 'Man is a dream about a shadow. But when some splendour falls upon him from God, a glory comes to him and his life is sweet'.[5] It is that paradox whereby the insignificant is accorded significance that explains the poet's choice of the sentence from Paul Claudel that serves as epigraph to *No-one*:

Et de ce néant indestructible qui est moi

where Claudel is asking 'What is this death that you have taken from me compared to the truth of your presence / And to this indestructible nothingness that is I?'. Though he himself would blanch at the suggestion, charisma and indestructibility are aspects of R. S. Thomas himself. They explain, for one thing, the warm affection with which he is viewed from within the Welsh culture that he belatedly joined, but now so proudly manifests and bravely represents. The only variation on 'no-one' and on the impersonal third-person 'he' in *No-one* is when the poet calls himself 'R. S.' The personal initials are what not only close friends but ordinary readers, students, critics, aspiring poets, distant admirers and even ideological opponents feel they have an agreed right to use when talking of his work, or even to R.S. Thomas himself. The 'liberty' thus taken is real liberty, based as it is on critical admiration as well as affection or a sense of solidarity. 'R. S.' is therefore the name that we, too, shall use from here on. From 'no-one' to 'R. S.' is a significant stretch on a road of self-discovery. Whether by design or accident, his own use of 'R. S.' starts exactly half-way through the text of *No-one*, and within only two pages of his comment, 'It was in this way that he came to know himself, with all his weaknesses' (p. 71). At the same time, R. S. himself has said, about his choice of '*No-one*' as a title, that 'the publishers would not have asked me to write an autobiography if I were, in all seriousness, no-one.' For anyone who has met him, he is proof of the difference between importance and self-importance. Only a writer who knows, at a deep impersonal level, that he is *someone* can afford to call himself 'no-one'.

2

The small boy in Holyhead shouting at presences at the head of the stairs, and discovering *nothing* and *no-one* more articulate than his own 'Boo!', was experiencing the beginning of the religious sense in childhood. Later, as priest and poet, he was to wrestle more strenuously with such unaccommodating absences. The small boy grew into one of our most memorable poets on the theme of the *deus absconditus*, the hidden God:

> It is this great absence
> that is like a presence, that compels
> me to address it without hope
> of a reply. It is a room I enter
>
> from which someone has just
> gone.

'The Absence'

Of course, not all supernatural intimations need be Christian, and the author of *No-one* is good on other mysteries along the way. In other words, he is good on *mystery*. He seems, for example, always to have had a consciousness of some 'otherness', even in himself. He doesn't know where he got the notion, one night as a small boy, of creating an effigy, dressing it in clothes and setting it on a chair in the shadows at the head of the stairs to await what must have been a hair-raising return for his parents (p. 31). And at university, during student dances, 'he would go outside and look through the windows at the merry crowd inside, and see it all as something completely unreal' (p. 38). The scene reminds us of the situation recorded in Philip Larkin's 'Reasons for Attendance'.[6] But R. S.'s outsiderness is very different from Larkin's social unease, which is culturally very much that of an *in*sider. These small points of accidental contact make us realise that, of the important poets who emerged in the late 1940s and 1950s, the two most clearly in counterpoint – because so often on the same tune of disappearing landscapes and lost identities – are the Welsh-nationalist-rural Thomas and the English-nationalist-suburban Larkin. They are both great elegiac laureates: Larkin of English-domestic banal, R. S. of Welsh-alternative loss. Even the religious/secular counterpoint pivots on a shared point, as in R. S.'s 'a room I enter // from which someone has just / gone' and Larkin's talk of rooms 'shaped to the comfort of the last to go',[7] the latter furnished no doubt with a three-piece suite, a radio and a vase. But the personal tune is sometimes in more straightforward harmony. It is interesting, for example, that the Larkin poem R. S. most admires is 'Faith Healing'.[8] It ties in with the moving description in *No-one* of how R. S. once took his father to a faith-healing meeting in the hope of restoring his hearing (p. 82). The episode is part of a section describing his relationship with his parents generally, and the Larkin poem is relevant in that respect as well. R. S. sees his mother as someone who, orphaned at the age of six, 'had been deprived of love'. In turn, her own inability, and that of her husband, to express their love for the boy is a theme implicit in *No-one*, a strong undercurrent in *The Echoes Return Slow* (1988), and the subject of a straightforward statement in a recent radio interview.[9] It is relevant therefore that the climax of Larkin's 'Faith Healing' is that very point. R. S.'s poetry is relatively thin in terms of sociological or autobiographical detail. Part of the importance of the prose is that it supplements that detail.

But it is the world of nature that gets the human world into perspective. R. S.'s month-by-month journal, *A Year in Llŷn*, comes naturally to mind when one reads Larkin's 'Forget What Did', a poem about 'stopping the diary' in order to forget the merely personal.[10] And in *No-one*, immediately after the episode where he chooses to view his dancing contemporaries through a window, R. S. affirms the relative 'littleness' of all domestic experiences when viewed at any distance. Nature provides that distance. He recalls a story by Maeterlinck, who described

> how, while descending from a mountain in the Alps, he saw below him a glorious valley under the summer sun. And to crown everything, there was a crowd of people out in the fields harvesting the hay. But as he came within earshot of the people, he found that they were quarrelling amongst themselves, using the dirtiest and most unseemly language. (p. 38)

R. S. always has this larger, natural perspective on what man thinks he is about. And even closer to, there are still things that remain mysterious, alternative. The unexplained figure at the frozen pond above Holyhead (p. 31), for example, or the equally mysterious man who stands 'like a shadow ... as if living in another world', silent and unexplaining, some ten yards away as R. S. converses one afternoon with a family of his cottage parishioners above Manafon (p. 101). The disciples' experience on the road to Emmaus as reflected at the end of T. S. Eliot's *The Waste Land* comes to mind – 'But who

is the third one walking beside you?'. R. S. has often been attacked
for his New Theology view that Christ's resurrection is essentially a
'metaphor' (p. 84).[11] Does he therefore not believe it happened literally? Either way, these inexplicable presences in the prose help
restore our sense of the mystery of quite literal things.

But, sixty years on, the small boy who had shouted 'Boo!' at the
presences at the head of the stairs also became the author of *Abercuawg*. This 1976 National Eisteddfod lecture explored the concept
of presence and absence in specifically cultural terms:

> People tend to think that the void is the original state, and that being is
> something that comes to fill that void. Mention is made of presence and
> absence. But we shall never become conscious of the absent as such; only
> conscious that what we seek for is not present. So only being is real.
> 'Nothing' is an entity that cannot be thought ... Try it. You can't. There
> is always something there. Fall back on language. Shout: NOTHING! It is
> completely meaningless. But shout: Abercuawg! and the echoes start to
> awaken.

'Abercuawg' – the place in a ninth-century Welsh poem where
'cuckoos sing' – is R. S.'s symbol for an ideal, eternal, Welsh-speaking
Wales. The place may never become reality in our time, or even in
time at all, but is the potential that gives meaning to all places and
times in which we *do* live. It is a recurrent echo in R. S.'s work of the
Wordsworthian idea of 'something evermore about to be'.[12] But
R. S. also knows that at one time a totally Welsh-speaking Wales *did*
exist. So, in a sense, the small boy at the foot of the stairs in Holyhead,
feeling instinctively that 'a house is not a dead thing' because 'it is
given to sighing, squeaking and whispering', is wiser than he knows.
The whole experience reminds us of the answer to the question 'What
is it to love a country?' that Waldo Williams poses in his poem, '*Pa
Beth Yw Dyn?*' ('What is Man?'), a poem echoed in 'And what is
life?' in *The Echoes Return Slow*. So what is it to love a country?

> *Cadw tŷ*
> *Mewn cwmwl tystion*
>
> It is to keep house
> In a cloud of witnesses.[13]

Apart from its religious reference (Hebrews 12:1), 'a cloud of wit-
nesses' is also a metaphor for the living witness of forebears within a

particular culture. R. S. sanely argues that we only know who we are by knowing also *where* we are. A particular place creates around us an unique culture that gives us not only our identity but also our vision and values. But a culture – that unconscious field of force in which everyone lives – lives itself daily at vanishing point. It surfaces into consciousness only when threatened or actually extinguished – a fact memorably registered in Edmund Blunden's 'Forefathers'.[14] It is like the moment when R. S., driving to his still relatively new home in Llŷn, gets out of his car and sees the amazing contrast of dark clouds throwing the peninsula into shadow while their own crests are all gold. 'I have never seen a sight quite like it,' he says, and then immediately wonders whether the original inhabitants of a ruined house at the side of the road also saw the same sights. 'Did they notice? Did they appreciate and marvel at the miracle of the creation? They perished. I do not know even the name of the house' (p. 169).

With a place or a culture, as with an individual house, we inherit squeaks and whispers and sighs. And to go 'abroad' in any real sense is to be aware of the squeaks, whispers and sighs of other countries, too. In a moving passage, R. S. recalls his visit with his wife, the distinguished artist Mildred Eldridge, to Mallorca:

> Each night there came the song of the cicada from the bushes in the hotel garden, and outside the town all through the night the crickets would keep up a noise like that of the nightjar. This was R. S.'s first glimpse of the Mediterranean and, looking down on its incomparable blue from the top of the cliffs, he recalled his schooldays studying Vergil's *Aeneid*, with its frequent references to the sea. Amidst the olive trees and the sound of goatbells everywhere, he had the feeling that he was in touch with a very old culture. One day he travelled up a valley and heard a goatherd walking the slope and talking in a normal voice, as if speaking to himself. But suddenly there came an answer from the opposite slope where there was another goatherd. So silent was the place that it was like a whispering gallery, enabling the two to hear each other, although there was something like two hundred yards between them. (pp. 86–7)

'Talking in a normal voice, as if speaking to himself': it is a marvellous image for the ease of communication within a culture. Compared to it, the famous whispering gallery of St Paul's Cathedral is mere tourist business. Reference to cicadas, olive trees and Vergil strikes echoing notes off a timeless, irreducible way of life. We may sometimes want to escape such hauntings. It is often healthy to do so. But, in R. S.'s own words, life is not worth living in 'a land without vibrations'.[15]

3

So there are religious and cultural dimensions to the prose. But they are also wonderfully grounded in the personal. R. S.'s parishes are milestones on a very individual return journey. From childhood to retirement, this particular journey completes a geographic 'oval' (p. 77), a circuit driven by the challenge of reinheriting Welsh Wales. From his childhood in Holyhead on Anglesey, he moves east to two curacies in the Marches (Chirk in Denbighshire and Hanmer in Flintshire), then goes south to Manafon in Montgomeryshire, south-westward to Eglwys-fach in Cardiganshire, and north again to Aber-daron and Y Rhiw in the Llŷn Peninsula of Caernarfonshire, before reaching in 1994 his present home at Llanfair-yng-Nghornwy on the island of Anglesey from which he started. The human forces driving such a journey are best read in the texts themselves, but they can be crystallised here by a short early paragraph from *No-one* that speaks volumes. The literal start was the childhood in Holyhead on Anglesey, but the internal start was an early memory of being with his father in Liverpool – of being, for the first time consciously, *outside* Wales. It is a memory that appropriately questions the nature of memory itself:

> How does memory work? It keeps hold of some things, while letting other things go to oblivion. It is one thing that remains. One day on the beach at Hoylake his father directed his attention to a row of mountains far away over the sea to the west. 'That's Wales,' he said, in English. (p. 28)

In the version in *Former Paths* in 1972 the Welsh mountains seen across the sea are 'grey-blue', and from the Anglesey of his childhood in the 1988 volume *The Echoes Return Slow* they are again 'blue shadows on a longed-for horizon'. A. E. Housman's lovely phrase 'blue remembered hills',[16] borrowed by Dennis Potter as the title for his finest television play, is relevant. Housman's image may not have been borrowed into the Welsh, but is the perfect image for any land softly remembered 'on a longed-for horizon'. What is sad, of course, is that R. S. as a youngster had no concept of the rich culture that the beckoning landscape represented. Hence the irony in that collapsed sentence, ' "That's Wales," he said, in English' – all the more poignant because the speaker is the poet's own father, whose own youth in Cardiganshire would have been Welsh-speaking. An entry in the *Encyclopaedia Britannica* once read 'For Wales, see England'. Ignorance of the sheer *otherness* of Wales is something R. S. spent the rest of his lifetime exposing.

No-one is structured by the way in which that outward Anglican career curves to follow an inward Welsh return-journey, to a place his parents had not prepared for him. But the return is universalised in that it is also seaward. The editor of a selection of Wordsworth's poetry, R. S. is himself profoundly Wordsworthian. He may not particularly follow Wordsworth in recognising 'In simple childhood something of the base / On which thy greatness stands'.[17] But he is certainly Wordsworthian in wanting to retrieve *any* source of human power that has been overlain – as poetry and religion have been by science, simple language by mere style, primary emotions by a 'refined, / But affected, sense',[18] pliant nature by concrete towns and cities, Welsh by English, living at the edge by the glamour of the centre. So when R. S., inland, yearns to return to places within sight of the sea (p. 43) it is because of happy childhood memories of the seaside port of Holyhead, certainly, but also with that seaward vision that, in the 'Immortality' Ode, the land-bound Wordsworth was also compelled to imagine:

> Hence, in a season of calm weather,
> Though inland far we be,
> Our souls have sight of that immortal sea
> Which brought us hither.

At the very end of *No-one* R. S. even quotes the Ode's final image of 'Thoughts that do often lie too deep for tears'. R. S. is Wordsworthian because his tears, like Wordsworth's, are those of something deeper than merely personal nostalgia.

And yet, on that journey, personal memories help to ground the larger vision, for example, R. S.'s memories, as a seaman's son at Holyhead, of 'gazing long at the sea' (p. 31), or of retired seamen 'gazing at the sea' as if 'expecting something to happen' (p. 30). Of course, the concern then was with arrivals and safe returns, not metaphysical departures. But those workaday memories help to desentimentalise the spiritual yielding that in the poetry so often takes the form of looking out to sea. In 'Sea-watching', for example:

Grey waters, vast
      as an area of prayer
that one enters. Daily
      over a period of years
I have let the eye rest on them.
Was I waiting for something?
               Nothing
but that continuous waving
      that is without meaning
occurred...
      There were days,
so beautiful the emptiness
it might have filled,
         its absence
was as its presence; not to be told
any more, so single my mind
after its long fast,
        my watching from praying.

The poet's return to the Llŷn Peninsula was drawn by this religious sense as much as by the attraction of a place where he could live his life in the Welsh language or by the appeal of actual childhood places. When R. S. reached Aberdaron in 1967, with Bardsey Island only two miles of dangerous water away, his journey had reached a promontory famous since the Dark Ages for literal pilgrimages, three of which, according to custom, equalled one to Rome. In Aberdaron the poet already felt he had 'reached the destination of his own personal pilgrimage' (p. 77). The very words merge religious journey with personal homing.

4

Saunders Lewis once remarked that he knew 'from teaching and from experience how difficult any language is to master so as to be able to hold controversy in it'.[19] The quality of R. S.'s Welsh has long since reached the level where he can hold controversy in it. The piece translated here as 'The Creative Writer's Suicide' is ample evidence of that. And the biblical exclamation at the heart of that essay – 'Woe is me that I was born! Who is wounded, and I am not wounded? For I bear in my body the marks of this battle' (pp. 22–3) – is the expression of a deeply political fact that underlies *all* his prose writings. It is the fact that his major art form, poetry, is for him possible only in English. Had he tried to be a Welsh-language poet, he would have been committing suicide as a creative writer. Though the other works translated here are not disquisitions on these questions, that is not to say they don't raise them. In fact, *No-one* contains a sustained meditation (pp. 91–5) on the politics of Welshness, even its theology, quoting as it does a text from Deuteronomy: 'The Lord did not set his love upon you, nor choose you, because ye were more in number than any people; for ye were the fewest of all people' (p. 92).

Unlike prose, poetry can be written only from the language that went in first. Themes, however, can find a natural passage between all forms, and it is interesting that R. S. has turned increasingly to autobiography not only in his Welsh prose, but also in his English poetry. Each poem in *The Echoes Return Slow* (1988) is accompanied by a piece of autobiographical prose circling around roughly the same experience. Those prose pieces could have been included in this volume, except that they cannot really be divorced from the corresponding poems that hold them in tension. In the same way, if one wants to see any of the 'ideas' at work in the present volume deepened, one should turn, not to the poet's more polemical prose (a medium in which he always expected to *lose* his argument),[20] but to the poetry itself.

But the prose still has its own vivid ways of recording experience. It is also good at fixing in the reader's mind the things and places on which the poet's memory depends. And in doing so it often taps back into poetry itself – sometimes into another poet's poetry. There is, for example, the underlying presence of Yeats. When R. S., describing the relative beauties of north and south Wales, rehearses those wonderful place names – Tregaron, Abergwesyn, Beddgelert, Nanmor – he feels he is 'naming the areas of Wales as a mother names her children' (p. 103). The simile is from Yeats's 'Easter 1916', where Yeats recites the names of the martyrs of the Easter uprising 'as a mother names her child'. The reference prompts R. S. to picture the emergence of a 'unified Wales', a concept grounded, here as elsewhere, in a love of actual places and place-names. It is a concept that he clinches with a specific mention of Yeats's play *Cathleen ni Houlihan*, whose heroine is the symbol of an eternally resurgent Ireland. Or take the following passage from the account of April in *A Year in Llŷn*:

April is the month of listening. Secretly, I find myself waiting for the song

of the blackcap or the grasshopper warbler, and of course, later on in the
month, for the cuckoo's double note. Every year without fail it is heard
by someone before it arrives, because people's ears are ready for it, and
when you're waiting there are other sounds that are very similar to it,
such as those of the collared dove, or even of mischievous children
imitating it. (p. 130)

Eliot's famous proposition that 'April is the cruellest month' is rep-
rimanded by being altered. 'April is the month of listening': R. S. is
urging attentiveness. This then modulates into an allusion to Wordsworth. When R. S. says that the cuckoo's song is sometimes heard
even before it occurs, 'because people's ears are ready for it', this
great Wordsworthian poet of our time is perhaps subconsciously
recalling Wordsworth himself:

> many a time
> At evening, when the stars had just begun,
> To move along the edges of the hills,
> Rising or setting, would he stand alone
> Beneath the trees or by the glimmering Lake,
> And there, with fingers interwoven, both hands
> Press'd closely palm to palm, and to his mouth
> Uplifted, he, as through an instrument,
> Blew mimic hootings to the silent owls . . .
>
> Then sometimes, in that silence, while he hung
> Listening, a gentle shock of mild surprize
> Has carried far into his heart the voice
> Of mountain torrents; or the visible scene
> Would enter unawares into his mind
> With all its solemn imagery, its rocks,
> Its woods, and that uncertain Heaven, receiv'd
> Into the bosom of the steady Lake.[21]

Like Wordsworth, R. S. is showing how intense expectation of one
sound makes us preternaturally receptive to others. How appropriate
therefore that both should use the image of a mischievous child
mimicking a bird's note. In this way, association of ideas links not
only self and world but also self and literature. With equal resonance,
an early memory in *No-one* evokes a rural version of the loneliness
of T. S. Eliot's Prufrock, who heard 'the mermaids singing each to
each':

Despite his mother's nervous and anxious nature, he was free to roam the island from earliest morning to sunset. He would gather flowers in the spring, and mushrooms in the autumn. He would climb the rocks and cliffs, gazing long at the sea and listening to the sound of the waves in the caves. There was one cave from which the cry of the seals came like the song of mermaids. There was unadulterated, endless pleasure to be had from being on his own like this. Was he preparing himself to be a poet? (pp. 31–2)

But the prose deals in more than hints and echoes. Though honest about the difficulty of deciding in what order things happened to the boy in question (p. 28), the prose works mark the milestones of an actual career. If the aim is to 'know' oneself in a conscious, discursive sense ('It was thus that he came to know himself, with all his weaknesses'), then prose is the right medium. And what is striking is how closely this self-knowledge involves knowing places. And knowing them for the first time. Not just in the sense of places newly arrived at, but of a new understanding of places longingly returned to. The first milestone in the 'public' career was Manafon – where the first poems about the bleak world of Iago Prytherch and of man's relationship to nature were born. And it was no less a milestone for Manafon itself. It is not an overstatement for R. S. to call the parish 'a region of small cottages and sheep, waiting for him to discover them' (p. 52). In an important sense, certainly in our time, he *created* Manafon. But he is not claiming, egotistically, to have put Manafon 'on the map'. Indeed, in *Former Paths* (p. 16), R. S. himself reminds us that Manafon's church registers went back to the Latin of the fifteenth century, and that it was already the parish of great literary priests – Ieuan Brydydd Hir, Gwallter Mechain and Penfro.[22] He describes Gwallter Mechain's '*Y nos dywell yn distewi*' as arguably the most perfect *englyn* in the Welsh language:

> *Y nos dywell yn distewi, – caddug*
>   *Yn cuddio Eryri,*
> *Yr haul yng ngwely'r heli,*
> *A'r lloer yn ariannu'r lli.*

> The night darkening silently, – the mist
>   Enshrouding Eryri,
> The sun set in its briny
> Bed, the moon silvering the sea.[23]

In this sense, knowing the place for the first time started to mean knowing it also for the first time in its own language. Manafon had lost its Welsh just as R. S. was regaining his. It is this experience of expectantly tracking a disappearing linguistic frontier that accounts for the shift in the poetry from rural concerns to political concern. It brought in, he claimed, an 'element of bitterness ... that would be there for many years' (p. 55). The concern was deepened in his next parish, Eglwys-fach, by his disappointment at discovering that the congregation was Welsh in neither attitude nor language – when the Welshness of the actual area had been one of R. S.'s main reasons for moving there. Then a further curve north-westwards to Aberdaron, at the tip of the Llŷn Peninsula. On arrival, there starts to grow in R. S.'s mind the repeated image of the peninsula as 'a bough of land between sea and sky', with the poet creeping out on it – as if seeking to extend the journey, even after arrival. When he arrived at Aberdaron in 1967, no sooner was the exile's geographical longing for the sea to the north-west satisfied than it was overtaken by a *temporal* longing for the actual places of his childhood, and of course that meant Anglesey (p. 88). Though R. S. stresses that you can travel back into childhood itself only through the imagination (p. 88), a further push north to at least the *places* of childhood was completed in 1994 with the poet's final move to Anglesey itself, for which he had felt a profound nostalgia ever since his first curacy at Chirk in 1936. And back at last on Anglesey, there is not only the delight of arrival at where he started, but also the knowledge of what he has brought with him. As in Llŷn and Eglwys-fach and Manafon, there is pre-eminently that sense of knowing a place for the first time in its own language. This is a knowledge far deeper than simply knowing that he himself is an older and a wiser man. Simply knowing more *facts* is something R. S. illustrates with an image from bird-watching. As a youngster on Anglesey he had heard the tumultuous noise made by the oystercatchers along the rocks at Holyhead. It was only later that he realised that their dramatic noise was only in aid of safe-guarding their young. 'That is one of the differences,' he says, 'that fifty years have made' (p. 147). As if in support of a deeper sense in which we know old places for the first time, there is the nice irony that many specific Welsh place-names have tended to follow him on his journey. For example, '*sarn*' (causeway) was the main part not only in the name of his retirement home at Y Rhiw in Llŷn (Sarn Rhiw), but also of many place-names in the Montgomeryshire he had left. 'Rhiw' itself had already been the name of the river that flowed past the rectory in Manafon, just as the Daron of Aberdaron is also the name of a river in Montgomeryshire. It almost gives a new application to the final line of the T. H. Parry-Williams poem that R. S. so admires: '*Duw a'm gwaredo, ni allaf ddianc rhag hon*', 'God save me, I cannot escape from this one.'[24]

He also recognises another irony in the journey – that the destination he reached in Llŷn was once, from the Anglesey of his childhood, a horizon. Places we want to get back to are often places we once wanted to get to. There are always other places, because every place is an end and a beginning. But, even given the mileage involved, the prose still displays continuity, the consistency within change of an actual traveller. Better than the image of a road, therefore, is that of a river, of sources that are always near. Of course, prose cannot capture the limpid continuities of a poem like 'The River':

> And the cobbled water
> Of the stream with the trout's indelible
> Shadows that winter
> Has not erased – I walk it
> Again under a clean
> Sky with the fish, speckled like thrushes,
> Silently singing among the weed's
> Branches.
>   I bring the heart
> Not the mind to the interpretation
> Of their music, letting the stream
> Comb me, feeling it fresh
> In my veins, revisiting the sources
> That are as near now
> As on the morning I set out from them.

A mottled, cobbled river-bed, looking as if it still retained 'the trout's indelible / Shadows' from a previous summer is an image as clear-eyed yet mysterious as Hopkins's 'rose-moles all in stipple upon trout that swim'[25] – which R. S. then emulates in the picture of trout 'speckled like thrushes'. The dappled world of cobbles and shadows is the perfect image for the variegated indelible experiences of a childhood that 'winter / Has not erased'.

The boast about revisiting 'sources / That are as near now / As on the morning I set out from them' cannot be felt on the pulse in prose as it can in poetry. Nevertheless, equally fine poems lie behind the prose. Though *No-one* is not meant to be a *biographia literaria* in the Coleridgean sense of a life refracted through literature and philosophy, R. S. has said that it is still 'something like Wordsworth's "Prelude" ... but less ambitious, and in prose; which is to say an attempt to outline the growth of a poet's mind; not a representative poet, of course, but a small poet who had to live throughout his life on tenterhooks through being an Englishman in his craft and a Welshman by instinct.'[26] Some of the classic English poems of this 'Welshman by instinct' are given their specific contexts in the prose of this volume; classic poems, and classic phrases, too. R. S.'s infamous description, for example, of Protestantism as 'the adroit castrator / Of art'[27] has a background here in his bold opinion that hymns, whether Anglican or Nonconformist, whether judged as poetry or as music, are third-rate (p. 83). Or if one thinks of 'the spilled blood / That went to the making of the wild sky' in 'Welsh Landscape', how naturally discovered the image now seems when we read in *Former Paths* of R. S., the young theological student, journeying home from Cardiff to Holyhead by train:

> the line from Cardiff to Shrewsbury runs along the Marches, with the plains of England on the one side and the hill-country of Wales on the other. I was often stirred on seeing these hills rising in the west. Sometimes night would start to fall before we reached Ludlow. Westwards the sky would be ablaze, reminding one of the battles of the past. Against that radiance, the hills rose dark and threatening as if full of armed men waiting for a chance to attack. (p. 10)

The reprimand in the most famous poem of all, 'A Peasant', that it is an 'affected' sensibility that takes objection to the gobbing, sour-smelling Iago Prytherch, is here again implicit in the eloquent tribute paid in *Former Paths* to the sheer craft and energy of Prytherch and his kind in working the land (p. 12). And, tying in with it, there is the description in *No-one* of the actual bleak November day out of which this seminal poem grew:

> For [R.S.], the countryside and its surroundings were beautiful. He wanted to continue to sing poems of praise to them. But how to reconcile with this the life and attitude of the farmers themselves? On a dark, cold day in November, on his way to visit a family in a farm over a thousand feet

above sea-level, he saw the farmer's brother out in the field, docking mangels. The thing made a profound impression on him, and when he returned to the house after the visit he set about writing 'A Peasant', the first poem to attempt to face the reality of the scenes around him. (p. 52)

No amount of contextualisation can explain a poem, but it is still good to have a context, and an occasion. It would be presumptuous to ignore them. It is like reading, at the other end of the emotional spectrum, Gerard Manley Hopkins saying about that amazing sonnet, 'Hurrahing in Harvest', that it 'was the outcome of half an hour of extreme enthusiasm as I walked home alone one day from fishing in the Elwy.'[28]

Or take another classic R. S. poem, 'Country Church (Manafon)'. This perfect lyric celebrates the brittle beauty of the church's river-stone construction, faced with engulfment by grass:

> The church stands, built from the river stone,
> Brittle with light, as though a breath could shatter
> Its slender frame, or spill the limpid water,
> Quiet as sunlight, cupped within the bone.
>
> It stands yet. But though soft flowers break
> In delicate waves round limbs the river fashioned
> With so smooth care, no friendly God has cautioned
> The brimming tides of fescue for its sake.

The vulnerability is registered anew in the prose, where the church is seen as 'a small hut in the fields', because seen there from a height that also reveals Wales's eternal hills. The rector of Manafon, we learn,

> would sometimes climb to the hilltops, and from one of their peaks a completely different world would open out in front of him. To the north-west, Cadair Idris was to be seen; to the north, Aran Fawddwy and Aran Benllyn, and to the north-east Y Berwyn – a prospect sufficient to raise the heart and make the blood sing. Turning to look down into the valley he would see everything in perspective, the people like ants below him, the church a small hut in the fields and the river like a silver thread flowing down the valley. The church was built of river stones, smoothed by centuries of water, and sometimes, when the light was strong, it was as if the water were still running over them. (p. 58)

5

In all this, it is the simplicity of the saying that appeals. The Welsh prose gives clear directions, but not just as a signpost or a headline might. It is worth, just once, looking at its expert tailoring in a brief untranslated passage:

Fedran nhw fyw efo'r syniad na fydd yna'r ffasiwn beth â Llŷn Gymraeg ar ôl y ganrif hon? O, meddech chi, mi fydd y wlad a'i henwau yma. Ysgerbwd. Ewch i'r rhannau o Gymru lle mae'r iaith wedi diflannu a'r enwau wedi cael eu llurgunio. Ysgerbwd o wlad yw hi. Er gwaetha'r golygfeydd gwych mae rhywbeth ar goll, na ŵyr neb byth beth ydi o, ond gwir Gymro. (p. 144)

It is often argued that, as long as place-names, landscapes, accents and something loosely called 'national character' survive, a younger generation need not worry that Welsh literature, and Welsh as a spoken language, might perish. In its understanding of the real nature of cultural identity, such an argument is obviously poor stuff, but it has an insidious grip in Wales today, and R. S.'s objection to it is sane and measured. And a certain measuring happens even in the prose style. Only the carcase of a culture survives in abandoned names, and at that point the sentence-lengths dwindle down to that one-word sentence – '*Ysgerbwd*.' ('Skeleton.') – then slowly expand again to achieve a fearful symmetry either side of that bare fact. We should be glad that R. S. did not forgo Welsh prose as well as Welsh poetry in his decision to avoid 'suicide' as a creative writer.

But even with its tensions and allusiveness, the prose is reassuringly consistent in terms of the person it communicates. It is interesting that, in an essay on his aims in writing *No-one*, R. S. should refer to Yeats's theory of the mask, the idea that a person can adopt many different, often antithetical, personalities: 'There is a world of difference between a man of action in the flesh and one who believes in living in the imagination. In this connection, Yeats showed that each one has his opposite side which tempts him to be otherwise'.[29] The plural title of the present volume – *Autobiographies* – is borrowed from Yeats, but not so as to evoke the plural identities that Yeats thought essential to the creative character. R. S.'s memories may take plural form – poetry, early memoir, autobiography, diary, confessional essay and so on. In turn, the different forms reflect a man who is both priest and iconoclast, English-language poet and Welsh nationalist, solitary bird-watcher and national polemicist. But in all these forms and capacities R. S. is throughout recognisably the same person, never tempted, in Yeatsian fashion, 'to be otherwise'.

Which is not to say, of course, that everything is on the surface. One should not, for example, pass by too quickly the brief early memory in *No-one* of Goole in Yorkshire – only a memory 'of a river flowing between banks that were all mud. But there were farms nearby. They would go to them to have tea in the orchards. The only trouble were the wasps that would come after the cakes and try to settle on his hands.' (p. 29). An idyll cut across by an invading insect is a recurrent memory. Indeed, the first two pages of *No-one* are positively dominated by insects. Their persistence in his memory reveals a mind aware early of fallen states, a sensibility not given to sentimentality. On the other hand, more romantically, tea in a different orchard in *Former Paths* (p. 9) crystallises a memory of early love. It reveals one of the most intriguing aspects of R. S.'s character. In so many ways a genuinely shy person, there is in him nevertheless a deep romantic ardour. It is what explains the Hardy-like, pent-up love-energy of his wonderful late poems to his first wife. The prose is full of rich human touches of this kind, that could easily have sustained elaboration. The priest's love-hate feelings towards his parishioners, for example; or his only-child's view of an absent, heroic sailor-father and an over-protective mother. This latter theme is there, highly pressurised, in the short prose pieces set alongside the poems of *The Echoes Return Slow* (1988), just as in this uncollected poem of 1973, called 'Autobiography':

> Two people cast up
>   on life's shore:
> can't you see the emptiness
>   of their pockets,
>   and their small hearts
> ready to burst with
>   love? Say 'feeling',
>   and the explosion
> not loud.
>   They come to
>   in a lodging, make love
>   in a rented bed.

> And I am not present
>   as yet.
> Could it be said, then,
> I am on my way, a nonentity
>   with a destination?
> What do they do
>   waiting for me? They invent
>   my name. I am born
> to a concept, answering
> to it with reluctance. I am
>   wheeled through ignorance
>   to a knowledge that is not
> joy.[30]

'A nonentity with a destination': clearly, the paradox that the word *'neb'* can mean both *no-one* and *someone* was already afoot in the poetry. But in the prose, of course, it is given softer lighting and a wider context. The stark view of the parents in the poem just quoted is in the prose softened and humanised. In *No-one* the mother's over-protectiveness is made poignant, understandable. On the eve of the young R. S. leaving home for the first time, he 'heard the sound of crying upstairs, and the voice of his father trying to silence his wife. Then in bed, after going to sleep, he awoke and felt someone kissing him over and over again.' (p. 36)

But one shouldn't underestimate the wit, either – a feature already too little recognised in the verbal play of the poems, and such an agreeable characteristic of the man himself. It is a dry humour, although always ready to run the full gamut of what constitutes a pun. Quite apart from the ironic potency of that apparently impotent word *'neb'*, there are other kinds of irony; sharp changes of tone, for example. There is a heartfelt lament in *A Year in Llŷn* that, because of Wales's lack of self-determination and of economic resources for academic projects, Welsh is not as well stocked as English with detailed names for different species of creatures and insects. The observation is prompted by R. S.'s concern to differentiate between a mouse and a bank vole, given that in Welsh the word for 'mouse' is part of both names. It was a bank vole, therefore, and not a mouse, that was killed by the cat belonging to a nearby farm. The point about our responsibility to recognise our fellow inhabitants on earth is perfectly serious, and is what justifies the trilingual glossary of birds' names that follows *A Year in Llŷn*. But the text modulates gently into a parting shot worthy of an eighteenth-century satirist: 'So the Latin name for the mouse that was killed by the cat of Rhydybengan Bach is *Clethrionomys glareolus*.' (p. 141)

With the same twinkle, the sudden extinction of falling stars in *Former Paths* (p. 5) is compared to the sharp disappearance of the fox in R. Williams Parry's sonnet of that name, 'Y *Llwynog*'. One needs to be aware that, in translation, a joke, too, can be extinguished. In that superb sonnet by R. Williams Parry, one of Wales's greatest lyric poets, it is the other way round, with the sudden disappearance of the fox being compared to that of a falling star. Such quick interchange is the very spirit of wit, so it is not surprising to find R. S.'s childhood memory of a cinema pianist accompanying a silent film and playing the piano '*nerth ei ddwylo*' (p. 8). The Welsh idiom is '*nerth ei draed*' – 'as fast as his feet (not his hands) could carry him'. But on the screen are 'Tom Mix and his wonder-horse' and 'cowboys and Red Indians pursuing each other across the plain'. To keep pace with them in a silent film, it was the pianist's hands that were crucial.

But it is the beauty of nature that really challenges the nimbleness of the words. Wales's profound cultural importance for R. S. is always underlain by her sheer physical beauty. Even early on, girls and sport only occasionally interrupt his attention to Wales's amazing landscapes. And from there on, those landscapes are given better billing than even language and poetry. This focuses the importance of *A Year in Llŷn*. As a month-by-month journal, it relishes that genre's need to engage with the changing seasons and to focus sights and sounds. The beauty of frosty starlit nights, the quality of light over water, or the different sounds that remind us that landscapes are heard as well as seen – these are things we will ourselves have often taken delight in. But there are also individual observations that will sharpen our attentiveness for next time; R. S.'s observation, for example, of the odd phenomenon that small clouds sometimes seem as if they are following the sun (p. 121). These delights do not self-consciously stud the prose, but are recorded with a simplicity that reveals R. S.'s unambiguous love for the very ground of Wales. It is a love that makes it natural that *A Year in Llŷn* should be also a journal of the *political* weather in Wales, a challenge to anyone who threatens her identity.

And above all there is the loving knowledgeable observation of birds. *A Year in Llŷn* more than justifies its avian glossary. R. S. once said that when birds figure naturally in poetry it isn't as Stone Curlews, Dartford Warblers or Lesser Spotted Woodpeckers.[30] But that is not to say that a passage cannot both name birds and be poetry, even in prose:

> May I tell you about an experience I had that shows how birds, and nature for that matter, will come to accept you, if you only cultivate enough patience to prove to them that there is no harm in you? I was in a thicket of willows. As there was a light breeze, I could hear the sound of the distant sea, but it was perfectly quiet amongst the trees. Gradually, I noticed the number of goldcrests that were there. The grove was full of them, flying hither and thither after the gnats. I stood perfectly still and they started to come closer. Some of them came within an arm's length on the branches, busily seeking their food, but hesitating nervously a moment to stare at the piece of wood that was different from the rest! They were so close I could see their dark eyes, like blackberry seeds. And the air was continuously full of the rustling of their wings, as they jumped from one twig to another. I almost expected to take one of them on my arm, but gradually they moved on in search of food, and complete silence returned to the trees, with only the sun's rays to remind me of the gold of their crests. (p. 145)

Once again we have the context for a famous poem: 'A Thicket in Lleyn' in *Experimenting With an Amen* (1986). But it is also an example of the incremental relationship between poem and prose, and poem and poem. 'A Thicket in Lleyn' doesn't name the goldcrests, but shares that perfect image of the birds' eyes as being like blackberry seeds. Conversely, the resplendent image that closes the poem, that of 'spray from the fountain / of the imagination', is not present in the description of the goldcrests in *A Year in Llŷn*. But the fountain image is splendidly there in the moving account in *Former Paths* of the large ash tree at the entrance to the rectory drive at Manafon (p. 15). In turn, this part of *Former Paths* has equivalents in other poems – in 'The Bush' in *Later Poems* (1983), where a tree's golden, falling leaves are related to the biblical burning bush, and in 'The Prayer' in *Laboratories of the Spirit* (1975), where it takes the form of leaves fountaining from 'the deciduous Cross' of Christ. In seeking an image for a once confident, plenary Welsh culture, R. S. draws on sources stretching from the burning tree of the *Mabinogion*, to Yeats's image of 'the abounding glittering jet' of self-delight,[32] to the bursting fountains of Waldo Williams.[33] In 'The Bush', for example:

> I have thought often
> of the fountain of my people
> that played beautifully here
> once in the sun's light
> like a tree undressing.

So the spectacle of the golden, unleaving ash tree at the gate of the rectory drive in Manafon in *Former Paths* (p. 15) is complex, however simply presented in the prose. One autumn its mass of yellow leaves was late being shed, but after a night of great frost, and in the brightness of dawn, the leaves started to fall. 'They continued to fall for hours until the tree was like a golden fountain playing silently in the sun; I shall never forget it.'

'I shall never forget it.' Memory is about thinking yourself back at the first place, but imagination is about *knowing* the place for the first time. Imagination, for one thing, brings into play the different person that you have in the meantime become. Any source worth revisiting is in this sense already very old, because not exhaustible by any one person's memories. At a certain level, the Welsh language of these autobiographies is for R. S. a resource, something that enables him to express certain controversial cultural or political truths all the more directly through the indirection of Welsh. But a mere 'resource' is exhaustible, just as the 'privacy' of Welsh as a minority language is in the present volume exhausted in translation. But in the original language of these autobiographies something very much richer happens. In the grain of the Welsh language itself are traceable a unique cultural history, a world-class literature, the consciousness of a race. It is only crass functionalism, or worse, that would deem the original language dispensable. As a word to describe the usefulness for R. S. of the Welsh language, 'resource' is clearly not the right one. But 'source' is. And the wonderful thing is how R. S. Thomas's Welsh-language prose, like his English-language poetry, makes us feel that the sources are still near.

JASON WALFORD DAVIES

References

1   Philip Larkin, 'Wants', *The Less Deceived* (Faber, 1955), p. 22.

2   Jenny Rees, *Looking for Mr Nobody: The Secret Life of Goronwy Rees* (Weidenfeld and Nicolson, 1994).

3   Edmund Morris, *The Rise of Theodore Roosevelt* (Collins, 1979).

4   Psalms 8:4.

5   Pindar, the end of the eighth *Pythian* Ode, one of the Greek poet's last and most celebrated works. The actual text translates: 'Man is but a dream of a shadow; but, when a gleam of sunshine comes as a gift of heaven, a radiant light rests on men, yes and a gentle life.'

6   Philip Larkin, 'Reasons for Attendance', *The Less Deceived* (Faber, 1955), p. 18.

7   *ibid.*, 'Home is so Sad', *The Whitsun Weddings* (Faber, 1964), p. 17.

8   Personal information. Larkin's 'Faith Healing' is in *The Whitsun Weddings* (Faber, 1964), p. 15.

9   A double-programme interview in Welsh with Beti George: *Beti a'i Phobl* ('Beti and Her People'), BBC Radio Cymru, 29 February and 5 March 1996.

10 Philip Larkin, 'Forget What Did', *High Windows* (Faber, 1974), p. 16.

11 See 'R. S. Thomas: Priest and Poet', a transcript of John Ormond's film for BBC Television, broadcast 2 April 1972, published in *Poetry Wales*, vol. 7, no. 4 (Spring 1972): 'I consider that the Resurrection is a metaphorical use of language, as is the Incarnation. We are not so hag-ridden today by heresy hunters as they were in the early centuries of the church. There's no doubt that we commit a lot more important heresies probably than by saying that the Resurrection and Incarnation are metaphors. My work as a poet has to deal with the presentation of imaginative truth. Christianity also seems to me to be a presentation of imaginative truth' (p. 53).

12 William Wordsworth, *The Prelude* (1805), VI, 542.

13 Waldo Williams, '*Pa Beth Yw Dyn?*', *Dail Pren* ('The Leaves of a Tree') (Gwasg Aberystwyth, 1956), p. 67.

14 Edmund Blunden, 'Forefathers', Robyn Marsack, ed., *Selected Poems: Edmund Blunden* (Carcanet New Press, 1982), pp. 26–7.

15 'The Welsh Parlour', *The Listener*, 16 January 1958, p. 119: 'But without the language the visitor must wander in an anonymous land, a land without vibrations'.

16 A. E. Housman, 'Into my heart an air that kills', Poem XL of *A Shropshire Lad*, *The Collected Poems of A. E. Housman* (Jonathan Cape, 1939), p. 58.

17 William Wordsworth, *The Prelude* (1805), XI, 330–31.

18 R. S. Thomas, 'A Peasant', *The Stones of the Field* (1946), reprinted in *Song at the Year's Turning* (Rupert Hart-Davis, 1955), p. 21.

19 Saunders Lewis, letter to Nina Wynne (20 September 1942), Wynne Collection, University of Wales, Bangor.

20 See p. 98.

21 William Wordsworth, *The Prelude* (1805), v, 390–413.

22 The bardic names, respectively, of Evan Evans (1731–88), Walter Davies (1761–1849), and William John Morgan (1846–1918). See also Notes and References, p. 178 below.

23 My translation. For a description of the *englyn* as a form, see Notes and References below, p. 178.

24 T. H. Parry-Williams, '*Hon*' ('This One'), *Ugain o Gerddi* ('Twenty Poems') (Gwasg Aberystwyth, 1949), p. 12.

25 Gerard Manley Hopkins, 'Pied Beauty', *Gerard Manley Hopkins*, Catherine Phillips, ed. (Oxford University Press, 1986), p. 133.

26 R. S. Thomas, '*Neb*', an essay on the volume, in *Llais Llyfrau*, Winter 1985, p. 5.

27 R. S. Thomas, *The Minister* (1953), p. 23.

28 Gerard Manley Hopkins, *The Letters of Gerard Manley Hopkins to Robert Bridges*, C. C. Abbott, ed. (Oxford University Press, 1935), p. 56.

29 R. S. Thomas, '*Neb*', *Llais Llyfrau*, Winter 1985, p. 5.

30 'Autobiography', *Wave* 7 (1973), pp. 36–7.

31 R. S. Thomas, 'Words and the Poet', *R. S. Thomas: Selected Prose*, Sandra Anstey, ed. (Poetry Wales Press, 1983), p. 84.

32 W. B. Yeats, 'Meditations in Time of Civil War' (*The Tower*, 1928), *Collected Poems* (Macmillan, 1952), p. 225.

33 See Waldo Williams, '*Mewn Dau Gae*' ('In Two Fields'), *Dail Pren* ('The Leaves of a Tree') (Gwasg Aberystwyth, 1956), p. 27.

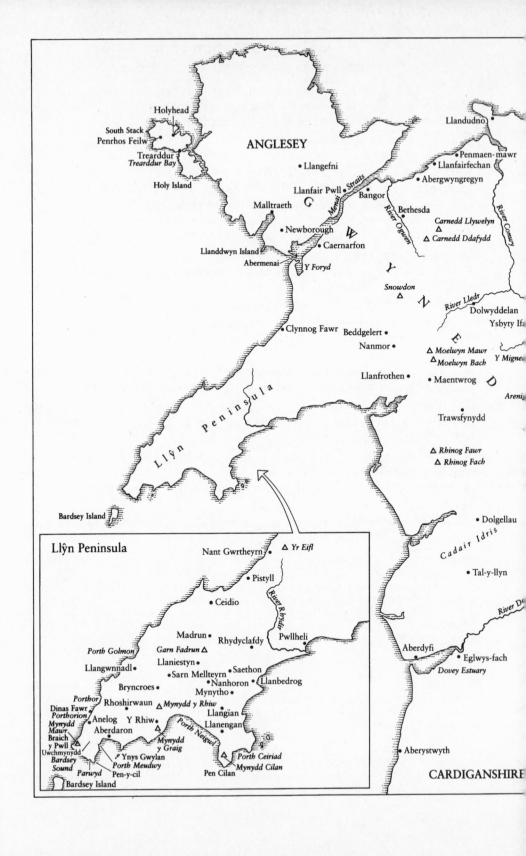

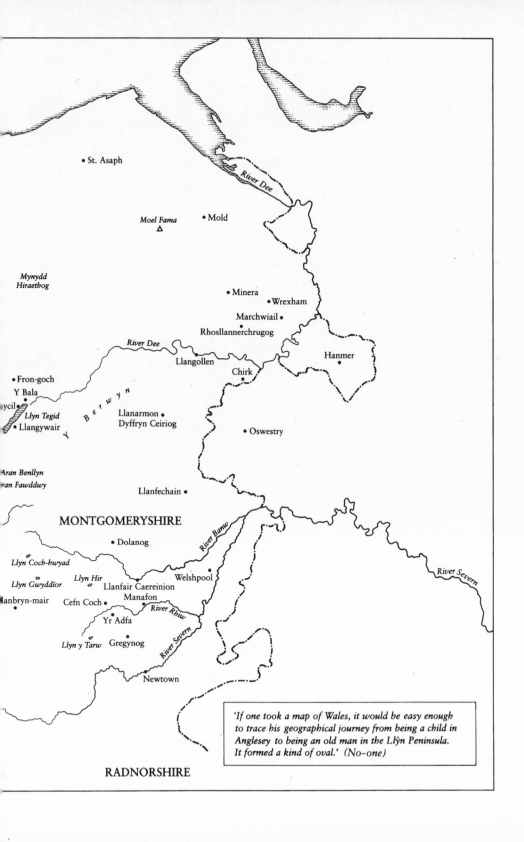

• St. Asaph

Moel Fama
△   • Mold

River Dee

*Mynydd
Hiraethog*

• Minera
• Wrexham
Marchwiail •
Rhosllannerchrugog

River Dee
Llangollen   Hanmer •
Chirk •

• Fron-goch
Y Bala
ycil •   *B e r w y n*   Llanarmon •
Llyn Tegid   Dyffryn Ceiriog
• Llangywair   • Oswestry

*Aran Benllyn
ran Fawddwy*

Llanfechain •

MONTGOMERYSHIRE

• Dolanog   *River Banw*

Llyn Coch-hwyad
River Severn
Llyn Hir   Welshpool
Llyn Guyddïor   Llanfair Caereinion
lanbryn-mair   Cefn Coch •   Manafon
River Rhiw
Yr Adfa •
River Severn
Llyn y Tarw   Gregynog

Newtown

> 'If one took a map of Wales, it would be easy enough
> to trace his geographical journey from being a child in
> Anglesey to being an old man in the Llŷn Peninsula.
> It formed a kind of oval.' (No-one)

RADNORSHIRE

At the End

Few possessions: a chair,
a table, a bed
to say my prayers by,
and, gathered from the shore,
the bone-like, crossed sticks
proving that nature
acknowledges the Crucifixion.
All night I am at
a window not too small
to be frame to the stars
that are no further off
than the city lights
I have rejected. By day
the passers-by, who are not
pilgrims, stare through the rain's
bars, seeing me as prisoner
of the one view, I who
have been made free
by the tide's pendulum truth
that the heart that is low now
will be at the full tomorrow.

                              R. S. THOMAS

FORMER PATHS

FORMER PATHS

It is towards the end of the First World War, and the place: the Wirral Peninsula, Cheshire. A little boy is playing on the beach. Over the sea towards the south-west there are tall grey-blue hills to be seen. His father points to them. 'That's Wales,' he says, in English. The boy lifts his head for a second and stares at them, before turning back to play with the sand. I am that boy on holiday from Liverpool with my parents. My father is a sailor, and we are living in Liverpool so as to be near him when his ship comes to the Liverpool docks from time to time. The Wirral is a lovely place to visit, and even when we are not on our holiday, it is possible to nip over the river Mersey for the day in one of the pleasure-boats.

I was born in Cardiff, but because my father was on deep water, my history for the first six years of my life was to move from port to port, with most of those years spent in England. Indeed, I was a town boy, and the first memories I have are of parks and the streets of big towns like Liverpool, with me going on the trams down to the quay to meet my father, or going on the ship itself and waiting in bed in his cabin while my mother and he were dining with the rest of the ship's officers. Another time off to one of the parks: it is the middle of winter, and the lake there frozen over. There is a crowd of people skating on it. Near the shore there is a bit that hasn't frozen. Along comes a priest, sailing along like a ship before the breeze. Suddenly, to my great amazement, he disappears into the pool. Others come at once and fish him out, soaking wet. He goes away, his bubble burst. The world goes on. It is lovely in the park in the summertime too. The breeze is full of the smell of roses. I bend to smell one of the flowers, but poor me! Some bugbear is waiting for me there! In an instant it is up my nose, and I start screaming all over the place. My mother rushes over to me, frightened out of her wits. Having blown my nose like a dragon into her handkerchief, here comes the enemy to light – a harmless little black fly! But the experience remains in the memory to this day, and it is always with trepidation that I smell a flower.

At the end of the war, when I was approaching my sixth year, we moved to live in Holyhead, where my father had found work on the ships that sailed between Wales and Ireland. I remember the day we arrived, a wet, dark December day. What town is worse than Holyhead on such a day? The taxi took us along the bare streets to our lodgings, with me staring despondently through the windows of the car. But the next day! A jewel of a morning. Every place gleaming, and the sea a wondrous blue. No doubt you know the *hen benillion*, the old folk-verses?

Ar noswaith ddrycinog mi euthum i rodio
Ar lannau y Fenai gan ddistaw fyfyrio;
Y gwynt oedd yn uchel, a gwyllt oedd y wendon,
A'r môr oedd yn lluchio dros waliau Caernarfon.

Ond trannoeth y bore mi euthum i rodio
Hyd lannau y Fenai, tawelwch oedd yno;
Y gwynt oedd yn ddistaw, a'r môr oedd yn dirion,
A'r haul oedd yn twynnu ar waliau Caernarfon.

One night of tempest I arose and went
Along the Menai shore on dreaming bent;
The wind was strong, and savage swung the tide,
And the waves blustered on Caernarfon side.

But on the morrow, when I passed that way,
On Menai shore the hush of heaven lay;
The wind was gentle and the sea a flower,
And the sun slumbered on Caernarfon tower.

That is a fairly accurate description of the type of weather to be had in Anglesey. Indeed, if someone asks you what kind of weather can be expected there, tell him, 'Oh, normally clearing towards afternoon.' It was the weather that was king in Holyhead. It was that which determined almost all my activities. I was a sickly child for the first part of my life. My mother believed that enough fresh sea air would make a new man of me. So for a year I did not go to school; the answer was the open air. I roamed the fields; I played along the shores; I fished for bullheads amongst the rocks. These were greedy creatures. I doted on the eager way in which they grabbed the bait. All that was needed was a piece of a limpet on a bent pin, drop it into a small pool and see the bullhead rush towards it from its hiding place to be hooked by me and put in a jam pot. I could have fished for hours, but one had to keep an eye on the tide. More than once I was caught, and had to jump ashore through the water. Then a hiding from my mother.

When the time came for me to begin school I met new friends, a family that lived at the other end of the island. The mother was a widow, with three children, a girl and two boys. The girl was three years my senior, but the lads were about the same age as me. They lived in Penrhos Feilw, and pretty quickly the home of that name became a place of magic and enchantment for me. The house stood on its own amongst the fields with the open sea about half a mile away. The boys had hiding places in the gorse where it was possible to hide completely out of sight of everyone, long tunnels leading through the gorse to some central chamber, and it was there that we sat like Red Indians to make our plans. My father and mother would visit this woman quite often, and while they were chatting or playing cards in the winter, we children would play in and out of the house. A special experience sometimes was sneaking out into the darkness and standing under the stars with the sea wind moaning around the silent house. And then we would walk home about two miles through the night with the gorse creaking on either side of the lane and the occasional shooting star rushing quietly across the sky and ceasing to be, like Williams Parry's fox. Safe in bed, I would go to sleep to the sound of the singing of a group of townsfolk who used to congregate sometimes at the corner of the street behind our house.

In summer I would make for my friends' home even more frequently. There was a good bay for swimming, Porth Gof Du, very close to them, and it was there that we liked to go. They were like porpoises in the water, and very soon I too learned to swim. It was an ideal bay, and completely private. There would very seldom be anyone else there. At full tide, the sea was some six feet deep in the small sandy cove that formed the bay. The water was crystal clear, and the whitebait and the sand eels would appear green in its depths. The bay faced east, and on many a morning I saw the sea gleaming like silver or gold in the sun. On mornings such as these our hearts would be light and full of mirth, and we would sing at the tops of our voices on the path through the heather to the bay. The sea there definitely had a certain magic, and the body would yearn to be baptised in it. At other times in the afternoon, when the cove was in shadow, having bathed hurriedly we would get dressed and go to explore the cliffs. My friends' heads were steadier than mine. Often I had to turn back, earning the reputation for being a coward. But gradually I too learned how to look over the precipice without too much fear, discovering that there was after all a fairly easy way down. A great thing was to be able to descend to some small beach far from everywhere, with the cliffs rising like a wall around us, and feel that no-one had ever stood there before. And the seagulls would confirm that feeling, circling overhead with a great tumult. Sometimes, to deny our claim that we were the first there, an iron ring would come to light. But we would quickly come to the conclusion that it was pirates who had placed it there! Are you familiar with the sound of the sea in a lonely rocky cove? There is no sound like it, or like the strange clank of the wave that penetrates to the depths of the rock. This is true solitude, and even three lively, mischievous lads would grow somewhat quiet on experiencing it. Then back we would go, competing to be the first to reach the top of the precipice; sometimes getting stuck by taking a different turning. On such occasions, there was nothing for it but to go back and start again, even though the top of the cliff was only about a yard or two beyond our reach. After a summer day like this it was a crown on everything to be able to walk home through the dusk that was full of the smell of the grass and the honeysuckle, with the nightjar singing incessantly in the bracken. The skin would be stinging where the sun and salt water had flayed it, but a glass of cold water before going to bed tasted marvellous, and the white sheets would be smooth and wholesome.

I have talked quite a bit about my friends, but of course there were many days when I would be on my own, since I was my parents' only child. But I did not feel myself to be lonely. I delighted in the open air, and often I would be out in the fields before dawn so as to have a few hours of pleasure before going to school. The feat was getting up and sneaking out without waking my mother who was herself quite a light sleeper. There was perfect freedom for me to go out, but had she woken, she would have tried to persuade me to go back to my bed, to have a bite to eat first, to wrap up warmly and so on. So, just as with stealing fruit, there was more pleasure to be had from escaping without anyone knowing, and returning by breakfast-time with a host of fascinating experiences – having seen a white stoat, having seen the moon setting over the water, and, towards Snowdon, the sun rising. Having seen; having heard. Very rarely would I walk along the road. I always preferred the other side of the hedge, with the result that my feet were wet far too often because of the dew or the rain. And although I denied this, the fact that I so frequently had a cold proved that it was my mother who was right.

One of the most engaging seasons in Holyhead was the time for gathering mushrooms. And at that time I wasn't the only one who used to get up early. How often I arrived at the cattle-field with the dawn in time to see a dark shadow about to leave the field with a basket full of mushrooms. I was sometimes so determined to be the first there that I would arrive at the field in the dark and have to pick up everything white in order to see whether it was a mushroom or a stone. And yet those early mornings were full of magic and enchantment. Have you ever touched a cold, dewy mushroom, and experienced its fresh smell? And nibbled it? The Welsh name, *caws llyffant*, 'toad cheese', is a good one. It has the taste of mild cheese, similar to Caerphilly cheese; something that disappears in the frying pan, no matter how careful you are.

I have already talked about some of my friends; but how did Rhodri come into my life, I wonder? After I moved to the grammar school, probably. The Penrhos Feilw family was a respectable one, and safe enough for me to make friends of. But Rhodri was from the town. He didn't talk with a pure accent. He wouldn't get up when my mother entered the room. So Rhodri was out of favour. But to me he was like a breath of fresh air from another world. He wasn't one of the riffraff; but wasn't one who was afraid of them, either. To me the riffraff were dreadfully frightening. They would lurk behind the walls and throw stones at me. They would challenge me to fight, and I didn't like that. If my father had had a greater share in my upbringing, it would have been otherwise. He had seen rough days in the old sailing ships, and he knew well how to look after himself. But his days at home were infrequent compared with his days at sea, and so it was my mother who shouldered the task of bringing me up, with consequences that weren't to the riffraff's liking. But Rhodri would run with them like a wolf with its pack. In the winter, when I was safe inside the house, with the curtains drawn against the night, I would hear some unearthly cry from outside, and the sound of feet galloping past. Rhodri and his posse on the trail. I once ventured to ask if I could go out to play. My mother became angry and asked with righteous scorn, 'What? With those?' I never asked again. But I was free to go to and from school with him and even to go for a walk with him, as long as night hadn't fallen. Rhodri opened up a new world for me. His head was full of skirmishes he had seen in the cinema. It was he who taught me that the rows of foxgloves weren't flowers, but wave after wave of Red Indians to be felled with our weapons – stones thrown, by Rhodri at least, with terrifying effect. We would play ball on the way home from school. One day I kicked the ball through the window of a house. I wanted to go to the door to apologise, but Rhodri grabbed my arm. 'Come on, you stupid idiot,' he said; and off we went, our hearts in our mouths. After reaching the street corner, Rhodri stopped to survey the scene. 'No-one in sight,' he said, laughing triumphantly. We pressed on, but poor me! The next day the headmaster comes to the classroom and asks me to go to his room. The cat was out of the bag, and my parents had to pay for the window. But it was poor Rhodri they blamed.

They were very unwilling for me to associate with him, though there was nothing I liked better than being in his company. His conversation was full of descriptions of the beating someone had received at the hands of his hero in a film. These were the days of Tom Mix and his wonder-horse, and I too got permission from time to time to go to see the cowboys and Red Indians pursuing each other across the plain. There was one cinema where they continued to show silent pictures when films with sound had come to the other cinemas. There was a piano there, and I can still see the pianist playing the instrument at full pelt by the weak light of the film and hear the notes getting faster and faster as the Indians overtook the wagon in which the blonde heroine was travelling. I can also hear the deafening applause of the town boys as the hero pushed the baddy over the precipice. And to close the film, there was the heroine waiting for him under a tree, wreathed in smiles. It was Rhodri, no doubt, who drew my attention to the girls. Sometimes one of his friends would join us for a walk. I would see them turning to look after some girl we had just passed and then starting to grin inanely and whisper to each other. 'Why didn't you talk to her?' they would ask. 'She was smiling at you.' To me, it was a terrifying idea. I was too shy to look at a girl, let alone talk to her. And yet, the little armed god was waiting for me.

There was another house out in the country, with a host of children, boys and girls. My mother would call there occasionally. One day we were there and, while my mother was talking to the woman of the house, one of the girls took me to one side and started to chat in a very friendly way about this and that. Gradually, I lost my shyness and began for the first time to bask in female company. I walked home with my mother like a person in a dream. The world had been transformed. I went to sleep seeing two black eyes beaming at me and hearing a soft voice tinkling. The little god's arrow was lodged fast in my heart. There was nothing that would do after that except walking the road, hoping to meet her by accident. Morning and afternoon during the holidays I was to be seen on my travels past her house. But I didn't succeed in meeting her. In the end there was nothing for it but to take a chance. I went through the gate to the door and knocked, trembling inwardly. A maid came to the door and told me that the family were in the orchard. Having gone there I found that the three girls were there with their father who had been ill. I was welcomed in a friendly and natural way, and I sat with them under the apple trees, with the bees humming and the birds singing and the long hot golden summer lengthening around us. How heavenly! I wanted never to leave there. It was enough just to sit and be able to listen to their melodious voices, glancing from time to time at my sweetheart. Also from time to time I said something, to show how extraordinarily daring I was. It speaks volumes for that genial man that he was kind enough to ask the silly idiot to stay to tea with them! And so it was for some months while the fever lasted. The beaches empty; the fields forgotten. There was but one road to travel along. If I went to the beach at all, it was only to write her name in the sand! I don't know how the matter came to an end – if it came to an end at all, since some hold that your first love remains with you throughout your life. Certainly, there was no quarrel, no disagreement. It gradually receded from my mind, and its place was taken by other things – sport in particular.

My father was a good cricketer, and I took after him. If you like nature, you can also like cricket, county cricket, I mean – the fine weather, the smell of the grass, and the sound of the wind murmuring in the trees. I wasn't as good a footballer. I was a fast runner, and I covered a lot of ground, but somehow the ball wouldn't do what I wanted it to do. I didn't keep my place in any team for long. But it was otherwise with rugby. This was the time when a rugby club was formed in the town, and I soon joined it. In this game speed is an advantage, of course. You have only to grab hold of the ball and away you go! But the drawback of it is this, as you know – if you have a swift winger, you have to work the ball out to him. But without a good centre, all is in vain. Being on either wing with Holyhead's team was pure idleness. And idleness leads to cold feet! If you want to be at your best in rugby, you have to warm the blood. I didn't develop into a good rugby player either. Something like cold feet always stayed with me, and after a short spell with the college's second fifteen, I retired and returned to my old habit of going for a long walk in the country, to gaze at the beauty of nature and to entertain the empty, prolonged thoughts of youth.

Time passed. The time arrived for me to leave Holyhead and take my place in the world. During my period in the theological college in Llandaff, I used to travel home on the train from Cardiff. As is commonly known, the line from Cardiff to Shrewsbury runs along the Marches, with the plains of England on the one side and the hill-country of Wales on the other. I was often stirred on seeing these hills rising in the west. Sometimes night would start to fall before we reached Ludlow. Westwards the sky would be ablaze, reminding one of the battles of the past. Against that radiance the hills rose dark and threatening as if full of armed men waiting for a chance to attack. To the west, therefore, there was a romantic, dangerous, mysterious land. But having reached home the thing would disappear from my mind for a while. At home there was an English-language life to be lived and work to be done for the next college term.

Having been curate of Chirk, between Wrexham and Oswestry, for four years, I decided to get married. The vicar did not want a curate who was married, therefore somewhere else to live had to be found. There was a charge in Maelor Saesneg that was vacant at the time, and since there was a suitable house, it was there that we went, in effect to the heart of the English plains – that part of Flintshire between Wrexham and Cheshire. And from there, some fifteen miles away, I saw at dusk the hills of Wales rising, telling as before of enchanting and mysterious things. I realised what I had done. That was not my place, on the plain amongst Welshmen with English accents and attitudes. I set about learning Welsh, in order to be able to return to the true Wales of my imagination. I progressed slowly, too slowly to be ready for a Welsh-speaking parish. I tried for two parishes, but the vicars refused to help me. I carried on, going to Llangollen every week to Iorwerth Roberts, to receive an hour's lesson from him. But there was no-one for me to talk to all week long, and progress was still slow. But within two years Manafon, a rural parish in Montgomeryshire, became vacant, and it was there to the rectory, on the bank of the river Rhiw, that we went. Welsh wasn't to be heard in Manafon either, but the place was in the heart of the hills, and when the floods came down from the moorland and the clouds flew past, I really felt that I had come back to Wales.

Manafon was an eye-opener for me. It was here that I became conscious of the conflict that exists between dream and reality. I was a little bourgeois, well-bred, with the mark of the church and library upon me. I had seen this tract of country from the train at dusk through romantic spectacles. I now found myself amongst tough, materialistic, hard-working people, who measured one another by the acre and by the pound; Welshmen who had turned their backs on their cultural inheritance and gone to trade in Welshpool and Oswestry and Shrewsbury; farmers of the cold, bare slopes who dreamed of gathering enough money to move to a more fertile farm on the plains. And yet it was an old-fashioned area to some extent. When I went there in 1942 there wasn't a single tractor in the place. The men worked with their hands, hoeing, shearing, gathering hay and cutting the hedges. The horse was still in high esteem. There was a smithy there; I can still hear the clang of the anvil and see the sparks flying. I remember the solitary beings in the fields hoeing or docking swedes, hour after hour. What was in their minds, I wonder? The question remains unanswered to this day.

Manafon was in a hollow. There was no village there, only a church, a school, a shop and a public house, and the surrounding hills rose to somewhere over a thousand feet. From the summit of the hills there were stunning views. Far to the north-west Cadair Idris was to be seen, to the north Aran Fawddwy and Aran Benllyn with Y Berwyn farther to the east. On a clear day Wales lay beneath your feet like a table set for your pleasure. If Anglesey is a place from which to see Arfon, the hill-country of Montgomeryshire is certainly a platform from which to see the splendour of Merionethshire.

Four miles up the valley on the edge of the moorland there was a chapel where Welsh was the main language of the congregation. I called on the minister and asked him to help me with the language. This was the Reverend D. T. Davies and I was given a welcome in his home. I struggled on. Sometimes after a meeting or a Whist Drive in Manafon, I would hear some of the people standing in the darkness and speaking Welsh, and I knew that they had come down from the smallholdings around Yr Adfa and Cefn Coch. I thought of them returning to their homes on the edge of the moorland. The dream was resurrected for a while, and the following day I would go for a long walk on that moorland and would meet some sheep-farmer tending his flock. Then venturing a word or two in Welsh, but thereafter having to slip back into English. Had I been able to speak Welsh when I went to Manafon, it would have been easier to entice them to use it, because many of them could still speak the language. Every farm and every family had a Welsh name, but most of the people had a Shropshire accent with a very strange admixture of Welsh idioms. But for someone who had an interest in language and who had to express himself through the medium of English, it was a treat to be able to listen to them sometimes. It was about the land and the livestock and the seasons that they would talk, and it was from them that I heard for the first time the coarse but beautiful words of the English farmer. It was also from them that I began to learn the facts of country life, so to speak. Their standards were simple and transparent. Man was there to do good work on the land. If the hay was ready to be carried in, it had to be gathered without delay. It was imperative that they tend the animals, for the sake of the profit that came from doing so. There wasn't a jot of tenderness or sentiment in it. If a lamb died, there was nothing for it but to fling it into the hedge for the crows to eat their fill of it. Religion was a matter for Sundays. And if there was an excuse for not going to church because a cow was calving, all the better. It was more convenient and more pleasurable perhaps to tend the sheep on Sunday morning, and by the evening the women were left to go to the service while the men stayed at home in case, you know, something should happen. But they were keen skilful workers. It was worth seeing their hedges mended or pleached. And because the farms were on the slopes of the valley, it was obvious to everyone how his neighbour was shaping up. 'Jones, Llwyn Copa, has planted his potatoes.' 'Ffinnant have tilled their five-acre field well.' Woe to him who bungled his work. The mess was plain for all to see. This interest in one another's work and affairs was innate. I would often be amazed at how good their eyes were. As I would be leaving the doorway of some farm, the woman of the house would say, 'Ho, Meri, Tŷ Brith, has already done her washing.' I would look to where she was pointing, and then, about a mile or two on the other side of the valley, I would see a row of clothes the same size as daisies. When someone went round to collect money for a good cause, they would scrutinise his collection book to see how much so-and-so had contributed. If a farmer with a hundred acres had given ten shillings, a farmer with fifty acres would give five. It was as simple as that.

There was bad feeling abroad in the parish: old enmities still existed, destroying the social life of the place; some dispute having arisen about someone's will, or someone having transgressed by design or by accident against someone else; and the trouble was often worse between members of the same family. Because of this it was impossible to hold some events, since if one family knew that members of the other family were likely to be present, they would not go there. It was also a strange parish in which to move about at night. Without either moon or stars it would be as black as a cow's belly sometimes, and if you passed someone or heard a small group talking quietly close to the hedge, there was no point in saying, 'Good night.' You wouldn't get a reply. It was as if you were back in the old days of the border battles, with the same old suspicion as alive as ever. And yet, I personally received great kindness from them. One of the mysteries of the place to me was why they were so unwilling to give money to any cause, including the Church, and yet willing to give me butter and eggs and farm produce. They were very pleased to see you in the evenings. It was there that I learned that it was no good visiting anyone except the sick during the day. From dawn till dusk there was endless work to be done on the farm. But after doing the milking, and feeding every animal, and cooping the hens, and washing, and making up the fire, they were ready to welcome you, and your wife with you if that were possible. After the birth of my son, it was impossible to get them to understand why we did not bring him with us, since their children were allowed to stay up until they themselves went to bed. I soon learned that there was no purpose in talking much about religion and things like that. The farm and personal life and old memories and the weather – those were the topics. Then at an appointed time, after a great deal of bustling on the part of the women, there came the formal, almost abrupt command: Come to the table. And for us at least, what a feast. Home-produced meat, home-baked bread, home-made butter, apple pie with a quarter of a pint of cream over it. And then turning back to the log fire on the open hearth, with the women yearning for a modern, ugly grate and us trying to persuade them otherwise. It was lovely sitting in front of the fire with its ribbons of flame, without the responsibility of having to feed and clean such a monster. Manafon was pretty primitive in those days. There was no water in the farmhouses, no electricity, no telephone. It was oil lamps that we too used in the rectory, and we got our water from the field on the other side of the river. The well would dry up in the summer and the supply to the house would cease. In the winter the pipe would freeze, and we would be back in the same situation. But what was lovely was to leave the farms after an entertaining and friendly evening, and emerge beneath the stars with only the sound of the river below us as we descended into the valley. After the light indoors it sometimes wasn't easy to find the path, and the farmer would insist on escorting us with his lantern. They were the same lamps we would see when the ewes were lambing in March. One night my predecessor lost his way completely, and after groping around for a quarter of an hour he went back to the farm for help.

It was in Manafon that I came to see the gap between town and country. Pavements and macadam constitute the environment of the town dweller, but fields and mud and dirt are the lot of the country-man. There was a smallholding on top of the hill, a long way from any track, let alone a road. The farmer there fell ill, and his cousin from Shrewsbury came to see him. She turned up in the village one evening in a fur coat and high heels, with a large, heavy bag. The shopkeeper didn't know what to do with her. 'This lady wants to go to Y Waun,' he said. 'I can't take her. Can you?' I agreed, and off we went over the wet fields and up the muddy track. The mud became worse and the lady more and more out of breath. I had to slow down considerably, even though it was I who was carrying her bag. Her shoes and stockings were covered with dirt. She was completely unfitted to venture into the country. I don't know if that journey was enough to prepare her for what awaited her. Most probably there would be hens under the table, and perhaps a little lamb in a box by the fire rubbing noses with a cat, with the lamp smoking and making a noise and a teapot full of strong tea stewing on the hob.

I said that the weather was everything in Holyhead. This was true to some extent in Manafon as well. It is true of the countryside in general, I think. One lives according to the seasons there. And of course, there is more variety to be had there than by the sea. The winters were very hard in Manafon. If there was snow about, we were sure to get it. In the great winter of 1947 we had the lane from the house to the main road filled with snow and we were unable to get the car out for nine weeks. Some nights it would freeze hard and one night that winter we had forty-two degrees of frost. I remember hearing the house cracking as the ice took hold, and by the morning it was impossible to see through the window, so thick were the ferns of ice on it. Oh, how we would welcome the spring after such a winter, with the trees starting to bud and the trout back in their habitual places in the limpid river. And then after a long and warm summer, behold the leaves starting to change colour, and for two months the valley would be like fairyland, the cherry trees crimson and the ash trees yellow. There was a large ash tree at the entrance to the rectory lane that would be completely yellow by November. One autumn the leaves remained on it longer than usual. But there came a great frost one night, and the following day, as the sun rose, the leaves began to fall. They continued to fall for hours until the tree was like a golden fountain playing silently in the sun; I shall never forget it.

And when the autumn came the foxes would begin to bark and the men would go after them. It was a very strange kind of hunting that existed in Manafon and the surrounding area. No horses, of course. The countryside was too mountainous. No, it was hunting on foot, until they lost the trail and the dogs, and wandered for hours in the dusk. Very often I heard the horn sounding out loudly on the hillsides about nine o'clock at night, as the huntsmen searched for their dogs. There was something odd about it all, as if the little people were busy hunting imaginary foxes amongst the clouds. And what a place for owls! On quiet nights of the full moon, the whole valley would be full of the cries of the owls, as if they had come there to hold an *eisteddfod* – which brings me back to the Welsh language. The minister of Yr Adfa left the area, and I was without a teacher once again. But mercifully I came into contact with the Reverend H. D. Owen of Penarth chapel, on top of the hill between Manafon and Llanfair Caereinion, and he and his wife Megan gave me a warm welcome in their home. It is mainly to them that I am indebted for being able to speak the language now. Progress was slow because of a lack of people to talk to, and you cannot take too much advantage of someone's hospitality. But every week for years I imposed myself on this kind family, and gradually I came to speak with less hesitancy and stammering. The first test came when it was arranged for me to give a talk to members of the chapel. I remember the evening: the chapel with its oil lamps, the wind blowing outside, and some twenty local farmers and their wives assembled to listen to that oddity – an Englishman who had learned Welsh. Mr Owen introduced me, asking the audience not to laugh if I made a mistake. Then off I went for about three-quarters of an hour like a ship driven in all directions by the wind. Somehow or other I reached dry land, and after a little discussion everyone went home. I myself walked home under the stars, murmuring some of the old *penillion telyn* over and over, whilst the wind answered me in the hedges. A few days later I met someone who had been in the audience that night. 'I was impressed, honestly,' he said, referring to my performance. I went on my way, somewhat doubtful. What did he mean, I wonder?

The odd thing about Manafon was that it appeared so Welsh even though the language was no longer there. It is true that the patrons of the public house at fair time went home late at night bellowing Welsh hymns abroad. But it was only on certain occasions that they used Welsh. It had disappeared from the village school since before the turn of the century, although it remained for a bit longer in the parish church. And of course, this was the old parish of Gwallter Mechain and Penfro and Ieuan Brydydd Hir, brilliant Welshmen, every one of them. It was this perhaps, and the peaty river flowing past, that gave a Welsh appearance to the area. It would often come to my mind as I listened to the sound of the river at night, how many rectors had done the same thing before me, for Manafon was an old parish, with the registers going back to the fifteenth century. Indeed, the early records were in Latin, before turning not to Welsh but to English. And even in the days of distinguished Welshmen like Gwallter Mechain, English was the language of all the records. Some of Man-afon's rectors were quite well known in their day, but the parishioners' memories of them were amusing. That Gwallter Mechain, for instance: Walter Davies to them. Although he was a poet and an *eisteddfodwr* of renown and an authoritative writer on agriculture, his reputation in Manafon in my time was as a conjurer. The old men of the parish liked to tell me how he put a man to stand on a stone in the river all night to repent of some wrong he had committed. But when I used to see the full moon rising yellow above Cae Siencyn, I preferred to remember my distant predecessor as the author of what is in the opinion of many the most perfect *englyn* in the Welsh language:

> Y *nos dywell yn distewi, – caddug*
> Yn cuddio Eryri,
> Yr haul yng ngwely'r heli,
> A'r lloer yn ariannu'r lli.

> The night darkening silently, – the mist
> Enshrouding Eryri,
> The sun set in its briny
> Bed, the moon silvering the sea.

THE
CREATIVE WRITER'S
SUICIDE

THE CREATIVE WRITER'S SUICIDE

In his book, *The Present Age*, Kierkegaard asked a profound and important question: does man have a right to let himself be killed for the sake of the truth? For Kierkegaard there were, as you know, three stages in the development of the personality, the aesthetic, the moral and the religious, and in accordance with this belief he gave up, early on in his career, any talent that he possessed for writing poetry, lest it should stand between him and the religious life. And because he asked this question in a religious context, it is obvious that it is not fitting for me to discuss it specifically today.* It is enough to say that he linked the question to the crucifixion of Jesus Christ. Because Christ was divine, was it right for him to allow the Jews to be guilty of killing him? God forbid that I should be guilty of blasphemy, but I should like to use Kierkegaard's question as a background to this little talk.

But having avoided the task of speaking as a theologian, it would be every bit as easy for me to succumb to the temptation of speaking as a philosopher by pursuing the word 'truth'. But we are all familiar with Pontius Pilate's contemptuous question. It is better, therefore, to let the philosophers ponder that one. And yet, although I am not myself much of a philosopher, I will say one thing, acknowledging the *petitio principii*: every person must pursue the type of truth that is true for him. This is not to deny that there is one basic truth; it means rather that there is one truth for the biologist, another for the economist, another for the creative writer, and so on. Are these aspects of the same basic truth? I cannot answer. But for a few minutes this afternoon, let us focus on the creative writer and ask, to begin with, what is the truth for him?

The answer, I believe, is that there is a level of excellence that he must aim for, come what may. His duty, his function, that which justifies his existence, is to exercise every literary talent he has in order to create a masterpiece in words, and with words. That is the truth for him. And

* 'The Creative Writer's Suicide' was delivered as a lecture at the Annual Rally of the Department of Continuing Education of the University of Wales, Aberystwyth, June 1977.

in pursuit of this truth he is prepared to expend all his resources even so far as to exhaust himself.

That is how I would tend to answer the question of members of the public who are always so eager to know how a poem is made – whether it is with the aid of inspiration, or after hours of difficult toil. It is true, of course, that different creative writers work in different ways, and that it is not every author who is willing to divulge his secret. Indeed, a writer can on occasion be quite whimsical in answering. If it is suggested that writing well is mainly a matter of inspiration, his tendency will be to emphasise the difficult toil. If the opposite is suggested, that some poem has caused him much effort, he will pooh-pooh the idea in order to show himself to be an inspired man. I do not for a moment wish to deny that there is such a thing as inspiration to help the author to write better from time to time. But we have also the testimony of many an honest writer to the hard work that is indispensable in the service of the muse. This is sometimes allowed to go to extremes, as in the case of Flaubert who would choose a new piece of paper for every sentence. Paper was, very likely, somewhat cheaper in those days. But we know also of the scores of versions of the same poem that a poet like Yeats would make, not to mention many other lesser-known poets. Yet, a true artist is prepared to endure all this, as long as he is given freedom to practise his craft. The only question that may arise here is: how free has he ever been?

This brings us to the pressure that there is, and that there has been over the centuries, on the creative writer. Kierkegaard's definition of a poet was that he is one who suffers. It is in his anguish that he opens his mouth, but the sound that comes out is so sweet to the ears of his listeners that they press him to sing again; that is, to suffer further.

Here we see the first temptation for a creative writer to commit suicide – by writing the kind of thing that pleases the public, rather than what he wants to write, in order to win prizes or acclaim. Who does not know about the old tricks an author is willing to play for the sake of the acclaim he will receive, until he loses every last grain of the originality that once belonged to him? And yet this, too, is a moot point, because if he is great enough, he will succeed in creating a masterpiece, while at the same time still pleasing the public, as Shakespeare did in his plays, and as the Welsh *cywyddwyr* succeeded in doing in their petitionary *cywyddau*. It is a matter of how intelligent and cultured the public is. Where such a public is to be had, it is possible for a creative writer to make a living and remain an artist of stature at the same time.

Where these conditions are not fulfilled, the only choice that remains for him is to make his money in another way, following the muse in his spare time, or to commit suicide as a creative writer.

But so far I have been generalising, taking it for granted that the circumstances remain more or less similar in every country, and that every creative writer is a member of an independent nation that has its own language, and that that language is responsive enough to every demand he makes upon it. But what is the situation in Wales? You know as well as I do, or you should know. This diabolical bilingualism! Oh, I know about all the arguments in its favour: how it enriches the personality, sharpens the mind, enables one to have the best of both worlds, and so on. Very likely. But to someone in Wales who has set his mind on being a creative writer, it is a millstone around his neck. That is to say, I am of the same opinion as those others who claim that it is from a one-language nation that the best literature comes. It is true that there are still creative writers in Wales who are lucky enough to have Welsh as their mother tongue, but they, too, are under pressure. There is not one of them who cannot speak English. In today's technological, industrial world, it could be argued that English is a richer language, a language more responsive than Welsh to the thousands of demands made upon it. Welsh is making a worthy job of it. But what Welshman has not blushed on discovering that so many words he had thought were Welsh are in truth derived from English? What Welshman is not ashamed to see the number of English words that daily settle in our language? Consider the *englynion* and the jokes that rely on an English word for their punch lines. Welsh abounds with them. If he were honest, what Welsh creative writer would not admit to having been tempted to write in English for some reason or other? And if he were to yield, this would be another example of suicide. But he need not lose heart. It is natural science, technology, and the other sciences that are responsible for most of the new English words that have to be translated into Welsh; but precisely because of this growing number, even the English poets have not as yet succeeded in creating much important poetry out of them. And I am doubtful whether they will succeed, either.

Nevertheless, that is not the only temptation for the creative writer in Welsh, nor the worst. Welsh culture, which to a great extent is inseparable from the Welsh language, is in mortal danger, as you know. In order to save that culture, an author is under pressure to write books and to contribute articles which are not the best work he can produce. But by so doing he may congratulate himself that he is a means of saving his nation from death, while at the same time busy committing suicide as a real creative writer. This is a problem peculiar to a small nation in a period of crisis because, in such a nation, it is amongst those who are most intelligent and most aware of what is happening that creative writers are to be found. It is they, therefore, who are in tune with the true need of the nation. This can lead to sitting on committees and travelling and making speeches and the like: honourable work, but not the work of a creative writer; for one thing, because it takes up his time, the most priceless thing he has. How many promising creative writers in Wales have committed literary suicide or impaired their true talent by choosing to respond to these demands rather than to the requirements of their craft? We were warned years ago by Saunders Lewis that we should expect from the creative writer or the scholar something different from what everyone else can give us.

Well, all this is true enough, and sad enough, but when we come to the Anglo-Welsh, as they are called – for the sake of convenience only, remember – the situation is a hundred times worse. An Anglo-Welsh writer is neither one thing nor the other. He subsists in no-man's-land between two cultures. For various reasons, he has to write in English. So, whatever is said to the contrary, he is contributing to English culture, and deserves the rebuke of his fellow Welshmen on that account. If he endeavours to make his work more Welsh he incurs the hostility or lack of interest of his English readers. There is no means of avoiding the former, and to surmount the latter countless footnotes must be employed – like those found in the work of David Jones – which destroy the effect, especially if the piece is a poem. Woe is me that I was born! Who is wounded, and I am not wounded? For I bear in my body the marks of this battle. Who in fact is this wretched Anglo-Welshman, except one who knows that he is Welsh, or who wishes to think of himself as such, but who is continually conscious that he speaks a foreign language? A North Walian is perhaps more conscious of this than the South Walian who hears English around him every hour of the day and every day of the week. A foreign language! Yes. Let no-one think that because there is so much English everywhere in Wales it is not a foreign language. Should it not strike more and more of us as an abomination that people whose names are Morgan and Megan and who live in houses called Nant y Grisial or Y Gelli speak English and are being conditioned to think like Englishmen? Aberdaron has its weaknesses, but it is completely natural, while I am chatting to one of the smallholders there, for me to hear him turn to his little girl and say,

'*Buddug, dos i nôl yr oen bach 'na*' ('Buddug, go and fetch that little lamb'). Yes indeed, if the Anglo-Welsh writer is honest with himself, he will have to admit that it is in a foreign language that he writes. If he is a true Welshman and one who is in tune with the spirit and traditions of his own country and nation, there will come the desire to learn the old language in order to reclaim his birthright. Very good! But that is not the end of the matter. There then comes the desire to write in Welsh, to prove to himself and to the public that he is a true Welshman. Vanity of vanities. There are examples of authors who have written prose of quality in a foreign language, as Conrad did. But where are the poets who have composed truly great poems in a foreign language? If an Anglo-Welshman was not fortunate enough to have Welsh as his second language when he was young enough, and to be able to live in a truly Welsh area, he will never become as good a writer in that language as he could be in English. And yet, the tempter is extremely cunning, one who can speak with a persuasive voice by showing how morally right the sacrifice is. But what has morality to do with inspired literature?

But let that be. An Anglo-Welshman who has experienced something of the virtue of English as a medium for poetry is hardly ever likely to yield to this temptation to commit suicide. The English language does its work thoroughly. Thanks to his upbringing, the Anglo-Welshman will prefer English literature. Speaking personally for a moment, I must confess, for example, that I cannot get much pleasure from *vers libre* in Welsh. Is Welsh as suited as English to that form, or is this some deficiency in me? Be that as may be, because the English language is in his subconscious, as it were, an Anglo-Welshman has an instinct that enables him to be self-critical while writing in that language. But in trying to write in Welsh he is unsure of himself and therefore dependent on others for criticism and correction. I believe it is too often forgotten that self-criticism is part of the creative process and that someone who is unable to do this thoroughly and directly is certain to fail as a creative writer, and more so as a poet. That is my main reason for not writing poetry in Welsh. Because I was thirty years old before I started to learn Welsh seriously, and as I did not have the privilege of being brought up in a Welsh environment, I possess neither the instinct nor the confidence that are indispensable to one who is bent on using language in the most skilful way possible, namely to write a poem. I have therefore refused to commit suicide as a writer. But if you must have an adjective to go with the word 'writer', it pains me to answer you. I have tried to steep myself in the history and traditions of Wales, but I am very conscious of the way in which today's cosmopolitan world has shattered those traditions. Yet I am equally conscious of the danger of a small nation congratulating its writers for the sole reason that they write in the mother tongue. Please forgive the Anglo-Welsh if they are able to see this more clearly than the Welsh themselves.

And yet, all this is in fact idle talk. In the Wales of today, there is no literary answer to the literary problem. The crisis that troubles the nation is caused by political pressure; it must therefore be solved politically. If you have kept Kierkegaard's question is mind while I have been speaking, you will have seen its relevance. He asked how could Jesus Christ allow the Jews to be guilty, so to speak, of his suicide. I, too, often ask myself: how can the Welsh be so heedless? How can they put up with circumstances that make it necessary for their creative writers to commit suicide? Every civilised nation takes pride in its writers. If a creative writer is to be tempted to commit suicide, the pressure to do so should arise from within him and not from without.

NO-ONE

NO-ONE

Et de ce néant indestructible qui est moi

Paul Claudel

Man is a prolific being; he has covered the face of the earth. Why fear barrenness, then? This very minute women are giving birth in every corner of the world. It was so in Cardiff on 29 March 1913; one birth among thousands. An addition to the pain of the world; a woman groaning and then a baby crying, and continuing to cry for a long time. There are diseases in this world, and little children fall prey to them. Meningitis! There are pictures showing a child who is not all there. But his clothes are pretty.

How far back can one remember? There was a door and a small child playing near it. Something happened. It was opened too suddenly by the maid. An arm was broken. There is a memory of the baby in someone's lap, and others around them making a fuss. The memory remains; the pain has disappeared. Then silence. If he did exist, where was he? According to the calendar, war came. The father was away at sea. He was followed by his young wife from port to port. The child would be ill sometimes. Doctors came into being; nasty men who would push a spoon down the throat. The child would hide behind the curtains. In vain. This was a port that had not been discovered by the Germans. But later, one night in Liverpool in the bedroom, with the mother preparing to go to bed, lo, the gas flame reduced to nothing, nothing but a blue spot in the glass sphere. The next day there was talk of a German zeppelin which had come very close to the city the previous night. In the absence of understanding, there is no fear.

But there was fun to be had, as well. The father's ship would sometimes come alongside the quay. The child would have to be taken aboard, and would be placed to sleep in his father's cabin. Ugh! Cockroaches! And the parents far away, enjoying themselves. It was in this way that fear became a part of his experience. And yet, there would be kind faces in the doorway from time to time, members of the ship's crew popping in to make sure he was all right. How can a child make adults understand the full terror of cockroaches?

Stories began to furnish his mind. His mother would read tales to him in bed. Princes and princesses became part of his imagination, along with dragons and giants. How a giant can snore! He would wake in the middle of the night to the sound of a giant snoring until the house was full of it. And it was in this way that the nightmares started. One night when he was older, a gorilla came to his bedroom. As it came through the door the boy jumped out of bed, screaming. His parents found him on the floor.

Liverpool was a strange town for a child, with two smells to it, the smell of beer and the smell of the docks. A smell can take you back further than anything else. To this very day the scent of lilac takes him back to one of the parks. One day he bent over to smell a bunch of pink flowers. But woe to him! A little black fly got into his nose, almost into his brain! He was frightened through and through and ran screaming to look for his mother. Isn't the world nasty to a little boy? Why did a much older boy have to attack him and hit him? Was it a symbol of the hatred of the crowd towards a coward and a budding poet? But others besides him would cry in Liverpool. Because of the proximity of the river Mersey the sound of the ships was often to be heard, and as if he were trying to imitate them he would sometimes have a bout of coughing that sounded very similar to a ship's horn. As Cilgwri was so close his mother would take him over the river in the ferry-boat to places like New Brighton and Hoylake. As the passengers came from the ship along the quayside in New Brighton, a one-legged man would climb a long ladder and dive down into the water after the pennies thrown for him by the crowd. Later on he would come to know of the things some people have to do in order to entertain others, such as putting their heads in the mouths of lions, or risking their lives walking tightropes far above other people.

How does memory work? It keeps hold of some things, while letting other things go to oblivion. It is one thing that remains. One day on the beach at Hoylake his father directed his attention to a row of mountains far away over the sea to the west. 'That's Wales,' he said, in English.

In what order did things happen to the boy in question? The timetable is uncertain. He is here; he is there. But when, nobody knows. He is in London watching the trains go by. Suddenly everything stops. He is too young to realise that this is the first anniversary of the armistice after the First World War. For some reason he is with his uncle in front of Wandsworth jail. There is a large crowd and the police on their horses. Why? He is in Cardiff, in Whitchurch. It appears that his father is playing cricket, because he comes to him and his mother in white clothes. Again in Whitchurch the boy boasts that he can run faster than a car. He is out with his aunt; a car comes past. The boy starts to run, but he is left far behind by the car. No matter; his faith is not shaken. His bubble isn't burst. He is in Goole in Yorkshire. His father is sailing between Goole and Antwerp. He is unwell here for weeks because of some unidentified illness. The memory he has of Goole is the memory of a river flowing between banks that were all mud. But there were farms nearby. They would go to them to have tea in the orchards. The only trouble were the wasps that would come after the cakes and try to settle on his hands. The others took no notice of them, but the wasps succeeded in ruining the pleasure of the afternoon for the nervous boy.

It was his father's work as a sailor that was the reason for the shifting from place to place. It was that work which in time brought the family to Holyhead, to settle there for the rest of their lives, even though his father did not like the place. He would still talk of his boyhood in Llandysul, Cardiganshire, where he would fish in the river Teifi with his back against one of the gravestones in the cemetery. At the time, the family ran the Porth Hotel in that town, but that did not last long. The father died comparatively young, leaving eleven children behind. It isn't surprising that the sons had to go to sea. Their father went round the world many times in the old sailing ships, and though he climbed the masts without falling, he had a terrible fall in Romania when he fell into the hold while the ship was at the quayside. This meant that he was in a hospital in the town for eighteen weeks, with no-one there able to understand English.

The family arrived in Holyhead immediately before Christmas, and three months later the boy celebrated his sixth birthday. He wasn't able to go to school because of some unidentified illness again, but he was left alone by the authorities because of his mother's promise that she would see to his education! He was certainly taught how to read and write by her, and in a year or two he was ready to go to some kind of school where the 'nice' people of the town sent their children.

What does Holyhead stand for? For the sea, of course, as it is an island, Ynys Gybi, Holy Island. Even though it is only a strip of water that makes it an island, the sea is still close enough and plays an important part in the lives of its people. There was a good harbour there, and before a storm it would fill with sailing ships of all kinds, until it was more like a forest. The sea became part of the child's life also, its noise, its smell, its ferocity on windy days. It was to be seen from his bedroom. At night the flashes from the lighthouse would dart through his room like the sails of a windmill. There would always be someone gazing at the sea, as if he were expecting something to happen. These were old sailors, their sailing days gone by. But there were also young men, waiting for their chance to go to the aid of a ship in trouble. There was a lifeboat, but the young men would be out in their small boats long before it was launched. In stormy weather, when the ship from Ireland was late, a fit of apprehension would seize the town, that wouldn't pass until the sound of the ship's horn, announcing that she had arrived safely, was heard. Sometimes his mother would see his father off, and while they stood on the quay the captain would call from the bridge, pretending to offer to take the boy with them. All this went on around the harbour and the docks, but there was another side to the island too, where there were only a few farms and scattered houses. In that area, there was one particular family, and the boy became close friends with the children. The mother was a widow, with two sons and a daughter. The house, Bryn Awel, came to mean something very special to him. He would love going there to play and sometimes to stay overnight with them. He would listen to the wind singing fiercely around the house, and first thing in the morning would slink from his bed to gaze at the white waves of the sea about a quarter of a mile away. Because he was in school by this time, there was nothing he liked better than to accompany his new friends on their way home, especially in the autumn when the sun was setting, the air chilly, and their heads full of plans for Guy Fawkes. Days in advance they would gather sticks and boxes and wood to make an enormous bonfire for old Guy. Oh, how he would look forward to that day, with its fireworks and the chance to be out in the dark, out of the sight and care of his parents. And then back to the house to have fun with the apples hanging from the rafters. And best of all, of course, the journey home under the stars, with the gorse creaking in the wind enough to turn the blood to ice, because memories of Hallowe'en and its ghosts were still within the recall of some of the old people. To a sensitive boy, ghosts were real enough – and how else is it possible to explain something that happened later?

It was winter, and though Holyhead was quite a mild place, a pond on the mountain had frozen over, with some snow around it. The three of them were there late in the afternoon, with night beginning to fall. In the middle of the pond there was a small patch that had not frozen. Two of them were looking down from a bank, with the third out of sight somewhere behind. Suddenly a figure appeared in front of them, running towards the edge of the clear water. The two shouted simultaneously, warning the other to be careful. But the next minute he joined them from an entirely different direction, and at the same time the apparition disappeared. The two would have been willing to agree that it was a dream, were it not for the fact that both of them had shouted simultaneously.

His parents would sometimes want to go out of an evening. 'Will you be all right on your own?' Of course he would. He hated admitting anything different. After they had gone, silence would take possession of the house. Slowly, he would realise that he was on his own. And yet, was he? A house is not a dead thing. It is given to sighing, squeaking and whispering. He would listen. Wasn't there someone upstairs? What was that noise, as of a man breathing? He would go to the bottom of the stairs and turn on the light. And yet the far end of the upstairs was in shadow. He would shout. No answer. He would climb the stairs, step by step, and having reached the top would listen again. Suddenly he would leap forward a step or two, thundering with his feet and shouting: 'Boo!' Nothing. No-one. He would come downstairs with some relief, and begin reading again in front of the fire until his parents came home.

A man's personality is a strange thing. It reveals itself in mysterious ways. From where did the boy get the idea of making an effigy, dressing it and placing it on a chair at the head of the stairs? And when his parents came in, there was the figure waiting for them in the shadows. And of course it was his mother who was the first to climb the stairs and have the shock of her life. Then screams and a great commotion, and his father reading him the riot act for such foolishness. And yet it was all quite innocent. They would have gladly stayed at home, were it not for the fact that he had assured them that he would be all right.

And he was on the whole a happy boy. At least that is what he told himself after reaching adulthood. It was the countryside that made him so. Despite his mother's nervous and anxious nature, he was free to roam the island from earliest morning to sunset. He would gather flowers in the spring, and mushrooms in the autumn. He would climb the rocks and cliffs, gazing long at the sea and listening to the sound of the waves in the caves. There was one cave from which the cry of the seals came like the song of mermaids. There was unadulterated, endless pleasure to be had from being on his own like this. Was he preparing himself to be a poet? How can someone become a poet? From where did the desire to write verses come from? In school he would compose a poem and pass it to his neighbour at the next desk, who, after reading it, would pass it back, whispering, 'Poet Laureate.' Was his neighbour being sarcastic? The budding poet would take the praise as his due.

How did Tennyson become his favourite poet? After winning a school prize and having to choose a book, he asked for a biography of the poet. Tennyson's early poems were full of references to the country-side, even though it was the countryside of England. The boy doted on the descriptions in 'The Lady of Shalott':

> In the stormy east-wind straining,
> The pale yellow woods were waning,
> The broad stream in his banks complaining,
> Heavily the low sky raining
>   Over towered Camelot.

He took Welsh in his first year in secondary school, a subject amongst other subjects. Nothing remained in his memory except one tiny stanza about an apple:

> *Wel, dyma lencyn bochgoch,*
> *er nad oes ganddo ben,*
> *mae'n hardd, mor hardd â brenin*
> *yn hongian ar y pren.*

> Well, here's a red-cheeked fellow,
> though without a head is he,
> he's handsome, handsome as a king,
> hanging on the tree.

Who took Welsh seriously? English was the language of the school except on St David's Day, when a concert would be held instead of lessons, and a play in the town hall in the evening. Many were surprised to learn on such days that a good number of the staff could speak Welsh, although they sounded pretty funny enough to children who were used to hearing them speak *yr iaith fain*, the thin language, English, on all other days. And, of course, the town itself. Was it called Caergybi? Not at all. It was Holyhead, as it is to this day, even in everyday speech. Thus life went on, like a film containing thousands of little events, most of them having vanished into oblivion by now. Here he is crying, having had a beating from a stronger boy. There he is singing at the top of his voice as he sees the waves galloping over the beach on a day of stormy weather, with the spray darting madly in all directions like a flock of seagulls. He is in the cinema; he is on a playing field; he is eyeing a girl without venturing to say a word to her, without touching her as bolder boys would do.

For anyone who lives in Holyhead, the most outstanding views are the mountains of Snowdonia, which stretch from Penmaen-mawr in the east to Bardsey Island in the west, over fifty miles of magnificent mountains, for the inhabitants of Anglesey a daily background. Oh, how the clouds rise in white clusters above their heads, turning golden and then red towards sunset! Then the snow will come in the winter to turn them white, while Anglesey remains green. How the boy would yearn for snow in order to have fun. But it was very rarely that hard weather came to the plains. He would remember the day the train came from London to Holyhead with a heap of snow on top of the carriages like some visitor from a magic land. Not that he wouldn't sometimes leave Holyhead with his mother and see the countryside flooded or under a covering of snow. She had relatives in south Wales, and she would greatly enjoy visiting and being pampered by them, because she was an orphan. The boy did not like the South. He did not feel at ease there. The relatives were Nonconformists, a bit puritanical. For a lively youngster, Sundays would be painful. The family didn't get up until late, but if the boy were seen taking a trivial book to bed to read on Sunday morning, he would be rebuked harshly for not reading the Bible or some other religious book. After two weeks of this he was more than glad to be able to come home to Anglesey. How lovely it was to hear the wind beating at the carriage after they had crossed the Menai Straits, and the climax of the journey was crossing Morfa Malltraeth, because the train would travel faster there than anywhere else.

The days of his boyhood were without end. He would play, he would race, he would go to swim in the sea, to row a boat, to fish. Some days in the summer he and his friends would swim in Porth Gof Du, with not a single living soul there to disturb their merriment. How they would sing as they walked over the heath with their swimming costumes under their arms! They knew exactly how to reach the inlet when the tide had filled it with green translucent water. And then they would play or climb the rocks to get warm. Sometimes when they were sitting on the rocks eating their sandwiches, a boat or two would sail in from Trearddur and stay awhile before heading for home. Occasionally their parents would accompany the boys, making something of a party, and when they had gone home, the lads from the nearby farm would nip down like scavengers to see whether there were any morsels left behind.

It was his friends who had the idea of going to Llanddwyn Island at the other end of Anglesey, but somehow, every time they arranged to go there, it turned out that he couldn't go. The place took on a significance similar to that of the lighthouse in Virginia Woolf's novel, but at last he succeeded in reaching it. That day, not only he and his friends but a crowd of people. While they were having tea amongst the rocks a sailing ship arrived from somewhere, and a bearded man came ashore and asked whether any of them had some tobacco he could have. No-one had any, as not one of them was a smoker, but they somehow felt glad that the man considered them old enough to smoke. That little episode was like something out of a novel about pirates. The boy did not foresee it at the time, of course, but he would revisit Llanddwyn Island more than once in the future.

If he remains at home too long, the desire to move away comes to even the happiest boy. He was offered work in the town by the father of one of his friends, but did not for a minute consider accepting it. Who put it into his head to be a candidate for Holy Orders? He wasn't by any means a regular worshipper in church. Indeed, his mother had the tactless habit of setting off for a walk on Sunday evenings just as the congregation would be making for the church. This embarrassed the boy, as it did when he accompanied his mother there. She would be certain to be late, with the result that they would have to walk the whole length of the church in order to find a seat. He would have fits of blushing during the service, imagining that everyone was staring at him. Indeed, one morning he became ill thinking about it, so that he had to leave. This was a blessing, because he was excused from church for weeks. But who knows in what way a man's fate asserts itself? We are familiar with the story in the Bible about God calling Samuel, and consequently we perhaps think that we must hear God's voice calling fairly clearly, if we are supposed to do a particular thing. But on reflection, of course, it is obvious that choosing a vocation depends on many things.

His mother lost her parents when she was six years old, and was brought up by an aunt and her husband, who was a parish priest. She was sent to a boarding school in England which had an ecclesiastical atmosphere, and as a result she had some attachment to the Church. So when she saw that her son had no strong objection to the idea of being a candidate for Holy Orders she secretly rejoiced and persuaded her husband to agree to the idea. And the son accepted that he would have to start learning Greek and go on to university, and because Bangor was the closest one, that it was there that he would go. All this was quite clear and definite. Now he had to be accepted by the Church in Wales as a candidate, to enable him to sit an examination to secure a grant or scholarship to pay for his higher education. He went down to Lampeter to sit the examination, where he met other boys who were doing the same thing. He would get to know these better at Bangor. He won a scholarship. Who heard of anyone failing? But getting the money was essential, as his parents did not have enough. His father had by now become deaf and had had to give up his work at sea. Be that as it may, the boy would hardly have succeeded in his A-level examination, even, were it not for the headmaster, Derry Evans, a man who possessed an innate gift for teaching Latin. The latter gave him an excellent foundation that enabled him not only to succeed academically, but also to develop into a poet, because of the emphasis on language. Through having to search for the right word to translate the Latin, he learned the need to do so in poetry as well.

But one must be honest: the boy had little interest in books. The open air was his main delight, with sport a very close second. Not that he was outstanding in any game, but he loved playing them, which is half the battle. But however fond he was of nature, no-one told him how fine a place Holyhead was for birds and flowers. It was later on, after his interest in them had deepened and matured, that he came to know about the sea birds that would nest in their thousands on the rocks around South Stack. It was there, later, that the artist Charles Tunnicliffe would come to study the peregrine falcons that nested there. And, had he only known it at the time, it was a splendid place to watch the birds go past in the autumn on their way south. He heard the birds around him unconsciously as it were. It was only later on that he would come to put names to the notes registered in his subconscious. These too would make *hiraeth* well up in him after he had moved far away from the sea. In the meantime he continued to enjoy Holyhead for other reasons, for the opportunity to go swimming in the summer, to go deep into the heart of the countryside on his bicycle and to wander aimlessly for hours in the morning before going to school. He would go to parties in the winter and meet girls there. In the summer his friends from Bryn

Awel liked to arrange parties on the rocks, and on the way home perhaps one of the girls would, with a laugh, take hold of his arm and with a leisurely step walk along with him. But it was the same old shyness that restrained him and none of them became his girlfriend. And, indeed, what did he know about sex? His parents weren't eager to enlighten him, and because he moved in refined circles he heard little about the facts of life. For a nineteen-year-old, all this was in the future and would many times make him a laughing stock, because sex is the greater part of the life and thought of so many people.

But the time came for him to leave Holyhead and head for Bangor as a student at the college. And his mother came with him! On the pretext that she was eager to see that he had good lodgings and so on, she came also to share his first day away from home. But mercifully, because he was totally unknown, the other students did not stand in ranks to make fun of the little baby arriving with his nurse. Those were his feelings at the time. It was later that he would remember how he had returned to the house the previous night and heard the sound of crying upstairs, and the voice of his father trying to silence his wife. Then in bed, after going to sleep, he awoke and felt someone kissing him over and over again. This is how a mother came to realise that she was about to lose the child of whom she had been too possessive. But although she had another day with her son before letting go of him, she had to catch the train back to Holyhead before nightfall, and the boy was left to spend his first night away from home in lodgings that overlooked the river Menai towards Anglesey.

It was October when the university term started, and the day after saying goodbye to his mother he went to the college to be registered, gazing with admiration and shyness at the multi-coloured company of different ages who were there to follow a university course. On the first Saturday night there was a dance to welcome the new arrivals, and he went there, and stood at the far end of the large hall with a group of his fellow students, gazing enviously at the self-confidence of the older students as they whirled around the floor with their partners. How long would it be before he learnt to push an indulgent girl up one end of the hall and down the other, and ask whether he could have the last dance, as an excuse to escort her home to the girls' hostel? The first time he did this he wrote afterwards to his parents to say that he had met a miracle of a girl, even though he had not succeeded even in finding out her name. He joined the rugby team and had the occasional game with the second fifteen, but his fate all along was to be chosen and then dropped, getting to play more often in away matches, because of his willingness to pay for a train ticket. He had no guts, no stomach. By playing on the wing and having to wait a long time sometimes before receiving the ball, he would get cold feet; but if he got to play with the forwards, he would more and more warm to the game and would play better because of it. He attended the lectures and made a half-hearted effort to join one or two of the societies, but his love of the open air remained stronger than anything else.

Bangor and the surrounding area were very different from Holyhead, of course. He recalled the time when he went with his parents for a two-week holiday to Dolwyddelan and Maentwrog on the narrow-gauge line from Llandudno Junction. As the train climbed up the Conwy Valley, and then along the river Lledr past Pont-y-Pant, he rushed from one side of the carriage to the other, marvelling at the beauty and strangeness of the countryside. The trees and waterfalls and the rugged slopes were so different from Holyhead. He had a foretaste of this while playing cricket in Parciau in Anglesey. During the break in play he went to the wood that encircled the field, and heard the wind murmuring in the branches and realised, unconsciously as it were, that there was another kind of natural beauty beyond that of Holyhead. He recaptured the experience in Bangor. One night he went out for a walk to Melin Esgob. There was a full moon and the stream sparkled under its light as it flowed past the narrow-gauge line that led to Llandygái Mountain. After walking for hours he returned to his lodgings with a new feeling of exciting freedom. He did not for a minute consider that the landlady took it for granted that he had been out with a girl.

Then, the mountains. He was by now within reach of the summits he had gazed at from afar throughout his boyhood. Now and again he would take a day off and catch a bus for Abergwyngregyn. Then climb towards Foel Fras and walk along Y Carneddau and down to Bethesda to catch a bus back to Bangor. The first time he did this, after climbing a hillock and seeing the summits in their glory before him, he burst out singing, '*Hen Wlad Fy Nhadau*', 'The Ancient Land of My Fathers', pitching his tiny voice against the majestic mountains around him. Another time, in February, in a spell of unusually warm weather, he climbed the northern slope of Carnedd Llywelyn, drenched in sweat. But after reaching the saddle between Llywelyn and Dafydd he found that the far slope was white with snow and that a freezing wind was blowing towards him, enough to take his very breath away. As he climbed, he had the impression that he was the only living being on the mountains, but after reaching the summit he saw that there were two black dots beneath him struggling up over the deep snow.

Compared with experiences such as these there was something unreal about his attempts to take part in college activities. It was some natural but unhealthy ambition that drove him during the week to look at the notice-board to see whether his name was included in the team that was to play on the following Saturday. Likewise with the girls at the dances. He sometimes asked a girl to come for a walk on a Sunday, but it was obvious that she did not share one grain of his interest in the natural world. Indeed, more than one hinted that a seat in the cinema some evening would be much more acceptable!

'Who does he think he is?' was the murmur he would hear from time to time. But he didn't know who he was. He was no-one. Sometimes during a dance he would go outside and look through the windows at the merry crowd inside, and see it all as something completely unreal. And yet something was stirring in him. He would contribute limp, sentimental poems to the college magazine under a laughably literary pseudonym. One day in the common room he heard the new editor declaring quite clearly that he wouldn't publish anything by this bloody pseudonym. What he did then was to write a poem, get a friend to copy it out in his own handwriting, and send it in under another pseudonym. It was a great if trivial satisfaction that he experienced when the poem appeared in the next issue of the magazine. This was only an introduction to the pettiness of social life when compared with the life of the open air. He was yet to discover Maeterlinck's story, describing how, while descending from a mountain in the Alps, he saw below him a glorious valley under the summer sun. And to crown everything, there was a crowd of people out in the fields harvesting the hay. But as he came within earshot of the people, he found that they were quarrelling amongst themselves, using the dirtiest and most unseemly language. An extremely relevant parable, as the boy later learned.

He had to go into private lodgings during his first year because there wasn't enough room in the old red house that served as a hostel. But by his second year the building was extended and a new wing and a chapel built. There was now room for twenty-one candidates for Holy Orders under the young Warden, Glyn Simon. From this time on, he came under more discipline. Everyone was expected to attend the daily services and to study diligently in the private rooms provided for all. After compline, the short service at the end of the day, there was to be no noise, and lights would be out by eleven. This led to amusing occurrences. The boy would occasionally play chess with Emrys Edwards, but often in the middle of the game the lights would go out. There would be nothing for it then but to finish the game by torchlight, a strange sight to say the least. The number of games on offer was countless. For some reason he began to play cards. Every Saturday morning in the winter he would go to the common room to play bridge for an hour or more, a bad and wasteful habit, and the only justification was that it helped to kill time before the rugby match in the afternoon. On one occasion on the way home after an away game, he was enticed by three others to play for money. Without being able to prove anything, he felt that he was being cheated. He lost a substantial portion of his meagre pocket-money, and that did it. The bad habit of playing cards was broken, and even after becoming a parish priest he would never divulge his ability to play bridge.

Through one window in his small room he could look across the river Menai to Anglesey, and sometimes in the evening he would hear a bell ringing in one of the large houses at the riverside, or listen to the owls answering one another on a quiet night. Here he would study every night, making his way like a caterpillar through the pile of Latin and Greek books that had been set for his degree course. His attitude was completely wrong. Instead of reading around the course and trying to understand his subjects, he submitted to one idea only: he had to pass. Therefore, instead of joining the learned societies of the college in order to broaden his knowledge, he studied conscientiously and narrowly, and used his spare time to go out into the world of nature as usual. He knew that keeping him in college was a strain on his parents' limited resources. The only activity he would take part in was the choral society; he had always liked music. He would remember the time when, as a young lad, he was put in a room to amuse himself with a gramophone belonging to someone else. Amongst the records there was one called *Reminiscences of Mozart*. He did not know who Mozart was, or even how to pronounce his name, but he greatly enjoyed the music, playing it over and over again. He did not understand music, but it was in the family. His father's mother had had a first-class voice, and she was earnestly encouraged to go to Italy to be properly trained. But she refused. His father also had a good voice, and would give an occasional recital in Dublin when he was on the ships. The boy became a member of the college choir, which meant that he practised as a bass every Friday night. D. T. Davies was the choirmaster, a man with the talent to draw the best out of his singers. The boy would sit in the back row with three adults, trying his utmost to sing as second-bass. When rehearsing Verdi's *Requiem*, he would growl the '*Dies Irae*' like a fifty-year-old, taking his share of the praise that was in truth being offered to the other three. The great night came when they were to perform the work in public in the Pritchard Jones Hall with the help of the three men from the town choir, the town's choral society and professional visiting soloists. Everything went well, but at one point during the performance, when the tenors were supposed to sing out loud and clear, there was silence from their side. During subsequent criticism of the performance the boy was thankful that it wasn't as a tenor that he had tried to sing!

Although Glyn Simon was somewhat effeminate in his manner, he was firm enough in defence of his convictions and would lay down the law without mincing matters to those members of the hostel who were not, in his view, pulling their weight. He was High Church, and the services in the hostel's new chapel had that kind of atmosphere. The smell of incense continued to linger about the chapel long after the administering of Holy Communion – Mass, to him. Two students were chosen to tend on him at every Mass, and when the young man's turn came, he would be annoyed by the Warden's manner of hurrying through the opening sentences, without leaving time for the two to say their words. He always preached well, and the young man would have something to ponder despite the Warden's whimsicality.

In the refectory there were two tables, one for the English students and the other for the Welsh. The boy would sit with the English students, as English was his language. But sometimes he would be drawn to sit at the other table. One or two of them would try to get him to say words like '*llwy*', 'spoon', and then burst out laughing because of his patois. The Warden himself was trying to learn Welsh, and would take the occasional service in the old language, but, unfortunately, the boy did not feel any desire to learn it. His background overpowered him, and he tended to be drawn to English-speaking friends and girls. And indeed even in those early days, when there were no more than five hundred students, it was English that was the prominent language. There were enough Welsh-speaking Welshmen, of course, but most were from the South, with their emphasis on rugby above all else. So the boy continued to live a thoroughly English life, as he had done at home. The only exception, perhaps, was the singing. The students would burst out into song at the slightest excuse. They would sing while waiting for the train to take them to another town to play rugby. They would sing around college; and the members of the hostel would sing while waiting for a meal, to the distress of the Warden who would accuse them of singing nonconformist hymns. But so the time passed until the final year came, and the boy started to worry pretty seriously about the examinations facing him. His memory was poor, but he had too many books to be able to revise them often. He had to read and try to remember them in readiness for the big day. But the strain of that year would remain with him for many years. Until he became a middle-aged man, he would continue to have a dream about having to face an examination without being ready for it. But he did his paltry best, and after waiting throughout the summer heard that he had graduated without much honour. Nevertheless, the way was clear for him to go on to the theological college in Llandaff, and having enjoyed the summer as best he could under the circumstances, it was there that he went with some of the other hostel students the following October.

He had been born in Cardiff, and yet he derived no pleasure from returning to the city. Indeed, in Llandaff he soon began to yearn for the life and background of the North. There was nowhere to go for a walk except along the main road. There were no mountains, no open ground. Worse still, the year was divided into four terms, which meant that he had to return in the middle of the summer to complete the fourth. Neither the college nor the routine appealed to him at all. After the hostel in Bangor the buildings were old-fashioned, the food uninteresting, the chapel nothing but some prefabricated hut and the Warden again effeminate, although a scholar and able to lay down the law as severely as Glyn Simon. The students did not take the college seriously. Although there was a day of silence every term, when everyone was expected to spend the day without talking, many of them would meet in the afternoon and go for a walk to have fun. The custom was to invite well-known men to mark these days, but only one of them said something that was destined to return to the young man's mind more than once during his career in the Church. That was R. O. P. Taylor from Ringwood in Hampshire. During one of his addresses he talked of some unnamed colonel in his parish who was a burden to him, and he referred to him as 'actually a very frightened man'. The boy was destined to meet more than one person who, if not frightened, was an utter nuisance in the parish. Everyone was expected to take services somewhere in the surrounding area in order to gain experience, but mercifully this was not compulsory, and so, with his usual cowardice, the boy succeeded in avoiding this. Only two occasions were to stay in his memory. Sometime during the year Kreisler came to give a recital in the city and the boy got a seat fairly close to him. Secondly, straight after the end of the autumn term the All Blacks came to Cardiff to play against Wales, and the young man stayed on to watch the game. It was touch and go until the final minute, when the winning try was scored by Rees Jones in the corner where the boy was standing. When he reached Holyhead late that night he had lost his voice completely.

Mercifully, the church system worked in such a way as to release him from the college's control before his due time, to the disgust of the staff who opposed his leaving before he had passed the second part of the general examination. He had before this been offered a curacy by the vicar of Rhosymedre, near Ruabon, but fair play to the Sub-warden of the college, he said that that type of parish would not suit him. 'I would rather see you go to the parish of Chirk,' he said. And so it transpired. The vicar of that place needed a curate and, being an influential man, persuaded the bishop to ordain him before he had passed the second part of the examination. The young man went to see him during the summer, was found acceptable, and went there in October to make a start on his first job and receive his first salary at the age of twenty-three.

Chirk is a border-country town between the hills of Denbighshire to the west and the plains of Shropshire to the east, and with two coal-mines. Most of the miners' houses were close to the A5 road, with another suburb about a mile and a half to the north-east, close to one of the pits. To the west was the Ceiriog Valley with the river rushing down between fairly high and steep hills to join the Dee about a mile or two from Chirk. At the other end of the valley rose Y Berwyn, a mountain of over two thousand feet. In the excitement of the new life opening up before him, the boy forgot about Holyhead and the sea for the time being. He had to stand in the pulpit and give a sermon for the first time in his life. For his first sermon he was sent by the vicar to Halton, the missionary church near the coal-pit already referred to. Then there was the matter of settling into his new lodgings and starting to build up his first library. Having arrived in the parish and seen the vicar's books, he realised that all he possessed were a few college books. He joined a book club in London which enabled him to have around fifty books on hire-purchase. For the first time in his life he owned books of poetry.

It was October and the trees in their splendour were starting to turn colour. He went to explore the countryside to the west and wrote a jubilant letter home praising the beauty of the area. His father's answer was that he should be a poet. But within three weeks the weather turned around, and there came the mist and the rain and the cold that were fairly common along the Welsh border, and the young man realised with a terrible suddenness where he was. It was in this way that the *hiraeth* for Anglesey and the sea began, a *hiraeth* that would influence him throughout the years to come.

Of course, there was some consolation. He realised that the country to the west was Wales, a quite different land from Chirk itself with its miners with their Shropshire accent, and the middle class that had settled in the houses outside the village. Before long a meeting of the clergy was held in the vicarage of Llanarmon Dyffryn Ceiriog, and he went there with the vicar. During the meeting, as he looked through the window, he saw the long spur of Y Berwyn rising against the sky, and a thrill went through him. He therefore started to wander more and more into this countryside, following the long ridge running from Chirk to Nantyr and beyond. He became friendly with a girl who was lodging fairly close by and who also owned a car, and she would sometimes take him further, as far as places such as Y Bala, and occasionally even back to Anglesey. This was the period of cheap petrol and it was possible to go for a whole day through north Wales for four shillings! The trouble was, having seen Anglesey once again, on the next day the old painful *hiraeth* would return, stronger than ever. But there was work to be done, and he started to get to know the parishioners.

It was here, for the first time, that he came face to face with the problem of pain. Some of the parishioners were very ill and required frequent visiting. There was the paralysed woman in her bed who was convinced that she was getting better. Every time he called she would half raise an arm to show that she was improving. Another, whose husband worked in the coal-mine, would take minutes to answer the door because she suffered so badly from rheumatism. Having returned to the kitchen, she would chat quite cheerfully for half an hour, sitting on a high stool to help her endure the pain. Then, there was a man who worked night shifts at the pit and who as a result suffered from stomach pains because he could not digest his food, a problem which, in turn, developed into an abscess. The curate was more than eager to help these people, but how? Slowly, by reading and thinking, he came to understand that this was one of the greatest problems to have troubled man since he started using his brain.

Soon he learned that his predecessor had been chaplain to the local branch of Toc H, a movement founded during the First World War. He agreed to do the same thing, and this meant meeting on a weekly basis in a small hut to conduct a ceremony of lighting and extinguishing a candle and also to discuss various subjects, and ending with a prayer. He himself started to give talks there, as well as to other groups. He found also that there were other middle-class men in the area who would be willing to talk about more substantial topics than usual, some of them experienced men who had lived abroad for a time. He loved to listen to them debating with one another, quoting examples from this or that country. Under these influences his interest in intellectual matters developed, and he started to take magazines, amongst them a monthly concerned with theosophy, published in India. Before long he built up enough confidence to write an article or two and got this magazine to accept them. Around this time Dr E. E. Thomas, rector of Marchwiail, started a series of lectures in the parish, and the curate became a member of his classes. Having got to know the lecturer, he mentioned with a mixture of pride and shyness the articles that had been published. The rector read one of them, and when he saw that the curate had referred to him, he praised it, urging him to stick at it. Better late than never. Gradually he was getting to grips with the subjects he should have covered in college.

In 1938 came the awakening. As the situation in Europe deteriorated there came into his hands a booklet by Hewlett Johnson, Dean of Canterbury, the 'Red Dean' as he was called, which blamed the capitalists for the condition of Europe. He delivered a talk about this booklet to Toc H and, following the enthusiastic applause he received, he preached on the same subject in the parish church the following Sunday. But afterwards, while discussing the subject with his vicar and telling him how he felt, the vicar turned on him, saying, 'Don't preach such stuff.' It was this that opened his eyes to a fact of which he would later become more and more aware: the Church was not willing to condemn war, only to exhort young men to do their 'duty' and then pray for them. But to a boy with ideals to uphold, the situation was clear enough: Christ was a pacifist, but not so the Church established in his name.

Meanwhile things went on in their usual way with parties and visits to the cinemas in Oswestry, combined with parish work. But under the influence of the beautiful and exciting country to the west he continued to write poetry – tender, innocent lyrics in the manner of the Georgian poets, because that was the background to his reading among the poets. Edward Thomas was one of his favourites and because the latter had written about the countryside, the budding poet tried to imitate him. The more 'modern' English poets, such as Hopkins, Wilfred Owen, Pound and Eliot had not yet broken through to his inner world to shatter the unreal dreams that dwelled there. And alas, the Welsh poets did not exist for him. Who was to blame? The desire to write was within him, but because of the nature of his education and his background, he could only think in terms of the English language.

The girl he had started to court was a recognised artist with experience of art school in London and also of Italy. Looking at her paintings, he identified with the artistic life. She had already exhibited her work in galleries in London, and he too yearned to prove himself in his field. He heard of an editor of a magazine in Dublin, Seamus O'Sullivan, who had the reputation of being kind to young writers. He sent him a poem or two, and before long one of them was accepted. He arranged to visit the editor when the latter was staying with his brother in Bryn-y-neuadd, Llanfairfechan, and he was able to spend a whole day in their company. Later he went to Dublin to see him, where he met other poets such as Austin Clarke who was considered to be Ireland's foremost poet after W. B. Yeats. As everyone knows, the Irish are talkers, and the young poet felt quite shy and taciturn in their midst, but their company satisfied some urge within him at the time.

Another author who influenced him at that stage was Fiona Macleod. One of his books came to his attention accidentally and it echoed the *hiraeth* for the west that he was experiencing at the time. He went to look for other books by the same author and for months he was under the spell of the Hebrides of which the author wrote. He was already familiar with the early work of W. B. Yeats in poetry and prose, and the two writers soon came to represent exactly the life that he would love to live among the peat and the heather on the west coast. He longed more than ever for this life, which, unknown to him, had almost ceased to exist, because the two writers were describing Scotland and Ireland as they had been fifty years before. He persuaded the girl to come with him to the Hebrides for two weeks' holiday, without knowing where exactly he was going.

First thing one morning in July the two set out for the north in a little Austin car, and after a pleasant, easeful journey they crossed the border at about half past two. The next day they went up into the true highlands, and here were mountains higher than any of the mountains of

Wales. There was some vague plan in the young man's mind to try and catch the MacBrayne ship from Mallaig for one of the islands, but because of the poor condition of the road, they came into sight of the harbour just in time to see the ship leaving the quay. There was nothing for it but to think of something else. The curate saw a boat by the quay and a seaman just disembarked from it. 'Are you going to the islands?' he asked, rather unhopefully. 'Which islands?' the other asked. He did not know. 'I live in Soay,' the seaman said. 'I'll take you there, if you want.' What luck! He went back to the girl and within half an hour he was saying goodbye to her and setting out for an island he had never heard of before.

Within an hour, having gone past the southern peninsula of Skye, they saw a little island in front of them, and the boat aimed for a small central beach. There was a small row of crofts along it. They landed and the seaman took him to his home. His wife wasn't too pleased to see that he had bought a stranger, and having had a cup of tea and a sandwich, the curate heard the sound of arguing in the kitchen. The upshot was that the seaman took him to one of the other houses, where a woman took him in and gave him a bed. She had two or three sons and a daughter, but somehow or other she found room for him in the little cottage. He was put in the parlour to have his meals, as a guest, but he would join the family in the kitchen for a chat before going to bed. Gaelic was the language of the home and he would listen to its sound in the kitchen, like water splashing, but after he had joined them, it was English that was spoken for the rest of the evening. The man of the house went to a drawer and took out a box of sweets and offered them to everyone. Suddenly there was quite a stir and the rumour went about that John Macdonald was coming to a *ceilidh*, their word for a *noson lawen*, an evening of entertainment. But it was quite a tame evening's entertainment. Macdonald passed in front of the window and stood in the doorway. 'Come in, John Macdonald.' A long silence after he had settled in the best chair by the peat fire. Then, 'It's a fine evening.' 'Very fine, John Macdonald.' And after about half an hour of that, Macdonald got up, bade them goodbye, and went home.

The first day was quite fine, but, unfortunately, after that the weather changed and the island's habitual rain started. The young man had not brought remotely the right clothing, and he was unable to go out very much because of the incessant rain. At night, having gone to bed right under the crooked roof, he would hear the rest of the family climbing the flimsy ladder to their beds, causing the cottage to shake like a basket.

He awoke in the middle of the night and went to the small window to gaze at the bay below him. The water was like glass under the grey light of the moon, with the sound of raindrops over everything. He tried his best to convince himself that he was in the Hebrides. But it was so different. By the end of the week he had had enough, and returned to the mainland to Mallaig. There he heard that his friend had gone to Canna, one of the other islands, a mile or two to the west. He sent her a telegram, imploring her to leave, and having got her back, he urged her to return to Wales. He had been completely disillusioned. He did not get one glimpse of Fiona Macleod's magical land.

And yet the dreams did not cease to be, and within a year he had better luck in Ireland. After the service on Christmas morning the vicar told him that, if he so wished, he was free for a week or more, and he jumped on his bicycle and headed for home. He reached Llanfair Pwll that evening and the next day he started out again for Holyhead. There he decided to cross to Ireland and try to visit the west. He called in on Seamus O'Sullivan and received from him a letter of introduction to one of the eminent men of Galway, Liam O'Briain, who was a professor at the university. He left Dublin on the train first thing in the morning, after a hard frost. But as the train neared the west the frost disappeared and everything was green. He reached Galway at half past ten, and went directly to the professor's house. The door was answered by a girl who showed him to a room. Soon the door opened and a short, strongly built man came into the room. '*Bore da*, Mr Thomas,' 'Good morning, Mr Thomas,' he said. During the First World War he had been imprisoned by the English in Fron-goch near Y Bala, where he learned some Welsh, but he was also professor of Celtic at the university. He offered his guest a large glass of whiskey, even though it was only eleven o'clock. He was, like many of his fellow-countrymen, an enthusiastic conversationalist and after lunch he accompanied the curate on his way to the west, talking all the while. After about four miles he said goodbye, giving the address of a house where he could stay that night, together with a hundred instructions regarding places to see and roads to travel along, and suchlike. The young man had noticed the number of carts that stood on the square in Galway, having come there with a load of seaweed, and as night began to fall, he was passed by cart after cart on its way home to the west. As each cart passed him the driver greeted him in Irish. This, and the smell of the peat in his nostrils, raised his spirits and filled him with new hope. This was the country of which Yeats had sung, a land of common folk, their language Irish and their

ways traditionally Celtic. After walking far, far into the dusk, he saw
the house Liam O'Briain had recommended to him as lodgings for
the night. He went to the door and explained his business. When he
mentioned the professor from Galway, the woman of the house said
with great dignity, 'We have the honour of knowing Liam O'Briain.'

When he awoke the next day and looked through a window, he found
that he was looking across the sea to the Aran Isles, and there came
memories of Synge and others who had described the harsh and primitive life of the islands' inhabitants. Having said goodbye to his hosts,
he walked on into a land that pleased him, with its lakes and rocks and
men riding on the backs of donkeys. He went to a house in Carraroe,
where a friend of Seamus O'Sullivan's lived, and asked whether there
was a suitable place to stay in the village. 'Do you want to catch a fever?'
the man asked. 'You had better stay with us.' And so it was for a few
days.

This man was a painter called Charles Lamb, and his wife was a
veterinary surgeon. Another girl was staying with them at the time, and
on New Year's Eve the curate went out with her to see the hundreds of
candles that had been lit in the window of every cottage and croft along
the coast and the lakes as a sign that there was a welcome for every man
and spirit that happened to be abroad at the year's turning. Having
welcomed the new year in this way the young man caught the bus back
to Galway the next day, noticing that the bus was filled with Gaelic
conversation. Within three days he was back in his parish in Chirk, a
very different place from the land far to the west.

Later that year came the Munich crisis. The main railway line ran
through Chirk, and while the discussions between Hitler and Chamberlain continued, hundreds of trains would go past during the night on
their way south, carrying weapons, no doubt, to defend England from
an attack by the Germans. Chamberlain returned with his piece of
paper, and the crisis passed. But the young curate wasn't familiar
enough with the way of the world to realise that Chamberlain was only
playing for time. He wrote in his innocence to his friends in Carraroe
insisting that God would not allow something as terrible as war. But
others knew better and the country began to get ready. And indeed
before the end of another year the nations of the world were at one
another's throats, and there came all the tribulations of gas masks, the
rationing of food and petrol and so on. The curate worked with others
for days preparing ration books for the areas around Chirk, and the

women began to gather black material to put over the windows to hide the lights after dark. And yet at the same time the curate and his sweetheart decided to get married, and the wedding was celebrated in Llanycil on the shore of Llyn Tegid, an area of which both of them had become very fond. It was a very small wedding, but he had asked the owner of the hotel where they were staying to invite a harpist to play for them and their parents on the previous evening, like a *neithior*, a traditional Welsh marriage-feast. But the owner was an Englishman and he did not succeed in getting hold of anyone, even though the curate had been told by Euros, when he came to know him, that there were plenty of harpists to be had in the surrounding area, if you only set about it in the right way. The vicar did not want a curate who was married, and so the problem of finding somewhere else arose. On the other hand they did not want to move into lodgings. At last he heard about a living in Maelor Saesneg which included a house. It was part of the parish of Hanmer, but the young man did not know at the time about that place's connection with Owain Glyndŵr. And yet, such information would hardly have been enough to ease his *hiraeth*, after he had moved fifteen miles further east. Now Wales and her hills were further away than ever, and he would gaze hopelessly at them over miles of flat, uninteresting land.

By this time the war had started in earnest, and although there wasn't much local danger, the parish was in the flightpath of the German aeroplanes as they made for Merseyside. Every night, weather permitting, the aeroplanes would pass overhead on their way in, and they soon started getting on the curate's nerves, not because of fear so much as disgust and despair at the thought that they were on their way to drop their fiendish loads on helpless women and children. At the same time he noticed that he wasn't showing enough confidence and fearlessness in the presence of the girl he had promised to look after. Although Merseyside was some twenty miles as the crow flies, as he stood in the doorway with his wife to listen to the sound of the bombs in the distance and to see the flames lighting up the sky, he felt the occasional puff of wind going through his hair and lifting his wife's skirt. Sometimes the Germans would drop a few bombs in the area, after seeing a light somewhere perhaps, but without injuring anyone, thanks to the open nature of the land. One night he happened to be looking through the window when he heard a bomb screaming on its way down very close by. He waited for the explosion, but nothing happened. The next day it was discovered that the bomb had plunged to earth within a yard or two of a zinc-roofed cottage, where an old couple lived. They were fast asleep at the time, without realising that anything out of the ordinary had happened! The curate decided to erect an earthwork against the wall of the parsonage, opposite the space under the stairs, as a shelter, should more bombs start to fall. One night when he was leaving the church, which was next door to the house, he heard a terrible bang very close by. He ran inside and urged his wife to come and take cover under the stairs, and there they were for hours, while the enemy aeroplanes circled above their heads. They heard afterwards that there were Italians as well as Germans, and that they were having difficulty as they tried to get close to Merseyside. Many bombs were dropped in the area that night, and the hill-country in the vicinity of Minera was set on fire. On seeing the flames, they started to drop bombs there as well, and a shepherd who lived at the edge of the moorland got the fright of his life. So hateful was it to the curate to think of the destruction occurring almost every night, and such was his *hiraeth* for the hills in the distance (Moel Fama could be seen quite clearly to the north-west), that he decided to learn Welsh as a means of enabling him to return to the true Wales.

There was very little petrol available for private purposes, but his wife had a class in one of the boarding schools not far from Llangollen, and after enquiring he learned of a teacher in that town who would be willing to give him a Welsh lesson on the same night. The teacher was Iorwerth Roberts, and it was to him that the young man went for a time, although his progress was slow without anyone with whom to practise the language. Mercifully, within two years he heard that a parish in Montgomeryshire was vacant, and went to see it. But after telling his former vicar about the parish, he heard that there were problems there, and the vicar said that he would prefer to see him in Manafon, which, unknown to the young man, was also vacant. He went to see this parish and before long, thanks to the influence of his former vicar, he had been appointed rector of Manafon.

Although Welsh was not spoken in this parish, it was in the hills and within reach of places such as Yr Adfa and Llanfair Caereinion. The language could be heard there, and even on the ridge between Manafon and Llanfair there was a chapel where services and *eisteddfodau* were held in Welsh only. There was also a Welsh chapel in Yr Adfa, and it was to the minister there that he went first for help with his Welsh. This was D. T. Davies, a man from the South, but after a while he moved, and the new rector went to the minister of Penarth, the chapel between

Manafon and Llanfair, and asked for his help. This was H. D. Owen, originally from Penrhosgarnedd. This was a blessing since it meant that the learner came to speak the language of the North. He was given a warm welcome by H. D. and his wife Megan in their home, and after struggling on for years at their expense he came to speak Welsh quite satisfactorily, although it took a very long time, as he did not wish to impose on these kind people too often. Meanwhile he had to learn the craft of being a young rector amongst rough and hardened farmers who expected more from him than he could give; while they in turn failed to meet his own ideals.

Manafon was in a small valley some five hundred feet above sea level. The hills all around it rose to something like a thousand feet. On the valley bed the river Rhiw ran past on its way to join the Severn six miles to the east. The rectory stood on the river bank, and the river sound could be heard at night like the blood running in their veins. 'Where is Manafon?' was the most common question posed by strangers. And yet this was the parish of Ieuan Brydydd Hir, Gwallter Mechain and Penfro, in their day three talented and famous Welshmen. As is known, Gwallter Mechain was a writer of *englynion*, a man of the *eisteddfodau* and an authority on the agriculture of his day. By now he was Walter Davies, and renowned above all else as a conjurer. A story was told of him making a man stand all night on a stone in the middle of the river for some minor misdemeanour! A brilliant and staunch Welshman, and yet, while inspecting the church's register, the new rector saw an entry early in the last century for the Easter Vestry which said, in English, 'Easter Vestry. No-one present.' In Penfro's time at the turn of the century the Welsh language in the church was holding its own, but the school had already turned to the English language, a sign of the parishioners' desire to see their children get on in the world!

There is a poem by Edward Thomas, 'The New House', which describes the feelings of the owner on his first move there. So it was with the new rector. At the head of the stairs, there was a large window. He approached it and looked across the river to the field on the other side of it and up to the bare ridge where the clouds were hurrying by. That very moment he foresaw the seasons before him, with the weather turning from rain to shine and from heat to snow. And so it came to pass. There was nothing else to see but the land and the sky under the changing seasons. Were it not for the river, it could have been quite uninteresting. But that river was like a living thing and as full of moods as a girl. In the summer it shrank to nothing, but in the autumn and winter would rise suddenly because of the rains and roar past, bearing with it all manner of wreckage. There was a cellar under the house, and in the autumn the rector said, 'I wonder if the water comes into the cellar?' He then opened the door and, behold, the water was within a foot of the head of the steps! It was also in the river that he would fish for the quite numerous trout. That is why his father was so pleased when he heard of his appointment to the parish, for there was nothing he liked better than to fish in a river. The river became a part of their life, sometimes quiet, another time rushing past, brown with the peat from its source. It was a region of small cottages and sheep, waiting for him to discover them.

Manafon scarcely existed. There was no village there, only a church, a school, a public house and a shop. The farms were scattered along the slopes, smallholdings on the whole, with the occasional more substantial farm. The people were English–Welsh, with Welsh names and a Shropshire accent. They became the subject of his poetry. For him, the countryside and its surroundings were beautiful. He wanted to continue to sing poems of praise to them. But how to reconcile with this the life and attitude of the farmers themselves? On a dark, cold day in November, on his way to visit a family in a farm over a thousand feet above sea-level, he saw the farmer's brother out in the field, docking mangels. The thing made a profound impression on him, and when he returned to the house after the visit he set about writing 'A Peasant', the first poem to attempt to face the reality of the scenes around him.

Was it because of the hardness of the people and their work, or because of some nicety in himself, that the tension arose that was to be a part of his spiritual and literary problems for so many years? At the time he was too young and too inexperienced to know that tension is an irremovable part of art. And yet two-thirds of him was in sympathy with these people who had to be out in all weathers tending the land and looking after the animals that were as unmanageable as the people themselves. These were times before the advent of television, without petrol to go to town except on fair-day. After long hours of hard work in all kinds of weather, what was there to do each night after eating but to nod at the fireside before climbing to their beds under the slates? What use was it speaking of the life of the spirit to people who lacked some of the normal amenities of the life of the middle classes? They were earth of the earth; their only interests were the farm, the animals, the prices, and the personal lives of their neighbours. The horizons of some of them lay no further than the far side of the slope of the valley where they lived. But the rector would sometimes climb to the hilltops, and from one of their peaks a completely different world would open out in front of him. To the north-west, Cadair Idris was to be seen; to the north, Aran Fawddwy and Aran Benllyn, and to the north-east Y Berwyn – a prospect sufficient to raise the heart and make the blood sing. Turning to look down into the valley he would see everything in perspective, the people like ants below him, the church a small hut in the fields and the river like a silver thread flowing down the valley. The church was built of river stones, smoothed by centuries of water, and sometimes, when the light was strong, it was as if the water were still running over them. Sunday after Sunday, despite their trials during the week, an assembly of people would come together to sing their unmelodious hymns and to hear the young rector tell of a world that existed only in his imagination, and the bell would awaken echoes in the wood of a time that never was. But sometimes he would invite a party from elsewhere in order to have some real music in the church. A madrigal choir from Welshpool would visit, and once, after a weekend course at Gregynog, a small orchestra came to play in the church. The sound of the strings suited the time of year to perfection, and when they came out of the church in the evening, it was beginning to snow.

The war was beginning to draw to its close. Because of the military conscription that threw thousands of young Welshmen into the midst of the English, a degree of nationalism arose amongst them. Even the English–Welsh from the South felt that they were of a different lineage from that of their fellow-soldiers. Some of them wrote to the papers and the magazines to express this feeling. Because of this, the periodical *Wales* was restarted under the editorship of Keidrych Rhys in order to give them a platform in English. The emphasis was on Welshness: stories with Welsh characters, Welsh expressions and quotations from the classic poets. The young rector's imagination was fired by such lines as:

> *Dyred i'r fedw gadeiriog*
> *I grefydd y gwŷdd a'r gog.*
> Come to the spreading birch tree
> To the religion of the trees and the cuckoo.

> *Stafell Gynddylan ys tywyll heno.*
> The hall of Cynddylan is dark tonight.

Sûn y galon fach yn torri.
The sound of the little heart breaking.

Therefore he, too, had to show that he was a Welshman by using names that could not possibly be English ones. He called his first character, the farmer he had seen docking swedes, Iago Prydderch, spelling it Prytherch so that his English readers would pronounce it correctly. He read in *Y Faner* an article by Saunders Lewis which finished with the words, '*O, flodyn y dyffryn, deffro*' ('Oh, flower of the valley, awake'). He was stirred through and through. He went to Llanfarian to visit Saunders Lewis without a word of introduction. He was received kindly and began to speak in English about his ideals and plans, but in no time at all was led by Saunders to soldier on in his imperfect Welsh.

Later a nationalist from Scotland, Douglas Young, came to address a meeting in Rhosllannerchrugog. The rector went there and met him after his speech. Following his review in *Wales* of the literature of the Scottish renaissance, the rector was invited to go to Scotland for a week to address meetings on the history and literature of Wales.

To help him in his efforts to learn Welsh he would attend the meetings of the ministers of Llanfair and the surrounding area, the Brotherhood as it was called. It was to Llanfair that, later on, Islwyn Ffowc Elis came. The rector called by one day to invite him to come for a walk to the moorland around Cwm Nant yr Eira, but Islwyn refused. He was too busy trying to serve his own Wales. The question was, were the two versions of Wales one? He had met Euros Bowen once or twice, and he wrote to him now for help with the Welsh language. He received a kind invitation to stay in Llangywair for a week. Walking along the shores of Llyn Tegid, he mentioned how the light would lie differently on the slopes of Arenig from the way it did in Manafon. Euros stopped and said in his convinced manner, 'This proves that you're a Welshman.' Euros was one for staying up until the early hours of the morning, but his visitor learned a great deal about Wales and the Welsh language that week. Euros was keen to take him to see Llwyd o'r Bryn, but on reflection, he decided that his torrent of Welsh would be too much for the learner.

Through his poems in *Wales* the rector became fairly well known as one of the Anglo-Welsh poets. He met people such as Gwenallt and Aneirin Talfan and Waldo. One day Islwyn told him of a plan to go to Trawsfynydd to prevent the army from extending its camp there. The thing was completely secret and they had to change the date because someone had talked. But the day came and the rector started first thing in the morning for Traws. On the way down to Dolgellau he noticed a small crowd standing outside a café, drinking coffee. D. J. Williams was amongst them. When he arrived, Gwynfor was there and Waldo and many others, but they were short of the hundred that had promised to come. However there were enough, and they began to take their places on the road to the camp in order to close it. They succeeded pretty well by arranging to change places from time to time. After Gwynfor explained at one point that four of them would have to follow the four in front, Waldo said, '*Wela i. Ar ôl bwyd yr ail bedwar*' ('I see. After food the further four').*

When the rector returned to his parish, the papers next day were full of bold headlines about the event. So a new element came into his work. From trying to understand the countryman in Manafon as a man, and making him a symbol of the relationship that existed between man and the earth in the contemporary world of the machine, he turned to taking an interest in the history of Wales, her political and social problems, and his own situation as a Welshman who had to respond and write in English because of his upbringing. This was responsible for the element of bitterness in his work, an element that would be there for many years. And yet behind and around everything there was the beauty and freshness of nature. Unknown to him, his experience at this time was the same as that of Wordsworth and Coleridge. There was a dew on things. An odour came from off the wet earth that would remind him of Holyhead, when he was a boy there. At night the valley echoed with the cry of the owls. The fox barked and the vixen screamed very close to the rectory, and the river ran past, murmuring to itself under the stars. In the evening he would visit his parishioners, walking across the fields towards some spot of light from the window, like a yellow flower on the hillside. Almost every week, through all weathers, he would walk to the home of H. D. Owen to practise the Welsh language, having done his homework from Caradar's books, *Welsh Made Easy*. Climbing from the hollow he would look down and see the hillsides sometimes white with snow, and the whole area hanging in front of him like an illusion. At Christmas-time he would lead the young people's club from farm to farm to sing carols, and the welcome they received was amazing, as if every farm were competing for supremacy with their

---

* The second sentence is an example of the impromptu composition of lines of full *cynghanedd*, the intricate system of alliteration and internal rhyme that characterises traditional Welsh verse.

neighbours. It didn't even matter if they had gone to bed. They had to get up and invite the singers in for a cup of tea. In order to reach one farm they had to descend into the hollow, cross a stream on a footbridge and climb the opposite bank. As they passed through the trees and up under the starry sky the beauty of the place took his breath away. And it would be something similar in March, when the men would be busy with the little lambs. The rector would look through his window at night and see the light of the lanterns twinkling here and there as the shepherds moved about the fields. And sometimes, while visiting one of the farmhouses, he would see a pet lamb huddling weakly in a box by the fire, like one of the family.

As hopes that the war would not last long increased, the rector's wife expressed her desire to have a child. He had not thought seriously about the possibility. How can no-one be a father to someone? But so it was, and one morning in August 1945, after a night of thunder, he stood in a room in the hospital in Newtown to gaze at the bit of flesh lying in a cradle next to his mother's bed. This was Gwydion. As he looked at him, the rector was struck by the calmness in his face; but when he returned to the rectory, the child showed *o ba radd roedd ei wreiddyn*, 'what stuff his roots were made of', by crying and refusing to sleep for some two years. A nurse was found for him, but after looking after him throughout the day, she could not stay up with him all night as well. His parents therefore shared the week by staying with him in turns. Many pieces of advice were given by the parishioners, but neither they nor the doctor were much help. For some reason the little creature continued to cry until he had all his teeth. Then he started to get better and the time came for the nurse and her own little boy to leave the place. The nurse's son had been good company for Gwydion, and great was the expectancy for him to come home from school to play with the little one. And never was there so much expectancy as in 1947, the year of the great snow. Towards the end of January the weather changed with remarkable suddenness and it started to snow. Within a day or two there was a white layer covering everywhere. And after the east wind had risen the path from the house to the main road was filled with six feet of snow. The rector had to start digging through it, and some of the parishioners did the same from the other side, until they met halfway, leaving a narrow passage between the walls of snow. Then it started to freeze hard every night, and very often even all day, to the extent that the rector could not get his car out of the garage for nine weeks. The wind on the hillsides was merciless, and everyone pitied the women who had to walk across the fields to the coop to feed the hens. To make things worse for the rector, he had to keep a fire going in the church to warm it throughout the period. The sexton who for years had usually laid a fire there had grown old, and as he was a heavy man and had to go down stairs under the church to light the fire, the rector had persuaded him to give up the work, in case he had a fall. 'We'll get someone else,' he said. But no-one had offered, and now the worst winter of the century had begun. In addition to this the pipes in the large rectory would freeze every night, and the whole morning would pass while he and his wife thawed them. Sometimes the heavy clouds would move and the sun would come for an hour or two. But the clear sky only caused a worse frost than ever. One night the temperature dropped to minus ten degrees Fahrenheit, that is, forty-two degrees of frost. The house would crack throughout the night as the frost tightened its grip, and by morning all the windows were covered with ferns of ice, which were impossible to see through. The water in the house was frozen, and even the river was finding it difficult to move. And through all this the little one had to be kept warm and amused in the house, since it was too cold by far even to think about taking him outside. Then, after a day of waiting, there would come the sound of a snowball hitting the window, and there was Roy, the nurse's son, having returned from school. There were snow-drifts of eighteen feet in Dolanog that winter, and there would be stories about the people of the moorland having to walk miles to the nearest village to buy bread. The birds nearly starved to death, the fields were full of the footprints of foxes, and the bark was stripped from most of the trees by the rabbits in their efforts to find food. When the thaw with its heavy rain finally came, the ice in the river cracked like a gunshot, and large white lumps started to race past the rectory. That exceptional winter was followed by one of the best summers of the century.

After the winter had passed, and with the lifting of the restrictions on motoring at the end of the war, a chance came for the rector and his wife to resume their practice of travelling around Wales. One morning a letter came for his wife from a college friend who was at the time staying in Nanmor. He had met an extremely interesting old man, and he wanted both of them to go over to see him. When they arrived, he took them up the hill to Carneddi, the home of Carneddog. When Carneddog discovered that the rector was a Welshman and a poet, he gave him a signed copy of his anthology. While they were talking together other people came to the door and Cynan and his son came in. Years later, this son moved to Holyhead as a doctor, and when the rector's father died, ap Cynan was the man who looked after him in the hospital.

But apart from Nanmor, which is one of the most beautiful areas in Wales, there were other places to visit: Cwm Twrch in Montgomeryshire, for example, in the parish of Garthbeibio, where the river ran down in a series of waterfalls to meet the river Banw. Then there was Tal-y-llyn, and the sea itself at Aberdyfi where they would sometimes take Gwydion to enjoy the waves. And as he went about like this, he started to form a unified picture of Wales, her mountains, her moorland and her foaming streams. He would enjoy travelling in his car to the edge of the moorland the other side of Cefn Coch to wander for a whole day over the moor-grass growing around such lakes as Llyn Coch-hwyad, Llyn Gwyddïor, Llyn Hir and Llyn y Tarw. It was by the side of Llyn Coch-hwyad that he heard for the first time the enchanting, heartbreaking music of the golden plover. And yet this bird was a symbol of the grievous condition of the country. During his travels the rector would come across a ruin tucked in under the moorland, with a little stream bubbling past, and perhaps, a rowan tree with its red berries where once there had been a garden. From an old tree near the house a carrion crow would fly from off its nest, emphasising how 'uninhabited' the building was. This word became a true description of most of the uplands of Montgomeryshire. People lived here once, living a life in Welsh, making their living from the land, cutting peat and holding cultural meetings in the local chapel. But they had gone, almost every one of them. There was no-one left to hear the curlew returning in the spring and to see the moorland white with cotton grass in June or the hedgerows yellow with the golden chain around Waun Clapiau. It has been said that more than thirty thousand people left Montgomeryshire between the two world wars, and now no-one visited these bald hills except the occasional wealthy farmer from the valleys who received a subsidy for keeping bullocks there. The rector began to write poetry longing for the old order, and for the poor and lonely life of the few who had remained. For example, a family was still living in one of the farmhouses, and the children had to walk two miles over the moor through all weathers before meeting the taxi that took them to the nearest school miles away. But in addition a political element came into his poetry, together with a great deal of bitterness because of the English oppression that caused these things to happen. But with the honesty of a poet he also saw the failings of his fellow-Welshmen, who had not sufficient backbone to rise and demand the right to govern themselves. All this led to the tension from which creative work arises. He asked himself about the condition and function of the smallholder in his fields. What was he thinking about, if about anything? Was he of equal value to the important, learned people of the world? What was nature to him? Did he seriously believe in God and in eternal life? He gave sermon after sermon to his congregation, trying in his immature, idealistic way to get them to see things as he did. Some of them would have to walk a mile or more to church, and when the time came for him to climb into the pulpit they were starting to doze.

By now he had found some pattern for living. In the morning he would study and sometimes write poetry; go for a walk in the afternoon or take his son out in his pram; and in the evening visit his parishioners, which meant supper with the family and hours of talking in front of an open fire. Then home through the rain or under the stars to the parsonage by the river. His wife would paint, and in the evening go out to her extramural class to help pay for a nurse for the little one. Getting a nurse for the house was the only way of securing time and quiet for her husband to study and for herself to paint, instead of having to spend every day looking after a peevish, irritable child – not by nature but because of some specific problem in his tummy for which no-one could suggest a remedy.

Time passed in this way until it was time for the young boy himself to go to school. Before he was three, the nurse returned to her home, taking her son with her, of course. This meant that Gwydion no longer had company, and he started to depend on one or two of the boys from the parish who would come to the rectory to play around the cowsheds. This was a preparation for the time when he would go to school to be one of them, but he wasn't allowed to eat school lunch with them. His father would take him up the road, fetch him at midday, and then take him back for the afternoon session. His parents saw no reason why he should accept the state's charity in this matter. These were innocent days for him, days for learning to socialise and to receive the elementary instruction of the primary school. But unfortunately within about two years it became obvious that he had learned all that the school could give him, and the problem of what to do next arose. Even if his parents were willing to leave him in the elementary school, he would have to move to the secondary school when he was eleven, and that wasn't a satisfactory school. It would also mean catching a bus that roamed around the countryside to pick up the children all over the place first thing in the morning and take them back at the end of the day, a journey of nearly two hours, not to mention the time spent in school. In the end it was decided that he had to go to a boarding school in Shropshire, a school which had a very good reputation. So his mother had to continue with her night classes to help pay the way. It was a turbulent time at first, and the little one nearly broke his heart through homesickness. But gradually he settled down and started to enjoy the sport and the company, and when the time came for him to move again, he won a scholarship to a school in the south of England, where he had to try to settle in once again among strangers.

By the end of about eleven years in Manafon the rector saw an advertisement in a paper saying that a bird observatory had been opened on Bardsey Island. The name and address of the founder and secretary of the venture was William Condry, Eglwys-fach, Cardiganshire. This was in 1953. He and his wife went over to Eglwys-fach, and the result was an arrangement to visit Bardsey in 1954. He and his wife had already been on a week's holiday in Aberdaron, when the boy was much younger. But in August 1954 they went as a family to spend two weeks on Bardsey. William Condry urged them to be sure to call on the Keating family in Plas-yn-Rhiw; and so it turned out. They received a warm welcome from these three remarkable sisters, and after staying overnight with them a relationship was established that would over the years develop into a friendship. They were unmarried sisters who had come to the area with their mother years earlier. They had fallen in love with the Plas and had restored it from a ruin to a dignified house with an extensive garden around it, and fine views of Mynydd Cilan across Porth Neigwl. They were enthusiastic supporters of the National Trust, and they used to try to get everyone who called by to join the organisation.

Having said goodbye to their new friends, the Thomases went on to Aberdaron to catch the small boat to Bardsey. Wil Evans, Cristin, was the boatman and within the hour he was ready to start from the beach. There was quite a crowd wanting to cross with their belongings, and Wil also brought the cattle-boat, to share the load. Unfortunately, while they were busy loading the boats, the cattle-boat was taken by the current and was holed by one of the rocks. No-one was sure how serious this was, so they started, with Y Benlli pulling the other boat. The rector and his son and some others were in the cattle-boat, and they hadn't gone far before the water began to rise in it. Signals were made to draw Wil's attention, and he started to head for Porth Meudwy. By the time they got there the water had nearly reached the gunwale, to the point where it was a miracle that the boat didn't sink. In Y Borth they set about putting a patch over the hole, and away they went again. It was, mercifully, a fine afternoon and everyone arrived safely. But alas! When people started to unload the cattle-boat, it was found that everything was soaking wet. The sea had got into the boxes and the food tins, and it was all ruined; the bread was like porridge, and the fruit and sugar and so on a sight to be seen. Wil had to cross again the next day to fetch replacements. But after the trouble everyone settled down to have two weeks' holiday in an unique place, and to learn something about the birds that went past and the ones that were drawn by the lighthouse on stormy nights. There was another boy staying at the observatory and Gwydion got on well with him, both pretending that they were famous ornithologists. The two weeks passed quickly enough and the Saturday came when they had to return to the mainland. Unfortunately the wind was quite fresh and the rector doubted whether it would be possible to cross. He went to Tŷ Pellaf to ask Wil, 'Are you going to cross today?' Wil spat, looked up at the sky and said, 'I'll give it a go.' Cold comfort for an inexperienced man like the rector. What if he failed? Would he be able to turn the boat round and come back? They left the small bay and began to struggle across the sea. The boat began to jump like a billy goat and wave after wave washed over it. One of the party, who had come with his newly wedded wife, took fright. 'Is this all right, Wil?' he asked. Wil looked at him and spat again. 'It'll get worse soon,' he said dryly. And worse it was. The little boat floundered in the big waves for an hour or more, creeping slowly over Bardsey Sound; and the lad at the helm had to slow down now and again to avoid hitting a big wave full in its face and perhaps filling the boat. The rector became very worried at the thought that he had put his wife and child in danger like this. But of course, unknown to him, Wil was well accustomed to such a crossing and was quite used to getting soaked to the skin.

At last Porth Meudwy came into view once again, and the party landed, more thankful than ever before in their lives. As he said goodbye to Wil the rector felt that he would never again risk it. But despite that he went many times again, until he knew every corner of this enchanting little island. And meanwhile he and his wife continued to go over from time to time to spend a day with the sisters in Plas-yn-Rhiw, and had to listen hour after hour to their innumerable stories. Then in 1954 William Condry sent a letter to the rector to say that the vicar of Eglwys-fach was retiring, and what about it? Manafon was in the diocese of St Asaph, but the other was in the diocese of St David's. However, the former bishop of St Asaph, William Havard, was by this time bishop of St David's, and the rector wrote to him to ask to be considered as the vicar of Eglwys-fach. And that is how it turned out. Before long he received a letter to say that he had been appointed and asking when he wished to move. His poor wife was in the middle of making a mural for the hospital in Gobowen, but she agreed to take her canvas down off the wall in Manafon, and move to the new house.

It was October when they moved, and unbelievably wet; and it continued to rain throughout that winter until June. But they had moved a great deal closer to the sea – for that is what was behind it all. Apart from the desire to secure a Welsh-speaking parish, the cold winters in Manafon had started to take their toll on them, until thinking about the seaside was as good as experiencing a warmer climate. Sometimes when they were in Manafon, a few herring gulls would fly overhead, making the habitual noise of seaside birds.

At other times, as he wandered on the moorland on the other side of Cefn Coch, he would perhaps meet a shepherd who would say to him, 'You can almost smell the sea today.' All this was enough to prod the old *hiraeth* that was always simmering within him. On top of this, Eglwys-fach was a Welsh-speaking parish, so that he would not always have to travel outside the parish to use the Welsh language. He would also have to give a sermon in Welsh every Sunday. He had been in Manafon for twelve years and had grown tired there. The farmers were so worldly. It was all well and good that they had an interest in the land and the animals, but they had little enthusiasm for things Welsh, cultural matters and the like. They were miserly with their money, but generous to him personally, giving many gifts of eggs and butter and bacon. Manafon had been a well-endowed parish before the disestablishment, and the people insisted on looking on the rector as still a rich man, even though the Church in Wales had been disendowed many years since and the parson's salary was the same as that of every other country vicar. But it was an easy way for the parishioners to avoid their responsibilities towards the Church. The rector was expected to be at the head of every list of donations, and they would then adjust the contributions according to the size of the farm: a farmer of two hundred acres giving two pounds, say, a farmer of a hundred acres a pound, and so on – as simple as that. At the end of the war, reports came that the children of Europe were very short of food. The rector decided that he would go to every house in the parish to ask for money for the fund established by Kate Roberts. It was a strange experience, as he went from farm to farm, to see the farmers and their wives snatching the book from his hands to see how much other people were giving. As he went from one to the other he would say by way of introduction, 'You know that the little children of Europe are starving, don't you?' 'You don't say,' would be the answer more often than not.

Of course, the hardship of the lives of some of them was heart-breaking. Pity would well up in him as he visited the sick in their comfortless beds under the slates. But one night, after taking the Sacrament to a sick man in his bed in a cottage at the top of the hill, as he was leaving the house he heard the laughter of the young people in the kitchen like the laughter of the devil himself, and the darkness and the raindrops falling from the trees added to his feeling of despair. And this is how things were. After pitying them, he would the next day hear some example of their callousness and hate, and how they were so ready to take even their relatives to court.

He was brought up in Holyhead, so he was used to a good deal of sunshine. But since Manafon was in a hollow, there wasn't any sunshine worth talking about in the winter. After waiting for it until eleven o'clock in the morning, he would lose it the other side of the opposite slope by two o'clock. The effect of this was that the pipes would not thaw before the sun had set, if they had not gone about it with cloths and hot water. In this cold, therefore, with the snow sometimes lasting for weeks, he would long for the seaside as he had known it in Anglesey. Having reached Eglwys-fach he decided that he would never again live in a hollow.

Eglwys-fach was in a pleasant part of rural Wales. It was a village on the main road, some five miles from the sea as the crow flies, with the river Dovey flowing past it. The hill-country rose immediately behind the main road, and foaming streams ran down the narrow valleys towards the few plains between sea and mountain. It was a Welsh area in its appearance, with the hills of Merionethshire rising in the north and the occasional glimpse of Cadair Idris from the high ground. After a storm, if the wind subsided, the sound of the sea could be heard from the west. And better than that, once every day the tide would come up the river and the tang of the sea could be smelt in the foam.

What he didn't know before settling there was how weak the Welsh language was in Eglwys-fach. It was a parish of several large houses, and every one of them in the hands of the English, despite the Welsh names on almost all of them. The Welsh who did not farm were only gardeners and maids to these people. And even amongst the common folk of the village there had been quite a bit of intermarrying with English people from places such as Herefordshire. In church all the emphasis was on the morning service in English. There was also a boarding school for boys there, and they would come along with their teachers. The boys formed the greater part of the church choir, and their parents would come to church on their frequent visits. Every Sunday morning the church would be full, not only of English people; the Welsh would also be there to experience some of the glory! But by the evening it was three or four of the faithful who came to Evensong.

The vicarage in Eglwys-fach was a smaller house than the rectory in Manafon, with its grey stones ruined by trimmings of red brick around every window. Having redecorated the interior, the new vicar spent a great deal of time getting rid of the red bricks by painting over them. As he went on with this work in the new year, his spirits were raised as he listened to the woodlark singing daily above the house. This is one of the most magical songs to be heard in Britain, and, listening to these melodious notes, there came to mind the Birds of Rhiannon and the old tale of how the listener would, on hearing them, forget time. He later came across the nest of one of these birds in the nearby field, but, alas, this sweet singer has by now become very rare in Britain.

Although Eglwys-fach was only a small rural parish, it was very different from Manafon. In Manafon there were only ordinary farmers, tenants mostly, but in Eglwys-fach there was an English middle class that was prepared to put more pressure on the vicar. His predecessor had been there for twenty-five years, and was held in high regard. He had christened and joined in marriage many of the parishioners, and could therefore be quite fatherly in his attitude. He was a safe, conventional man, and therefore popular. His successor was led to believe that there were high expectations of him, because he was young. But before long he found that there were many factions in this small parish and that no small skill was required to keep them from quarrelling with one another and, worse still, from feeling displeasure towards him. There were two landowners who divided the parish into two parts. There was the boarding school and its staff, the villagers, large and small so to speak, and the Welsh-speaking Welsh, half of those being

Nonconformists. And between them there was the vicar, like an Aunt Sally, should they wish to treat him as such. He had had enough of Manafon's crudity. But on looking back, he saw that the farmers there had more of an excuse for their harsh behaviour. They had not had much education or experience of the civilised world. But here in Eglwys-fach was a stratum of people who had had both, and were therefore less able to plead ignorance. The vicar gradually learned of mankind's old weaknesses, such as snobbery, jealousy and love of money. But he also recognised the challenge that was in front of him. He now had a more sophisticated congregation, and his sermons had to be carefully planned to deal with the new situation. He could not continue to talk of the world of nature all the time, but had to try to face some of the problems of the day, and of the mind of man. But he kept to the pattern of living that had become second nature to him by now, studying in the morning, walking in the afternoon and visiting his flock in the evening. And in addition to this, of course, there was the task of finding time to write his poems.

Immediately before leaving Manafon he had met James Hanley, the novelist, who was at the time living in Llanfechain in the north of the county. When he heard that the rector's poetry had not been published in London he promised that he would do his very best to right the wrong, and on his next visit to the city he contacted Rupert Hart-Davis who said that he would very much like to publish it. Until then the poems had only been published by small presses in Wales. Since he was introducing a new poet to the English public, Hart-Davis insisted on having a preface to the book by John Betjeman, and he invited the rector to London to meet them both. The parishioners had heard in advance that their new vicar was a poet, and great were their efforts to get hold of some of his work in order to try to discover what kind of strange man it was who was about to descend upon them. But now, with the publication of the work in London, it became easy enough for them to buy a copy if they wished. It was in this way that things went on, with him a recognised poet, a parish priest, and a bird-watcher. His work as a vicar was conventional enough, and included holding bilingual services, visiting his people, helping from time to time with the work of the school and attending the social and fashionable events of the middle class. One of the attractions of the parish, before he arrived, had been its proximity to Aberystwyth with its library and university. Soon after he settled there, a professor from Cambridge came to lecture on Chekhov, and the vicar went to hear him, expecting a feast. But alas,

The lecturer did not raise his head from his little book for a whole hour, the dryest lecture the vicar had ever heard. His enthusiasm for attending lectures disappeared. And he did not have much joy in the library, either. The books were there, of course, but he soon realised that he wasn't a scholar, prepared to spend hours in that large arid place, when a blessedly sunny day was calling him out of doors.

Greater joy was to be had with the birds. The river Dovey as it joined the sea was an area well known for its birds. The owner of the estate that extended alongside the river was Hubert Mappin, a wealthy and generous man, who was also an ardent churchman. As he wandered on this estate, the vicar had peace and quiet to forget about the tiny troubles of the parish. He also knew that the owner was in complete sympathy with him.

Apart from the local birds – some of them quite rare, since they only drop in on their way to or from their breeding place – Cardiganshire was home to the kite, a bird that doesn't nest anywhere in Britain outside Wales. William Condry was already a member of Pwyllgor Gwarchod y Barcud, the Committee for the Protection of the Kite, and the vicar joined too. This meant that the nests had to be found in the spring in order to keep an eye on them to see how many chicks would come from the nest later on. A landowner on whose property a kite had succeeded in raising a brood would receive a financial reward from the committee, but the vicar preferred to try to keep the location of the nest a secret, if it wasn't too close to the farm. The less people knew about the nests, the better. As he roamed around Cardiganshire he became familiar with a new part of Wales. What is more attractive than the little oak trees to be found along hillsides in the vicinity of Pontrhydfendigaid and Tregaron, with a little stream slipping past and the pied flycatcher and the redstart singing their bitter little songs from their twigs? And it would be there, more than anywhere else, that the kite would nest, in a fork in a tree. A thrill would go through him every time one of these golden-red birds arose from some trees in April, proving that its nest was sure to be there somewhere. Once, as he came quickly over the crest of the hill he saw a nest some ten yards in front of him, and the bird sitting on it. The bird did not rise, and neither did he move, but stared straight into the sharp eye of the kite as it stared back at him.

Protecting kites in Wales has had an interesting history. From being a quite common bird in the England of the Middle Ages, it had retreated to the remote hills of Wales, and by the beginning of this century its numbers had fallen to three or four pairs. Early in the century one or

two English people started to take an interest in them, and some of the
farmers and shepherds of Cardiganshire would remember these people
by name. By the time the protection committee was formed, the number
of kites had increased somewhat, but they continued to be in danger.
Most of the members of the committee were English, with Captain
Vaughan, a former member of the navy, as chairman. Very often, when
speaking with the farmers, it was difficult for them to understand what
you meant, until you used the English word 'kite'. It wasn't an uncommon experience, either, to hear a farmer denying that they were in his
area at all, with one of them flying above him as he spoke! But there
were honourable exceptions. There was a shepherd living at the head
of one of the valleys who would keep a diary to count how many times
he saw a kite in his own area, and this was a help to those who came to
look for their nests in the spring.

Adding his experiences in Cardiganshire to those he had in north
Wales, the vicar was able to form a unified picture of Wales itself, and
when someone asked him where the area or spot was that he had written
about, the answer, of course, was that it didn't exist. When he was in
Manafon he took the hill-country of Montgomeryshire as a background to his poems. While he was in Eglwys-fach, his mind tended to
return to the same place; but slowly the land of Cardiganshire was also
influencing him. In addition, this was the period, in the 1960s, when
the political situation worsened, and some of the younger Welsh people
began to use more direct methods against English oppression. Men
such as Emyr Llywelyn were treated quite abominably by the police,
and the poet from Eglwys-fach responded by writing poems that were
more patriotic. Of course, he was accused of narrow-mindedness by
the English critics. This was the period of some of his most bitter poems
against the English. But he did not act directly, remembering Saunders
Lewis's advice when he said that one should not expect too many
actions from a writer, because it is through his work that he is able to
influence others.

As was his custom, he would escape to the countryside in the afternoon to forget about the small troubles of the parish. But one cannot
escape completely. People's words and ideas continue to run through
the mind, and he had enough of these from the English of Eglwys-fach.
There was no-one like the Englishman; such a blessing he had been to
the rest of the world! 'I would like to hear someone other than an
Englishman saying that,' would be his answer. But he was a voice in the
wilderness, apart from Gwydol Owen in the post office. When Chur-

chill died, many of the English thought that the vicar was at fault for not praying for him in church. When Kennedy was killed some of the self-important people came to church in black clothes to show that they were of the same lineage. When there was a fashionable wedding or funeral they would come to church in clothes they had hired from Moss Bros! The fact that this agitated the poet's mind was proof that he was looking for new subjects. And the fact that he was still writing about the heart of the countryside without still living at its centre would be bound to create a rift in his art. He had in the past drawn his characters mainly from this source, but now, apart from the occasional character such as Hubert Mappin, the type of man that was most evident in Eglwys-fach was not to his liking as a subject for poetry. The tendency, therefore, was to write occasional poems rather than poems which arose from a more specific point of view. However he had two breaks as a result of winning a literary prize that forced him to travel overseas. Until now he had held that Wales was sufficient for him, and that he did not wish to go anywhere else. But after accepting the prize, he decided that he would go to Scandinavia first, to see the birds in September migrating past Falsterbo. It was a fascinating experience seeing thousands of birds of prey moving first thing every morning for about two hours. He also had a chance in Denmark to enquire about Kierkegaard, the Danish theologian, although he did not get time to find his grave. Then in 1966 he decided to visit Spain. He had read a book about a wilderness in southern Spain called the Coto Doñana, and nothing would do except to see the place, which was also a nature reserve. He persuaded Bill Condry to come with him, and first thing one morning towards the end of April the two started in the vicar's little car on their long journey, intending to camp as often as possible in order to keep the costs down.

After landing in France everything went well until they reached Arcachon on the other side of Bordeaux. Having camped the previous night they were on their way when they saw an interesting bird. Out of the car they came, taking their binoculars, but in no time, even though there was no warning to be seen, officers from the air force arrived and arrested them for spying! The rest of the day was spent answering silly questions from the air force and the police, who had come all the way from Bordeaux to cross-examine these two dangerous men! At last the farce was over, and they were free to go on their way, but they lost a whole day to no purpose at all.

Crossing the border between France and Spain made a deep

impression on the poet. One minute they were in the neat countryside of southern France. Within a short while they were driving down a bare, poor street with rags hanging from the windows to dry in the strong sunshine. They had reached Spain, the land of the sad-faced knight. Having gone through this village they saw the barren land stretching to the horizon; and so it was for hundreds of miles except for the occasional city on the way. The first city they stayed in was Burgos. On the outskirts of the town there was a campsite, and there they stayed overnight. But it came close to freezing that night, and before dawn the poet got up to go for a walk in order to get warm. He walked towards the east to meet the sun and his blood soon warmed. The nightingales were singing in the cold of the morning and the wryneck was making a mournful noise in the bushes. Then, as he came to the top of the hill, he saw the sun rising red, and the impoverished peasantry started to head for the fields. The dawn always has a special magic, but now in an unfamiliar country like Spain it was exceptionally enchanting. Migrating birds were rather scarce to begin with, but after they had passed Valladolid there was no shortage at all, with birds of all kinds to be seen flying and perching on the wires, many of them totally new to R. S.

Waiting ahead of them was Andalucía, a mountainous province of white homesteads which displayed the influence of the Moors. They were greatly tempted to drink from the foaming streams that came down from the mountains to the villages, but R. S. insisted that they fill a cask provided by somebody reliable and put tablets in it, for fear of fever. The beauty of some of the villages was quite treacherous, Grazalema especially so. But they were warned before arriving not to touch the local cheese because of the goats' milk in it.

One evening they came to the top of a pass and stopped to look around for somewhere to camp. They saw a building that looked like an old cowshed and went towards it through the heather. The crickets were singing as a great choir, filling the air around them, and creating a magical atmosphere. They went to the door of the cowshed and listened, and there came a sound from inside as of something breathing – an animal or a man? They went away very quietly and pitched their tents further down the pass; at least that is what Bill Condry did, but R. S. prepared his bed in the open air since night had fallen. He got very little sleep that night. Sleeping out-of-doors in a foreign country was such a strange experience that he was full of imaginings of all kinds, and he awoke several times during the night and saw the moon moving along the crest of the black mountain in front of him. By morning his bedclothes were wet from the dew, but within ten minutes after the sun had risen they were completely dry.

Having arrived at the edge of the nature reserve, the Coto Doñana, they discovered that there was no road for the eighteen miles to the *palacio* where they were to stay for a week. Some vehicles did travel over the sand through the wilderness, but their tracks were too deep for the Mini. Having ventured for a mile or two they became stuck in the ruts, and there was nothing for it but to be dragged to the *palacio* by one of the large vehicles. But having arrived, they had a wonderful week on the reserve. Bill Condry had been to Africa, but this was R. S.'s first experience of being in the middle of a wilderness. There were eagles, kites, shrikes, herons of all kinds and hundreds of other unfamiliar birds, and Bill Condry was fortunate enough to see a wild boar with its young. Every morning R. S. would set out on a journey to a new part of the reserve, with the southern sun striking him mercilessly. Every night he would return to see the mosquitoes rising in black columns as the sun went down. And at night the unfamiliar sounds of the wilderness would come to them as they lay in their tents, the strangest sound of all being that of the red-necked nightjar, which sounded like a horse trotting.

Within the week it was time for them to start on the long journey home, and having been dragged over the sand once again, they turned the nose of the car northwards. Door to door, they were away from home for a day or two short of a month, and R. S. would remember the journey for the rest of his life.

Later on, thinking about the experience he realised how the trip had shown him again *o ba radd roedd ei wreiddyn*, 'what stuff his roots were made of'. In taking their tents with them it was as if they had agreed to remain out in the heart of the countryside and to turn their backs on the culture of Spain. By doing this, of course, they missed the wonders of the Prado, the cathedrals, the monasteries and the architecture of places such as Granada. But R. S. was like that. Even though he was very fond of music and art, he would never be comfortable in academic and learned company. It was a certain shyness, along with a poor memory, that made it difficult for him to enjoy himself in a literary gathering, and given the choice between a meeting of that sort and the chance to go out into the countryside to enjoy the world of nature, it was the latter that he would choose every time, as Bill Condry would, too.

It was in this way that he came to know himself, with all his weaknesses, because it is, of course, a weakness not being able to speak knowledgeably and eruditely about intellectual matters such as literature, art and philosophy. No-one can avoid the company of learned people without being the poorer. At the same time one must remember the difference between scholars and creative people. It is easy to spend a whole day on a lyric and to fail in the end. But in the same space of time a student or a scholar will have perhaps read a whole book, and remembered it too. The creative mind usually has a poor memory. It will forget the things that are on the surface of life, but unbeknown to the poet other things sink into his subconscious to form there a matrix or pool from which he can draw at some time in the future. It is in this way that so many successful poems come into being.

Before he went to Spain R. S. heard that the vicar of Aberdaron was leaving the parish. Since he was already the tenant of a cottage in Y Rhiw on the estate of Plas-yn-Rhiw and also so fond of the Llŷn Peninsula, it would make sense if he succeeded the vicar of Aberdaron. The trouble was that Hubert Mappin was ill and unlikely to recover. R. S. did not feel like leaving him in his current state, especially since Patricia Mappin was a churchwarden. But as it happened, Aberdaron remained vacant because of a lack of applicants, and after the death of Hubert Mappin there was nothing to prevent R. S. from going. He wrote to the bishop, was accepted, and in May he and his wife moved from Cardiganshire to the Llŷn Peninsula. The appeal of Aberdaron was that it was so similar to Holyhead, if one forgot about the town of Holyhead itself. The vicarage was exposed to all winds, but was, because of this, also in the eye of the sun. The herring gulls would stand on the chimney-stack the same as in Holyhead, making their noise, redolent of the sea. And from the windows of the vicarage the sea was to be seen, about half a mile away. He also soon learned that Welsh was the language of the majority of the parishioners, the flowing and open language of the Llŷn Peninsula. So for the first time in his life R. S. was now in a parish where he could use the language with almost everyone, every single day.

After the usual trouble of moving furniture and seeing his books on every rise of the stairs, he set about the work of painting the interior of the house white, work that was not unpleasant in May with the strong light filling every room and the cry of the whimbrel to be heard from outside as these birds went on their way north to breed. He never had a house that satisfied him, and there was something missing in every church – a lack of taste or architectural deficiencies – but his wife's advice as an artist was a help in improving the situation somewhat. While they were in Eglwys-fach, they heard of a blacksmith in England called Alan Knight, and asked him to make a beautiful chandelier of wrought iron. This was a great asset for the church, and when they saw their chance in Aberdaron, they succeeded in persuading the warden to place a similar one there in memory of a relative of hers. Because both of them were so fastidious, R. S. asked himself many times during his career, wouldn't it have been better if he had left the heart of the country-side in order to reap the artistic advantages available in the main centres? But he knew the answer almost before asking. If he had to choose between a magnificent cathedral and a small country church, it would be the latter he would choose every time. As far as the cathedrals were concerned, with their ostentation and their war banners, and the organ thundering fit to shatter the roof – these always smacked of the nationalism and militarism of England. For him, the English for the most part were a people who continued to dote on such things. But it was the small, plain, unassuming things that appealed to him. That was what stirred him in Manafon to write about the smallholder in his tiny fields. That was why he wrote an article for a periodical like Y Fflam, praising Nonconfirmist places of worship such as Soar-y-mynydd and Maesyronnen. But the fault that he saw in Nonconfirmity was that it had started in plain but beautiful buildings like Maesyronnen, and, after becoming respectable and beginning to win wealthier people as members, had tried to put a shine on things and finished up with grand and tasteless places. But to be fair, this wasn't the fault of Non-confirmity alone. When he went to Eglwys-fach and saw how much needed to be done to the church, he visited many churches in Car-diganshire to look for ideas, but alas! Nothing of worth was to be had anywhere. Aberdaron was the first church with a bit of character to come under his care. It wasn't perfect by a long way. It too had been worked on over the centuries, but some features from the early period continued to give it a special quality. And its position at the edge of the sea was virtually unique. From his lectern inside the church the vicar could see the waves breaking on Ynys Gwylan across the bay; and sometimes during Communion first thing in the morning, when there was silence inside, there would come the sound of the wave breaking on the beach close by. The contrasts created by the presence of the sea have a special charm. For instance, Christmas is completely different near the sea from what it is in the heart of the countryside. One also usually thinks of the call of the owl as an inseparable part of wooded land. But that is the song of the tawny owl. There is also the little owl, and sometimes on quiet nights, between the sound of the waves murmuring on the beach, this owl's doleful call is also to be heard, especially in March.

And yet, quiet days were rather rare in Aberdaron. The wind was the main feature of the place, with its boisterous music filling the vicarage almost every day. It would blow from the north-west for days sometimes, whistling under the front door and making it very unpleasant to open the latter to whoever came by. The walls of the house were clad in slate, an attempt to keep out the driving rain, but one morning there rose a strong wind from the south-east snatching slate after slate from off the house like cards. This was the type of weather that R. S. had been used to in Holyhead, but it was somewhat grievous for a delicate person such as his wife.

For some people, life is a matter of looking back, and although that is not natural in a young man, it was R. S.'s tendency because of his *hiraeth*. He had lived at home long enough, and it was nice to be able to leave Holyhead and start a new life. But even in the college in Llandaff, and more so again in Chirk, he began to remember the sea and the whole atmosphere of Anglesey. Even in Chirk he was within reach of the hills and Welsh areas; but after marrying and having to move from there to Maelor Saesneg, he longed not only for the sea but also for the hill-country, so tediously flat was the dairy land around him. Being appointed rector of Manafon did something to allay that *hiraeth* by bringing him back to the hills. And after twelve years in that place, there was no *hiraeth* for the area while he was in Eglwys-fach, but his muse continued to feed on it for a very long time because of its fruitfulness as a subject for his poems. Having reached Aberdaron, however, not only was there no *hiraeth* for Eglwys-fach – it wasn't the source of many poems, either. To tell the truth, his muse had dried up. Having kept on writing for a quarter of a century about the life of the countryside, and later about the condition of Wales, he had milked the subject pretty dry, and it was fortunate that he changed publishers with his next book. His first publisher, Rupert Hart-Davis, had given up publishing years previously, and his business was bought by other publishers who, in R. S.'s opinion, were without much real interest in poetry. He therefore turned to Macmillan with his new book, a book that displayed new subject-matter and a new style.

However, his mind continued to ruminate on his experiences in Eglwys-fach, and foremost amongst those was the question of personality. His hold on his identity had been weak from the start, but that did not matter much in Manafon, as there was so little need to show it amongst the common folk of that parish. But having come to Eglwys-fach more pressure had been put on him to conform to the conventional type of parish priest. This, of course, meant that everyone there played some part, consciously or unknown to himself, competing against one another to appear a man of substance who could look back on a successful career. The people of the armed forces wanted you to know that they had been 'someone' in the forces by retaining their rank after retiring. The others wanted to convince their neighbours that they too were of account by giving sherry parties and the like. They were petty people, people who tried to create a bit of a storm in a teacup. But to what extent were they conscious of this? Can a man face life if he feels that he is no-one? There was a series on BBC Radio at the time, and R. S. suggested the possibility of having a discussion on this subject. It was done, but without much success. The members of the panel failed to get to grips with the problem. Take a man who is a bit of a character, with his amusing or tiresome traits, and his comical whims. Time was when he was young and to all appearances fairly normal, if there is such a condition. But he started to behave oddly. Did he do this on purpose, being conscious at first of what he was doing, and then forgetting as the habit took hold of him? A friend of R. S.'s, when he was in Eglwys-fach, would tell of his experience of a cousin of his. When the two men were younger they were friendly, indeed very close to each other. But the cousin, who was in the army, started to get on in the world, reaching the top of his profession and becoming a very important man. R. S.'s friend admitted to him that he could not be doing with him after that. He was so full of his job and importance that he could not remember the affinity that had once thrived between them. Is this more common in England and among the English than in Wales? Wales lost her leaders centuries ago. But there is still a ruling class in England, the product of the public schools and the armed forces, perhaps. The Englishman has more confidence, and therefore tends to be more overpowering. R. S. was quite fortunate. Because he was of a tolerant nature, and had chosen the unremarkable parishes, so to speak, he had little trouble. But if there is to be trouble, then it will raise its head where there is someone in the parish who likes to think of himself as a squire. And if he is accepted in that 'role' by others, this gives him the right to have his own way. One of the first men he will try to bring down is the vicar, since the vicar's function is to keep the peace in the parish, not drive people into head-on collision with one another. The worst ones for doing this, perhaps, are officers of the armed forces, and fate plays into their hands since in the armed forces the chaplain is subordinate to them in rank. It is very difficult for an officer who has retired to convince himself that he has done so. And there is the vicar in front of him to remind him of his superior rank. And since R. S. saw Christ's message as a totally pacifist one, trouble was sure at some time to raise its head. By remaining out in the heart of the countryside during the years of the war, he had avoided many of the troubles that would have arisen in the towns, with so many of the young people in the forces, and their parents coming to church on tiresome national prayer-days, expecting to hear prayers for victory and for the safety of their children. You cannot make these people see that praying for one man in a war means that you wish the worst to his enemy. And yet, trouble did arise from time to time, especially in Eglwys-fach. And often, in order to keep the parish more or less united, the vicar would give in to some extent, except in matters of major principle. But the question stayed with him: what kind of people were these deep down? There is some etiquette amongst the middle class that insists that a gentleman is always gentlemanly; but behind closed doors, as it were, and in private conversations, the habit breaks down, and malice and jealousy and cruelty come to light. This is understandable, since man is a sinner. But amongst people who claim to be Christians in that they attend the services of the Church, it could be expected that they would then be humble enough to apologise. But R. S. did not encounter one example of this throughout his career, and so the memories continue to be sour.

A creative artist has to be painfully honest with himself. He has to look as objectively as possible at his creations. What is the point of pretending that the poem is a good one, if it is not? But can the same honesty be expected from other people? Are not so many of life's activities means of escaping from such self-knowledge? How many people could persevere, if they knew in their hearts that they were quite unimportant and did their work often in a quite untidy way? As a result there is the whole pageant of mankind with its fantasies, its whims and its tricks. The world loves its own concerns. People come in their thousands to stare with a mixture of admiration and envy at the winners of medals, or those who have enough money to be able to put up a show in the presence of others. That is the way of the world. Shakespeare saw this, and Ellis Wynne of Y Lasynys, perhaps. That is why sermons are still needed, if there's an audience there to hear them. Over the centuries millions have listened to these truths. As Shelley said, it is not through lack of counsel and knowledge that the world went astray. But having listened, how many have gone even as far as Agrippa, who said to Paul, 'Almost thou persuadest me to be a Christian'? No, the world, including the majority of the members of the Church, is still not converted, because they do not believe in Jesus Christ when he says, 'Woe unto you, when all men shall speak well of you!' If R. S. had thought of being the vicar of one of the large towns, the glimpse of mankind that he had in Eglwys-fach would have been vitally important early on in his life. But since he wasn't like that, neither a novelist nor a dramatist, he saw it all as an unpleasant experience that only deepened his love of the countryside and the world of nature. And because of this, it wasn't only his ministry that failed, but his poetry too, because of its lack of human scope. In Manafon he tried to write about the people of the country, searching for a symbol of mankind. There was, therefore, an objective element in his work; but having reached Aberdaron, since there was no sustenance for his muse in looking back on Eglwys-fach, he turned increasingly to the question of the soul, the nature and existence of God, and the problem of time in the universe.

Writing about the Llŷn Peninsula is pleasurable work, but the majority of the people of Wales already know about it. Llŷn was for centuries on the route to Bardsey Island, and was therefore well known to the pilgrims who believed that three pilgrimages there were equivalent to one to Rome. Llŷn was an important part of the Celtic Church, with Aberdaron one of the mother churches of Wales. The churches of Clynnog Fawr, Pistyll and Llangwnnadl were all on the pilgrims' route, and with places such as St Mary's Well and Y Gegin Fawr still standing this period is remembered to this day. That is the atmosphere that is to be felt there. And some come in search of it. But having had time to settle there, the vicar found that there was also another aspect to the area. In the summer the peninsula was full of tourists, with Aberdaron packed, the English licking their ice-creams, or queueing to buy a newspaper to bury their heads in. Mynydd Mawr was opposite Bardsey Island, and not far from the ruins of Mary's Chapel and its well. The views were miraculous, but the most common sight was the rows of cars and the motorists with their heads in newspapers swallowing the petty news of the materialist world. And above all this the air force would practise astoundingly noisily almost every day. It became obvious to R. S. that there was a tension here. On the one hand there was the eternal appearance of the heather and the rocks and the sea, but overhead and everywhere else were auguries that the twentieth century was demanding attention even to the extent of destroying everything that was left of the Middle Ages.

R. S. felt that he had said what he had to say about the political situation of Wales. He had tried to write as a Welshman, even though it was in English that he did so, but there was an element of strain because of the kind of life he had to live. But finding himself in a totally Welsh community in Aberdaron, he no longer felt it necessary to emphasise his Welshness, only to accept it as a completely natural fact. Welsh was the language of the majority of the inhabitants, and there was no question of anything else in their homes or in their meetings. He had reached the destination of his own personal pilgrimage. Standing on the summit of Mynydd Mawr on a fine day, he could see Holyhead in the north and imagine himself as a child forty years before, playing on the beach there. Forty years distant in time, and only forty miles the distance. If one took a map of Wales, it would be easy enough to trace his geographical journey from being a child in Anglesey to being an old man in the Llŷn Peninsula. It formed a kind of oval from Holyhead to Chirk, out to Maelor Saesneg for a few miles, and starting to turn back in stages past Manafon and Eglwys-fach, a pretty limited circuit to correspond to his limited experience of life. How would things have turned out if he had been able to speak Welsh from the beginning? A futile question. But what he became more conscious of in Aberdaron was the fact that he had to write poetry in English. The conflict was more acute, although it was too late to do much about it. Many people asked him during his career in the Church whether there was a conflict between his role as priest and his role as poet, but he did not see one. But it was very different in the case of the languages involved: living in a traditionally Welsh area such as the Llŷn Peninsula, speaking the language every day, and yet expressing himself in a foreign language. For that was how he viewed the language on the lips of the visitors. Silently, he cursed their language. But the longer he remained in the area the greater the danger he saw to the Welsh language. It was this that turned him into more of a patriot than ever before in his life, if not in his literary work. Consider, I ask you, the audacity of an English woman on her way out of church after Morning Prayer, turning to the timid vicar at the church door and saying, 'I'm sorry we didn't pray for the queen!' And he not ready enough with the correct retort: 'Woman, be thankful that you had a service at all in your foreign language.'

'Aren't the English kind to the Church?' say the Welsh. But now he had an answer. 'So they should be, having an English service so far from home.' This was the tension in his life as a Welshman in the Llŷn Peninsula, the resort of the tourist. But there was another tension that had to do with his work as a poet. For the inhabitants, the age of the area was to be seen in its religious connections with the Celtic period. And yet, gazing on the pre-Cambrian rocks in Braich y Pwll, R. S. realised that he was in contact with something that had been there for a thousand million years. His head would spin. A timescale such as this raised all kinds of questions and problems. On seeing his shadow fall on such ancient rocks, he had to question himself in a different context and ask the same old question as before, 'Who am I?', and the answer now came more emphatically than ever before, 'No-one.'

But a no-one with a crown of light about his head. He would remember a verse from Pindar: 'Man is a dream about a shadow. But when some splendour falls upon him from God, a glory comes to him and his life is sweet.' So strong was the light in Braich y Pwll; the sun shining on him, the bees humming, and the sea flowing past like a huge blue river. Sometimes he would think that he had always been there, part of the unbroken chain of being. This was the subject of some of his new poems, which appeared under the auspices of his new publisher, Macmillan. It is so easy to believe in God when you are on your knees with your eyes closed, just as it is easy to be a Christian far away from the clamour and the trials of the world of people. But the memory would come of him on his knees in the church porch as far back as Manafon. He was neither inside nor outside, but on the border between the two, a ready symbol of contemporary man. To a thinking person, there are two aspects to the sea, the external and the internal. Or, if you like, it is both a mirror and a window. In the mirror is to be seen all the beauty and glory of the creation: the colours and the images of the clouds, with the birds going past on their eternal journey. But on using it as a window, an endless war is to be seen, one creature mercilessly and continuously devouring another. Under the deceptively innocent surface there are thousands of horrors, as if they were the creator's failed experiments. And through the seaweed, as if through a forest, the seals and the cormorants and the mackerel hunt like rapacious wolves. What kind of God created such a world? A God of love? The question was formerly asked by Tennyson in his long poem *In Memoriam*. Some people have argued that we humans cannot comprehend the feelings of animals. True enough. But it isn't only animals that are prey to the ruinous forces in life. People, too, are prone to being tortured by bacteria so small as to be invisible. There is something frightening in the fact that a great genius like Schubert or Keats can fall prey to forms so low down the chain of being. Many poems on this subject appeared in R. S.'s new book from Macmillan, with the modern influences represented by the machine making sudden appearances through it all. But a poet is a chameleon. His privilege is to be able to change his mind and his attitude. For an honest person, it isn't possible to hold always to the same position. Face to face with a mystery as awful as this, how can anyone be absolutely certain one way or the other? That was Job's problem, mute before his God. That was Blake's question, 'How do you know?' If a mortal being such as man could comprehend God, what kind of God would that be? In Thomas Aquinas's doctrine, God reveals himself according to the creature's ability to receive that knowledge, but of course never revealing all.

The glory of west Wales is its changeable weather. This is distilled in the old traditional verse 'Nos a Bore', 'Night and Morning', which describes the difference between a night of wind and rain on the banks of the river Menai and the heavenly quiet on the following day. Likewise in the Llŷn Peninsula. What is more exciting, more likely to lift the heart after a period of stormy weather, than seeing the blue start in the west, before slowly spreading over the sky to allow the sun to appear and the sea itself to turn blue? This is a symbol for the lifting of a burden from the soul after a period of despair. This is what makes the Llŷn Peninsula a marvellous area in which to live. Like Anglesey, the Llŷn Peninsula is one of the first places to sense a turn in the weather following a day or two of wind and rain. And in the winter, because of the effect of the Gulf Stream, it is like a platform from which to see the far mountains, white under snow. And even if snow comes to the peninsula, as it does occasionally, it doesn't remain long because of the salt water there.

The Llŷn Peninsula is a place to return to. Having been in England for a while, R. S. would reach some spot near Bryncroes, where the sea would be visible all around him, emphasising the fact that he lived on a peninsula. On fine days the peninsula is like a long branch suspended between sea and sky. From there in the winter one can see Ireland with the snow white on the Wicklow Mountains, and sometimes in the summer from the summit of Mynydd Mawr almost the whole of Wales is visible, from Snowdon and Anglesey in the north as far as the Preseli

Hills and Carn Ingli in the south. And what is more lovely than seeing the sun rising in spring above the Rhinogau, filling the land of Llŷn with golden light? There is no magic like that of the dawn. It is as if you are viewing the world as a baby does in its cradle, completely innocent, before humankind awakes and rises to go about its wicked work.

Aberdaron was without a vicar for a year, so the people were glad to have even someone like R. S. Nor did he hide the fact that what he had done, more or less, was come there to retire. It is necessary to be clear on this matter. In each one of the parishes he had been in, R. S. did his work as conscientiously as possible. He was not popular, nor a distinguished preacher. But he would visit his parishioners regularly, especially the sick. For example, in Manafon, one particular old man was confined to bed for nine years, before dying at the age of ninety. The rector visited him almost weekly, and listened to the same old stories week after week. No-one else was willing to go there to live in the past like this. But the rector would read the Bible to him and administer Communion to him, and it appeared that this was a comfort to the old man, who in his day had been a bit of a lad. Even so, R. S. would arrange his time so as to have a fair amount of freedom. He would study in the morning, feeling that at that time of day a priest's proper place was in his own room. This involved sacrificing quite a lot, as the morning is the time for seeing uncommon birds. This was particularly true in Aberdaron, especially in the spring and autumn when the birds would be migrating. But he would make an exception from time to time, especially in the autumn, when he would get up before dawn to see the smaller birds moving down the peninsula towards Bardsey, or sea birds driven closer to land by a great storm from the west. Calm was what was needed to see the smaller birds, and stormy weather to see the sea birds. But even on occasions of this kind, despite the temptation, he would feel uncomfortable about loitering too long, because he wasn't vicar of Aberdaron mainly in order to observe birds!

But so long as rural parishes such as his existed he did not feel his conscience pricked at all. There were always plenty of able and ambitious priests who longed to go to the large towns, a means of escaping the heart of the countryside, which they neither knew nor loved. But because of his unadulterated love for the countryside, throughout his career R. S. chose the care of small parishes, thereby securing the conditions that are essential to a poet, namely time and peace. Had he become vicar of one of the large towns, a thousand and one small matters would have absorbed his time. And like some justification of his desire, he was never throughout his life offered 'preferment'. And mercifully, in Aberdaron, amongst gentle and friendly people, he did not suffer the minor troubles that had been part of his experience in each of the other parishes.

His father died in 1965 in the hospital in Holyhead, at a time when R. S. was convalescing after treatment to his shoulder. He knew that his mother expected to be allowed to come to live with them, but he was unwilling to have her. She was a difficult person to live with, and it would not be fair to his wife. His mother's home was in a small row of houses, and therefore in a community. She had friends, which would not be the case if she moved to a new out-of-the-way place like Aberdaron or even Eglwys-fach, where he was at the time. There wasn't much wrong with his mother's health, but by 1969 his wife had become very ill. She had a disease that left her feeble for the rest of her life, and also damaged her sight. It became almost impossible for her to drive a car.

R. S. would go over to Holyhead fairly frequently to see how his mother was, sometimes calling on Charles Tunnicliffe on his way home. He would always find him busy making his incomparable illustrations of wild birds. His mother would also come to stay in Aberdaron from time to time, but he didn't see eye to eye with her. When this started and who was to blame, who knows? He would remember the difficulties there had always been between his father and her, although they had at intervals been happy enough. But it was she who insisted on being mistress, taking umbrage if she did not have her own way. As has already been said, she lost her parents when she was six years old and was raised by a relative who sent her in due course to a boarding school. She felt therefore that she had been deprived of love, and this did not add to the wellbeing of her home. And since his father was a sailor and often away from home, it was his mother who played the major role in R. S.'s upbringing. Looking back, with himself now a man and the father of a child, R. S. would remember that his mother had looked after him when he was young, but as he grew up, she remained too possessive of him, widening the gap between them. Nevertheless, it has to be admitted that it is a strain on both sides when, as it turned out in his case, a child remains at home until he is twenty-three years old, because of the length of an ordinand's training.

He was perhaps closer to his father, except that his father became deaf relatively early and was unable to hear his son's voice. He was a man who had seen the world and its ways, and he would perhaps have shared his experiences had he been able to have a normal relationship with his son. He had been a good singer and was therefore fond of music, and it was a great pain for R. S. to see him with his ear to the radio trying to hear the music. During his period in college R. S. heard that someone by the name of Pastor Jeffreys was coming to Bangor to hold a faith-healing meeting. He persuaded his father to come along to ask to have his hearing restored. Beforehand, R. S. prayed as he had never prayed before. In the hostel chapel there was a great crucifix hanging above the altar; and R. S. was for a time to be seen on his knees before it, praying for his father to have his hearing restored. And he did, for a while! On the night, the man arrived, and a great crowd assembled, his father in its midst. When his time came, he approached the man, and after the meeting, on their way to the station, he declared with great joy that he could hear a thrush singing. But, alas! after he had gone home, he slowly returned to his old condition. His wife was silly enough to accuse him of losing his faith. But who can understand the whole complexity of such things? Faith can doubtless create miracles, but there are many other factors at work, surely.

But in her turn, Margaret Thomas's time also came to an end. Ever since R. S. could remember she had complained; so he could never be sure whether the cause was illness or her pretending as much. But one day in Aberdaron he received a telephone message saying that his mother had fallen outside her house in Holyhead, and that the neighbours had found her. He went there and brought her back to Aberdaron. But within a few days it became clear that she was deteriorating, and having got the doctor it was decided that she had to be taken to Bangor. She was then moved to Llangefni, and there she died. The whole business left an unpleasant feeling in R. S., but he didn't know what the right answer would have been, if there was one at all. Strange, and perhaps crucial, is the relationship between a mother and her son. But the story was at an end. Although R. S. did not believe in the practice, he raised a modest stone in honour of his parents, because that would have been their wish. But the inscription would not have been commendable to one or other of them, because it was in Welsh.

'Although he did not believe in the practice'! What kind of priest was R. S? He was raised respectably enough. Although his father had experienced a rough life on the sea he was remarkably conventional and sociable. It was a real pain to him to get dirt on his shoes while going for a walk over the fields. But despite all the conventions, his parents had little taste for the finer things of life. The kind of order that existed in the Church in Wales in the 1930s has already been mentioned. Every 'important' parish was in the hands of priests who were getting on in age, and it was on them that the responsibility lay for instructing their curates in the ways of the world. And even if some of them knew something about the latter, how much did they know about taste in the arts and in poetry? And what would their paltry knowledge of such things be good for in the case of a curate who would have to spend the first half of his vicariate in the midst of the spiritual apathy of the bigoted common folk of the Wales of the 1930s? But once a young curate got his feet under him in one of these parishes, he was far enough removed from the grasp of the Church authorities to be certain to develop a quite independent and unconventional spirit. After years in such circumstances, R. S. would view with something less than enthusiasm the costly gravestones with their false words, or the unthinking rituals of the Church's conventional members; the monuments to the wretched youths killed in war; the pretentious, ugly gravestones that defaced so many graveyards in the heart of the countryside. All this only deepened the feeling within him that no memorial was necessary except for a plain wooden cross solely to indicate where your mortal remains were, for the sake of the family.

And consider the church services. How many people knew how to worship, kneeling and closing their eyes and offering themselves to God? The mark of Nonconformity was on too many of them. Despite his respect for so many Nonconformist ministers, R. S. was amazed at their attitude, presumptuous almost, towards the deity. When they prayed, they were too often as if under the impression that God was eavesdropping outside the door. And the music! God help us! How many church congregations can sing? How many organists can master their instruments? Talk about *cythraul canu*, the jealousy amongst musicians; in Manafon it was rampant. That is one thing that compensated him on going to Eglwys-fach. Patricia Mappin could play the organ and choose classical pieces to perform before the start of the service. But even then, R. S. was never fond of hymns, third-class verses set to similar music. Something he greatly preferred was chanting in the manner of the monks, but he himself wasn't enough of a musician to teach the congregation that kind of singing. That was another deficiency in his training at the theological college.

But if he was unconventional in his attitude towards the services and practices of the Church, how was it with his theology? As already mentioned, people liked to ask him whether there was any tension between his two offices as priest and poet, and he would deny this through insisting on seeing Jesus as a poet. But what confused people was his use of the word 'metaphor'. In a television programme he said that the Resurrection was a metaphor. So he didn't believe in it? But, of course, his point concerned the question of language. We do not have hard historical evidence for the resurrection of Christ. What we have are the words of the authors of the gospels and Saint Paul. They had a strange experience. They believed that the risen Christ had appeared to them. Accordingly, they sought to transmit their vision to future ages through the medium of words. If we have not had a vision of the risen Christ, we have to accept the verbal evidence of the Evangelists. But language is a symbol, a description of something in terms of something else. And, for R. S., that was the meaning of metaphor too.

Another aspect of Christianity was its rural background. Jesus ministered in the countryside. The basis for the greater part of his parables was the world of nature. His similes were natural ones. He compared the growth of the Kingdom to the growth of the seeds scattered on the land. The spirit moves just as the wind blows, with no-one knowing whence it comes, nor whither it goes.

For R. S. a glimpse of the blue sky through the bare trees was the same as looking at a stained-glass window in a cathedral. Going into the quiet and beauty of the moorland was like entering a more beautiful church than any he had ever seen. And looking on morning dew in the sun was like listening to the heavenly choir singing glory to God. He was doubtful whether, in an industrial town, he could have worshipped and continued to believe. That is, the countryside was indispensable to his faith. But, mercifully, he never had to put the thing to the test. He was free to preach a Christ of the countryside to the people of the countryside. The Christmas snow would come to sharpen the evening star in order to remind him of the one that once stood above the manger. The winter would roll away to give way to the spring, just as the stone was moved from the tomb to allow the risen Christ to appear. During Whitsun the strong wind would blow through the valley like the coming of the Holy Spirit. And at night in March he would see the farmers out in the fields with their lanterns helping new life into the world in the form of a little lamb. That was R. S.'s priestly work in Manafon, preaching the mysteries of the kingdom of heaven as they were revealed in the world that encompassed his parishioners. And since he lived in the countryside, as a poet, the other side of his function, he created poems about the countryside and about the people who lived and worked there.

Obviously, things changed in Eglwys-fach. There were many boys in the congregation. It was essential not to preach above their heads, but rather to mention standards, the challenge that would face them as they grew up. And in his poems he gradually turned away from the themes of the Welsh countryside, first to more directly nationalist topics, and then to poems on occasional subjects, but it was obvious that he had started to mark time, expecting a new direction to open up in front of him. But from the point of view of preaching, it wasn't the young men in Eglwys-fach who compelled him to avoid complexity. The need to do so started as soon as he went into the heart of the countryside. Welsh farmers are mainly people who work hard throughout the day and doze in front of the fire at night. They are not readers. So it is essential to keep fairly close to the land while preaching to them. This, too, affected his poems. These were on the whole simple and sincere, although they were not always as simple as some would insist. This was at once a weakness and a strength. Since the poems were neither sophisticated nor erudite, they were open to the scorn of knowledgeable critics. And yet, as some people put it, there is an element of simplicity in all true art.

He knew before going to Aberdaron that there would be English services in the morning, but he had not thought all that much about it. What he had not foreseen was their popularity. It was fashionable among the visitors to go to English Morning Prayer. So, in the summer, the service would be something like what it was in Eglwys-fach – that is to say, quite a crowd of English people present, with a fair handful of Welsh people enjoying their company! And as he would not know who would be there, it was essential to think fairly carefully about what he planned to say. It is a habit with some people while on holiday to go to church half hoping that they may receive some answer to their questions or their doubts. Many former worshippers have lost their faith because of the popular but over-simple presentation of science and technology. R. S. would attack these dogmas quite consistently, seeking to counteract their injurious influence on the majority of people. Here again this was perfectly harmonious with the new field of interest opening up in front of him as far as his poetry was concerned.

In 1968 R. S. and his wife went to Norway on a journey by car through the central part of that country. The main aim of the journey was bird-watching, but, as Tunnicliffe had told him beforehand, it was necessary to go quite far north in order to see the best birds. This was quite true, but they had an interesting enough fortnight, except that Norway was rather too similar to the hill-country of Wales. And yet, while climbing over the Jotunheimen, they had some idea of how it would be in the winter. It was July; but even so, the pass over the mountain had only recently been opened, and in the valleys tens of feet of snow still remained. After a fortnight amongst monotonous pine trees, it was no sorrow for the two to head for home.

Unfortunately, by the new year his wife had become ill before she had had much time in Aberdaron to do more than restore the garden and give it a new look. It was a long and painful illness and the side-effects were almost as bad as the disease itself, leaving her weak and ultimately affecting her eyesight. While she was in hospital in London, in order to raise her spirits and give her something to look forward to, R. S. arranged a vacation for both of them in Mallorca in October 1972. They went under the auspices of a company that arranged bird-watching holidays, and the two had to take a night-flight from Heathrow. What a new experience it was to look down on the Continent at night through the small window of the aeroplane! They crossed the French coast, with the lights of the towns visible below. Then darkness came for miles, suggesting that they were flying over the Alps. They reached Palma safely and went on a journey of an hour or more in a bus in the thick of night. At last, at approaching two o'clock in the morning, the lights were visible of the seaside town where they would be staying, and having reached the hotel everyone went to bed quite sleepy. They also had an interesting enough fortnight in the north-eastern part of the island, with the weather marvellously warm, although it was the end of October. Each night there came the song of the cicada from the bushes in the hotel garden, and outside the town all through the night the crickets would keep up a noise like that of the nightjar. This was R. S.'s first glimpse of the Mediterranean and, looking down on its incomparable blue from the top of the cliffs, he recalled his schooldays studying Vergil's *Aeneid* with its frequent references to the sea. Amidst the olive trees and the sound of goatbells everywhere, he had the feeling that he was in touch with a very old culture. One day he travelled up a valley and heard a goatherd walking the slope and talking in a normal voice, as if speaking to himself. But suddenly there came an answer from the opposite slope where there was another goatherd. So silent was the place that it was like a whispering gallery, enabling the two to hear each other, although there was something like two hundred yards between them.

An unpleasant aspect of the island was the residents' eagerness to shoot the birds. '*Coto*' signs, denoting shooting reserves, were everywhere. When R. S. mentioned this to one of the hotel staff, his reply was that birds came there in their thousands in the winter. Well, of course they do. The Mediterranean and North Africa are some of the main wintering grounds for birds of the north. But if they succeed in fleeing the cold of winter only to be shot by Spaniards, Italians and the like, then this, along with pesticide chemicals, will be sure before long to reduce their number significantly. Man has over the ages killed birds and animals; but with the new weapons and the pesticides he will in no time have an effect on them that his forefathers, throughout their history, never had. The Welsh are no worse than others in this respect, but their lack of knowledge and their lack of interest in the world of nature is a cause for concern. All power to the Welsh books and the programmes in the media which make a praiseworthy attempt to remove ignorance. In the old days, country children used to have time to familiarise themselves with nature while walking to school. But today, being provided with transport, they would be completely without contact with nature were it not for the interest of some of their teachers.

After the visit to Mallorca, life in Aberdaron went on quite without event. The main feature was the weather. To say this sounds pure cliché, but since R. S. had spent most of his life in the countryside, he was very conscious of the weather and given to delighting in its various changes. He learned much about the weather from his father who had a wealth of sayings and fables concerning it. And, like Holyhead, Aberdaron was exposed to all kinds of weather. The vicarage was in the teeth of every wind, and yet, during the eleven years that they were there, there was no snow or frost, only a little hoarfrost on the occasional night. But the sea was the thing. R. S. would take great delight in going out during a storm to watch the waves, as he used to do in the old days in Holyhead. When the wind was strong enough from the west and north-west the foam would rise like a fountain higher than the summit of

Bardsey on the eastern side, and Bardsey Sound would be like a stirred cauldron if the tide were running against the wind. It was easy to imagine the predicament of the sailing ships long ago, and how the inhabitants of Bardsey would be cut off, sometimes for weeks. Wasn't there a story about Ifan, Môr Awel, who once crossed in a boat to fetch help for a woman about to give birth? The people of Aberdaron were amazed when he landed, as it was no weather for anyone to venture into Bardsey Sound. And even in fair weather, the sea had to be respected. Wil, Tŷ Pellaf, would concur completely when R. S. told of the treacherous wave that came from somewhere, totally unexpected. When he was in Ireland, he heard of a woman sitting on a cliff in County Clare far removed, as it would seem, from the reach of the sea, but a higher wave than usual came and swept her into the sea and drowned her.

Mention has been made before of the comparison between the Llŷn Peninsula and Holyhead and of how R. S. would remember that he was living on a peninsula that, when he was in Holyhead, used to be on his horizon. By reaching Aberdaron he got rid of the old *hiraeth* for the sea and the west. What possessed him now occasionally was the *hiraeth* of time; the memories of his youth on Anglesey. But he knew that yielding to that was completely futile. Youth was much further away than Anglesey. Reaching the latter was only a matter of two hours in his car, even if it had changed out of all recognition. But there was no way of reaching the past except through the imagination, as he realised. During his career he spent most of his time amongst the elderly, and, as is well known, their tendency is to talk endlessly about the past. And, indeed, that is Wales's weakness. Don't most of us, when we have passed the period of our youth, tend to talk about the past? It is a bad sign. Hasn't Wales got a future? I fear that it is only a few brave people who believe in it.

The big question is this: in changing, do things change for the better? There were changes in the Church that were not to his liking. Committees had been engaged in considering the question of the reunification of the denominations. A commission on the liturgy had been busy considering changes to the services and retranslating the Scriptures. Since Welsh was for him a second language, R. S. did not feel that he was qualified to assess these new versions. But it was a different matter where English was concerned. For good or ill, this was his mother tongue and the language he had to write his poetry in. He wasn't content at all. He therefore clung to the King James Bible and to the

1662 Book of Common Prayer, considering the language of both to be indescribably superior, and, as far as he could judge, that was the case with the Welsh ones, too.

On the question of unification he felt very uncomfortable. He had been friends with Nonconformist ministers throughout his career, taking part in their services and fellowships from time to time. And, obviously, he was greatly indebted to one of them, H. D. Owen, for helping him to learn Welsh. He also admired their stand against war, and their loyalty to the old language in places like Aberdaron, where it would have paid them to provide for the English. But he had never felt comfortable in a chapel. There was a lack of taste, a lack of atmosphere. He knew, too, about the deficiency of the chapels' order of services. Such things made it impossible for him to worship satisfactorily in a chapel or to receive Communion there. In Aberdaron, only one building recommended itself, because of its position and traditions, as a suitable place to worship in, and that was the parish church. With the decline in the membership of all the denominations, there was enough space in the church to include everyone. All the other places of worship could have been closed, saving the cost of their upkeep. But this would hardly have been fair to the other denominations; and the churchgoers would not be so ready to see their own place of worship having to close, had the boot been on the other foot. So the vicar did nothing but retain the status quo, which meant, as long as John Morris was headmaster of the primary school, his complete cooperation. Each Christmas and Thanksgiving the children would come to the parish church to take part in the services. And at the start of every term, the vicar would go to the school to conduct an opening service. The governing body of the Church in Wales had ruled that a clergyman was free to retire at sixty-five if he so wished, but had no choice about going at the age of seventy. R. S. wasn't keen to remain as vicar to face the reformed services, along with the complications that were bound to arise following the attempt to unite the denominations. At the same time he was fond of the vicarage. While Sarn-y-Plas, the cottage in Y Rhiw was too small, there was plenty of space in the vicarage. Along the walls there were his wife's paintings, and in many of the rooms thousands of books of all kinds – excellent furniture. It would be more convenient to stay on and, having reached compulsory retirement age, to remain and do voluntary work in the parish. He wrote to the bishop to ask whether he wanted to appoint a successor. If not, R. S. would be willing to stay on in the living on the conditions mentioned. It was a disappointing answer that he received. So he wrote back to give the required notice of his intention to retire at the end of six months, when he would be sixty-five. He also determined to retire in the full sense of the word, and did not apply for the bishop's licence that would have enabled him to minister in the diocese. So it is that, seven years later, the parish of Aberdaron is still without a vicar.

The day arrived, and some of the furniture was moved to Sarn-y-Plas. But he had to get rid of two-thirds of his books owing to lack of space for them. Nor was there room for his wife's paintings on the stone walls of the cottage. When R. S. left Manafon, a journalist visited him to ask what he had achieved during his twelve years there. 'Nothing unusual,' was the answer. On Easter Sunday 1978 his insignificant career came to an end. If another journalist had asked the same question, the answer would have been the same. But this time no-one came, and a day or two later he found himself staring through the window of his new home across the beautiful but fierce waters of Porth Neigwl.

The date on the gable-end of Plas-yn-Rhiw is 1613. The likelihood is that Sarn Rhiw, as it is called by the local people, is of the same age. When the Keating sisters first saw the Plas it was a ruin. It was through their care that the place was restored and once again turned into a home. They became well known in Llŷn for their efforts to safeguard the natural beauty of the area. This meant that they opposed every attempt to develop the Llŷn Peninsula through establishing more and more caravan parks and the like. This aroused the enmity of many of the local people, who used to think of them as English newcomers without sympathy for the welfare of the locals. But the sisters continued to develop the work of the National Trust, with some of the cottages on the estate being handed over to the Trust. They also worked tirelessly to win new members to that body, boasting that each year it was they who recruited the greater number of these. In the old days R. S. and his family used to stay in a cottage called Fron Deg on the slopes of Mynydd y Rhiw. Out of their generosity the sisters offered them this cottage as a gift. But it was unusually small, without a lane of any kind leading to it. It wouldn't be a suitable place to which to retire, when the time came. So R. S. expressed his thanks and explained the reasons for not accepting. The next thing, to their great delight, was to be offered the tenancy of Sarn Rhiw, another place where they had once or twice stayed. The tenancy was a long one that would extend far enough into the future to include Gwydion's lifetime too.

Sarn-y-Plas stands on a wooded slope above Porth Neigwl. The local stone is called dolerite, and a single small piece of it is surprisingly heavy. Some of the stones of the house itself are huge. How the builders managed to get them into place to begin with, no-one knows. They certainly had a talent that has by now disappeared. From this cottage one can always hear the sound of the sea, as it is only about a hundred and fifty yards away. And sometimes on a still night there comes a sudden tumult from the beach, as the surge from the far Atlantic reaches the end of its journey. From his study window R. S. could see Cadair Idris on the far side of Cilan, bringing back memories of the time when he would climb it to admire the alpine flowers to be seen amongst its rocks in June. From the garden, when it was fine, if one walked only a few yards, Snowdon was to be seen, often white under snow in the winter, when the rest of the countryside was green. Between Snowdon and Cadair Idris one could see other hills, the hills of Merionethshire, such as Y Cnicht, Y Moelwynion and Y Rhinogau. 'What a place for writing poetry,' the visitor would say. Quite true, but because of the quiet rather than the views. There you have the main prerequisites of the creative mind, time and silence.

After rising in the morning the sun would shine into the rooms of the cottage through the small windows. Unfortunately, it would disappear quite quickly after lunch behind the trees surrounding the house. That was a loss after the vicarage at Aberdaron which was in the eye of the sun from sunrise to sunset. And yet the trees gave shelter to many more birds. The rooks would nest there in spring. The song of the tawny owl would be heard in winter, and sometimes in May an occasional migratory bird would call by and sing briefly before continuing on its journey north. And of course, from the beach at all times came the cry of the gulls and the other sea birds, and often a herring gull would stand on the chimney stack to yowl, as they used to do long ago in Holyhead. This is a noise that characterises seaside towns, and R. S. would remember once again that day in Manafon when three herring gulls flew over the valley, stirring in him a painful *hiraeth* for the sea to the west. Porth Neigwl was an exceedingly dangerous bay for the old sailing ships, and though he was so much inclined to praise the past at the expense of the present, seeing the waves rolling in so fiercely R. S. would give thanks that the machine had arrived, to save ships from being at the mercy of such seas. In the old days in weather of this kind the lifeboat would be launched time after time.

R. S. was henceforth free to live and write without any restriction placed upon him by the responsibilities of the office of parish priest. He was never a member of any political party. By all means, a priest should be interested in politics and, if necessary, deal with it in his sermons. But it is hardly fair to use the pulpit to preach party politics, with the congregation having no opportunity to ask a question or to answer back. Even so, if the majority in the congregation are members of a particular party, they see no fault in a preacher who supports their own cause. But if the preacher's convictions are different, then comes the criticism that maintains that he should stick to preaching the Gospel!

From the point of view of politics, patriotism was one of his favourite topics. He would see a need for reminding the Welsh-speaking congregations who they were and encouraging them to be proud of their nationality, remembering the labour of the valiant Welsh in the past to pass the language on to them. A verse particularly dear to him was that from Deuteronomy, the seventh verse of the seventh chapter: 'The Lord did not set his love upon you, nor choose you, because ye were more in number than any people; for ye were the fewest of all people'. An encouraging message for a small nation such as the Welsh; but no doubt his words on the whole fell on stony enough ground. When he first came to the parish and started mentioning Cymdeithas yr Iaith Gymraeg, no-one had heard of it. Or that was the impression he had, unless they were feigning. But there was one member of the Welsh congregation who happened to be different. Amongst the few who sometimes came to Evensong there were two who were not from the parish itself. When he came to ask, he heard that the husband was a 'detective', and that he and his wife had a cottage in the village, although they lived in Pwllheli. 'Huh,' he said to himself, 'what have I to do with the damned police?' But as he got to know the genial couple, he found that they were patriots of the true sort without any connection with the police. The man, Jack Roberts, had worked for a firm in London, and because the work had taken him here and there in Europe, he had mastered five or more languages, including Welsh, Russian, French, Spanish and English. He had a fairly good knowledge of Breton, and was also trying to get to grips with Basque. English is at the end of this list on purpose. It was, of all languages, the one he hated most. And since his wife Siani was a Welsh woman, he was under no compulsion to speak English.

After retiring, R. S. continued to visit these friends. At first, Evensong was still held in the church at Aberdaron, and if this family were there when R. S. went over, he would go home with them for a cup of tea and a chat. And naturally one of the main subjects under consideration on each occasion was the Welsh language, how it was in mortal danger and how weak were most of the Welsh-speaking Welsh in the face of this threat. R. S. had already noticed when he was a vicar how the undertakers would come to him after a funeral to pay the costs, take out their bilingual chequebooks, and having been informed of what they owed, start to write the cheques in English. Likewise the carpenters and builders. It was English-language invoices that all of them had, with the items entered in English throughout. And the more he took to noticing it, all the more English he saw: the shops, the post offices, the garages, all of them almost without exception in countryside and town alike conducting their business in English. On reflection, R. S. had no doubt that it was Cymdeithas yr Iaith Gymraeg that had woken him up to the situation. The story was true that he had heard as far back as Manafon when he had just started learning the language, about some minister having to leave the area under his care because he was too much of a Welshman. He couldn't believe the story at the time, but having been in the Llŷn Peninsula for some years he could easily credit it. This is the split in the Welshman's soul. In areas like Llŷn, Welsh is his mother-tongue and he speaks it fluently and naturally. But when it is a question of opening a shop, starting a business, keeping a hotel, or opening a camping area, there's nothing for it but English every time. In Parry-Williams's words:

> Cei ganmol hon fel canmol jŵg ar seld;
> Ond gwna hi'n hanfod – ac fe gei di weld.

> You can praise this one [the Welsh language] like
> praising a jug on a dresser;
> But make her a necessity – and you'll see.

It was in this way that he came to understand that the language had to battle on two fronts: against the oppression of the English state and its civil service; and also – the shame of it – against the Welsh themselves.

He experienced a monstrous example of this when he was vicar of Aberdaron. After some patriotic Welsh people had brought pressure to bear on the government, bilingual registers were given to the Church in Wales for registering marriages, with an order from the Registrar

General in London to make certain that it was English that appeared first in the register, and if the priest so wished, he could leave the Welsh out of it altogether, but not the English, on pain of death! The prejudice was clear, and R. S. protested to the Registrar General – but in vain, of course. Deanery discussions were held, and a letter was sent to the same man, with the same result. R. S. kept on protesting and encouraging more opposition; but in the next meeting of the clergymen, the Rural Dean said that he did not want to take the matter forward. In the meantime he had visited the churches and examined the registers, and nowhere but Aberdaron was registering marriages in the two languages. It was too much trouble, obviously. And there was a ready excuse to hand: you cannot keep the young couple waiting while you're rewriting the details in this old Welsh!

But it is true what Parry-Williams said. When the sickness of the Welsh people is revealed, they get angry. Worse than the enmity of the English towards the foreign language in their midst is the enmity of so many Welsh-speaking Welshmen towards their mother tongue when it becomes essential. That is what explains the malice against Cymdeithas yr Iaith. These brave young people have exposed the servility and apathy of the older Welsh generation, have shown that they have real love for the Welsh language to the extent of being prepared to make sacrifices for it, and have as a result reaped all the spite and enmity of that former generation. As is said, there is no war nastier and more injurious than civil war; and it is obvious to the sharp-eyed observer that, if there were plans to throw the English yoke from off their shoulders, it would be the Welsh themselves who would be amongst the first to betray those plans to the authorities.

The English are old hands at dealing with subjugated nations; they have had centuries of experience. Consider the violence in Ireland. But if someone's little finger were injured in Wales, the English would at once set about convincing us that we were the most uncivilised nation in the West. And yet on the sly they have respect for those who oppose them with force. If only the Welsh stood as one, the situation would start to improve overnight, as it were. The traditional answer from the English that has been so successful in the past is: it is completely impossible. That is the answer to the perfectly reasonable request to have a car licence disk in the two languages. But after some influential Welsh people threatened to take action, it was found that the thing was completely practicable. And to be fair to the English themselves – how much real objection would they have to seeing the Welsh language come first in our public life? It would be an added attraction when they came here on holiday, giving the impression that they are in a foreign land without the effort of going abroad. But the Welsh do not see this, and so lose out.

A question that ties in with this crisis, and one that caused R. S. considerable perplexity, was how to win something approaching freedom or self-rule, when so many things are set against it. One mustn't be naïve. The English state doesn't want to give Wales her freedom on a plate, as some optimistic Welsh people expect. The Referendum of 1979 showed that clearly enough. The offer was presented to the Welsh in such a way as to ensure its refusal. The sadness of the thing is that the only way to win freedom is through fighting for it. That is the lesson of history. Though R. S. was a pacifist, as was fitting for a priest, he knew of no example to the contrary, except India. And to this day it is the people who have used violence who have made the deepest impression on their oppressors. How many leaders of governments in Africa and India are there who were not in English prisons for some period, before succeeding in throwing off the yoke of their oppressors?

R. S. had been a pacifist on principle ever since finding himself at Chirk directly before the Second World War. He couldn't recommend violence even in the Welsh cause. Unfortunately, the Englishman respects violence, as he respects those who oppose him. The problem is not a simple one by any means, and it tormented him all the time. The vicar at Chirk knew him well enough to advise him not to accuse the farmers in Manafon of cruelty towards the animals. Farmers are used to the dirty side of life. Killing is part of their way of life. Catching and killing rabbits was a weekly necessity in Manafon, on account of their great numbers at that time. On a threshing day, before reaching the bottom of the rick, the men and the boys and the dogs would prepare for an attack on the hundreds of rats hiding there. The young rector would himself see the birds of prey hunting, and the weasel and the stoat going about their bloody work. And how beautiful those birds are, and how agile the small animals that hunt. Anyone who has seen a peregrine falcon falling like lightning on its prey is sure to experience a certain thrill that makes him feel quite humble. These are the masters of the world of nature. One of the unfailing rules of that world is that life has to die in the cause of life. If there is any other way on this earth, God has not seen fit to follow it. This is a doctrine that plays straight into the hands of the strong. As far as this world is concerned, Isaiah's vision of the wolf dwelling with the lamb, and the leopard lying down with the kid, is a myth. The economy doesn't work like that. And too often in this world, the race is to the swift, the battle to the strong. Of course there are spiritual and moral values, and if man is not willing to sacrifice his life for them, of what worth are they? That is the justification for the just war, and to a militaristic nation like the English, every war fought to 'defend' England is just; which brings us to another matter.

R. S. was rector of Manafon when the war came to an end. He and his wife went through the strange experience of having the house full of refugees from Hackney in London, people who were just as barbaric as the cursed enemy. A busload of them came to the village and it was on the rector that the responsibility fell for placing them in their new homes. But when some of them saw the farms along the hillsides that were to be their new homes they refused to go there, arguing that they had been assured before leaving London that they would be together at the end of the journey. The upshot was that the rectory family received more than their share of these ragamuffins. In the evening, the young mothers would leave their small children and go to the pub to drink, with R. S. having to drag them away from there. When they heard that there was a hospital for injured soldiers at Gregynog, three miles away, off they went there to flirt, although their own husbands were in mortal danger on the Continent. They arrived in May, when it was fine, but as soon as the days started to get shorter in early August, they became discontented with their lot and wanted to go home. R. S. warned them about the flying bombs that had newly started, but in vain. They insisted on returning. 'If you go, you will not be allowed to return to us,' he said again. And away they went. Within a few days a message came that someone wanted to speak to him on the telephone in the post office. And who should it be, but one of the girls who had newly left. They wanted to return, of course. The rector took her address and then went to enquire of the authorities whether they would be allowed to return to someone else, if he refused to take them. The answer was that they would. So he wrote to them to say that he was unwilling to receive them. Had he been certain that they would not be allowed to go elsewhere, he would have had to welcome them back, but that would have been a pain to both himself and his wife, so wild and uncivilised were they.

When the nuclear bomb was dropped on Hiroshima, the rector prepared to protest publicly in the church on the following Sunday. But the Japanese surrendered immediately, and everything was forgotten in the joy and thanksgiving that peace had returned to the world. He had little interest in politics, and did not follow the troubles between Russia and the West after the war. But the instincts that told him to protest after the dropping of the bomb were completely right. It should not have been dropped at all. But apart from that – or maybe because of it – the international situation went from bad to worse, with the two sides starting to add regularly to their stockpile of nuclear weapons.

These things were happening while he was in Eglwys-fach, without his paying them much attention. But by the time he reached Aberdaron they were so bad that there was no way of ignoring them. He wrote a letter to the press exposing the lie that it was possible to defend a country and win a war by nuclear means. Yet he retired from his living before being drawn into the local anti-nuclear movement. A public meeting was held in Pwllheli with the aim of forming a local branch of the Campaign for Nuclear Disarmament, and before long he was co-opted as a member of the committee. He started campaigning himself by writing more and more frequently to the press, giving interviews to the media, and giving addresses as a guest speaker at the occasional rally or protest. The situation was from the very start completely clear to him. Everything was changed by nuclear weapons. There was no defence against them; and because their effects were so indiscriminately destructive, it was completely immoral to threaten to use them against any other country. As has been said before, he was troubled by the element of power and violence in the creation, but he realised that even war, though often so horrible in its results, had hitherto kept within some limits. But it always created more evil than good, without succeeding in solving the problems that caused it. And nuclear weapons showed once and for all that it would never again be possible to try and solve them in this way. The bomb was a *reductio ad absurdum*. The human brain had succeeded in inventing the ultimate weapons that could not be used without destroying oneself as well as the enemy. The days were gone when a nation, like a selfish child, would seek to have its own way through violence. From there on international problems had to be solved through peaceful means. But this was far too simple for the great powers who were used to the old traditional methods of threatening and boasting and deceiving, while at the same time depending on a system of espionage, in order to steal a march on the other side; in other words, using brinkmanship, hoping that the enemy would yield out of fear.

Tied in with this was the question of Wales, a small peaceful country that each St David's Day would broadcast a message of peace to the world. Despite this, and despite the fact that every county council, in accordance with the wishes of their electorates, had announced that their land was a nuclear-free area – making Wales the first nuclear-free country in Europe – their announcement was pooh-poohed by the government of the day which said that it, rather than the local councils, was to operate in such matters. So much for democracy in the enlightened Britain of the day! So once again, as a result of the Act of Union of 1536, Wales was in danger of being dragged into another of England's wars. Her folly in refusing the paltry measure of home rule offered her in the Referendum of 1979 was now seen clearly enough.

The battle continues. The activists won the argument, but lost the battle, owing to the stubbornness and cunning of the great powers who have the propaganda in their own hands. So heartbreaking is it, late in the twentieth century, to see the same old tactics that succeeded in the past, when things were completely different, being employed again. Each side blames the other, and through lies and playing around with statistics in an unprincipled way, they convince their ignorant and oblivious people that the only way to solve the problem is to steal a march on the cursed enemy by producing more and more horrific weapons, until they have enough to kill every man jack over and again a hundred or a thousand times.

Here is R. S. towards the end of his life having to battle against every old man's temptation, despair. The tendency was always in him to look back and to see the past as superior. In the Wales of long ago the Welsh language was safe. There was a brotherhood and a community here. Heavy industry had not reached south Wales to plunder and deface it, making the nation top-heavy. Architecture was better, more in accord with the beauty of the environment; and the craftsman still took pride in his work. One other blessing was that the country was relatively free from the injurious effect of the Englishman's presence. R. S. always saw the industrial revolution as Wales's main disaster. He well knew that he would lose every argument if he sought to reason in prose. But having to live amongst the results of such a revolution was an utterly unpleasant experience. In the past the Llŷn Peninsula had been for him a country of enchantment. From Aberystwyth it was to be seen far to the northwest as a row of most attractive hills. Almost every country has a charm on being seen from across the sea, and it is not easy to remember that a quite ordinary life is lived there, as everywhere else. In his imagination the associations of the Llŷn Peninsula were those of history and spiritual retreat, but having arrived he found that it was an air force practice area. The deafening roar of the aeroplanes was certain to kill any attempt to live in the past. The Llŷn Peninsula is a traditionally Welsh-speaking area; but because of its beauty and its beaches, and because the industrial revolution has given birth to the motor car, it is full to overflowing with visitors every summer, so that it is almost impossible to live life in the Welsh language there. And by now in winter, because of the hundreds of street lights that have mushroomed all over the place, the night is full of artificial light. The stars and the sea and the outline of the peninsula are no longer to be seen, with the result that the beauty and natural solitude of the heart of the countryside have disappeared. To R. S. as a member of the anti-nuclear movement, it appeared that the government was encouraging everybody to use more and more electricity to justify the demand for more atomic power stations, for the plutonium to be had as a result. And since the ordinary man hates the dark and wants to tame nature, he is ready enough to play into the government's hands in this way. By night England and Wales turn into a sea of light, destroying the old element of mystery that long ago was so characteristic of the countryside. Imagine a man fifty years ago alighting from a train at a small station somewhere in the heart of the Welsh countryside at night. The first thing that would reach his ears from the darkness would be the sound of water falling from above. And on looking in the right direction he would see the dark shadow of the mountain between him and the sky, and he would be aware that he was not in England. That has gone for ever. Wales today is a land of pylons and wires, a land of television masts and police poles, a land of new roads full of visitors rushing to the sea, where the planted forests and the caravan parks are fast swallowing the remaining open ground. In the face of all this, R. S. well knew why he had become more and more interested in birds. Since the spirit of the countryside had weakened, since its beauty was being destroyed by modern developments, one of the few pleasures remaining there was to see some of the creatures still going about their traditional business. Birds existed millions of years before the advent of man. They are beautiful and full of life, and have adapted perfectly to their own needs. Man has for ages yearned to be able to fly, and at last he has succeeded at the expense of exhausting the earth of its resources and polluting it, and of filling the sky with unbearable tumult. Twice a year millions of birds rise into the air without much noise, without any harmful effect on the environment, to winter in warmer countries for a few months and to return in the spring to raise a new family. The majority of the small ones will migrate at night to avoid their enemies, but sea birds will also move during the day, giving one an opportunity to see them, especially when the weather is stormy, and they are driven nearer land. From the middle of August to the end of October the Llŷn Peninsula is a good place for seeing these on their way south. Thinking of these migrations, looking at the stars at night and bearing in mind the millions of small bodies on their way to a country they had never seen before, R. S. would marvel at how miraculous the creation was. And spending an hour or two looking over the sea hoping to see a migratory bird, he came to see the similarity between this and praying. He had to watch patiently for a long time for fear of losing the rare bird, because he did not know when it would come by. It is exactly the same with the relationship between man and God that is known as prayer. Great patience is called for, because no-one knows when God will choose to reveal Himself.

Of course, there are thousands of other birds in the world apart from the small number to be seen in Wales. Indeed, in Britain there is only one bird that chooses to nest only in Wales, and that is the kite. That is why R. S. was a member of the Committee for the Protection of the Kite. Mention has already been made of Wales's beautiful habitats, and indeed there are plenty of birds here to satisfy anyone if he only practises patience. For example, on a fine day in May, on the moorland extending from Y Migneint as far as Llanddewibrefi, when the golden plover was singing enchantingly above the blue lakes, R. S. used to feel that if there were no places like these in heaven, then he didn't want to go there. There are plenty of other beautiful places in the world, of course, but there is no more beautiful place than the mountains of Snowdonia as they can be seen from Anglesey on a clear day, when the sun is setting, turning the clouds above them from white to gold, and from gold to purple. And because Wales is so beautiful, R. S. would like to satisfy his *hiraeth* by recording some of the prospects he has seen during his lifetime.

When he lived in Chirk the *hiraeth* for Anglesey would sometimes get the better of him, and then there was nothing for it but to persuade his friend, who later became his wife, to take him home for the day, hoping that nothing of importance would arise in the parish in his absence. On one occasion, perhaps in November, they travelled to Holyhead, picked up his mother and went out to the coast beyond Penrhos Feilw, the place he was so fond of when he was a boy. It was a fine, sunny afternoon, with the wind lifting the foam from off the sea and driving it towards the town. Amongst the feathers of foam there was a considerable group of gulls, also circling in the wind. As the sun set, the foam and the gulls turned pink, and this, along with the sea turning purple and the wind singing wildly melodiously in his ears, would be among his permanent memories. On another occasion, in the summer, they went to Berffro and to Porth Gwyfan, and while they were sitting on the rocks, a crew of local lads came there to fish. It was a very fine evening, and as the fishermen walked over the rocks with their long fishing-rods rising like spears against the background of the mountains, they were like an old classical tapestry. As they started to fish, some exciting word arose amongst them that sounded to the non-Welsh-speaking R. S. like 'mikrish'. He later came to know that the word was of course *mecryll*, mackerel. And after coming to Aberdaron he would himself for some years go after these tasty fish.

One must then move to Manafon. It isn't possible to call that a par-ticularly beautiful place. But it was in a valley between wooded slopes, and since it was far enough from the sea, there was no salt water to shrivel the leaves before their time in autumn. So the autumn would extend over quite a long period, with the leaves turning colour very slowly, the ash trees turning yellow, and the cherry red, while the birch trees turned golden brown like a leopard. At the end of the lane from the rectory to the main road, there was a very large ash tree. The leaves remained on it very late one autumn, and all yellow. But one night in November it froze hard until, when morning came, everywhere was white. There was no wind, but as the sun rose above the hill, the leaves began to thaw in its modest warmth and then fall. For two hours or more it was as if a golden fountain were playing there, as the leaves fell to form a thick carpet covering the road.

Though the hill-country of Montgomeryshire is so sparsely popu-lated, there was the occasional cottage or smallholding, sometimes with an old man living there and working as a shepherd for wealthier farmers in the valleys. With the streams running past, peat smoke rising from the chimney and the trees red with the berries of the mountain ash in August, R. S. used to delight in meeting some of the smallholders in order to practise his meagre Welsh. One afternoon as he was conversing with the family close by their cottage, another man came from some-where and stood like a shadow some ten yards away. He said nothing, but remained standing there, as if living in another world. For R. S. that, too, became a wonderfully beautiful memory.

In this hill-country there also grew rows of golden chain, and these would be amazingly yellow amid the bareness of the hills in June. And having wandered for hours in the silence of the moorland, when R. S. returned to greener places, the song of a blackbird would strike his ear with a certain directness that made it seem as if he had never heard it before. One day towards the end of the war he was up on the heath when he saw two men amidst the moor grass cutting peat. He approached them for a chat, but they had quite a fright on seeing him appear as it were out of nowhere. 'We thought you was German,' one of them said.

This wasn't as funny as it appears, because there was a rumour abroad that a German plane had come down a few days previously. Early one morning one of the New Zealand planes came down in the middle of the moorland, killing its crew of four. Within an hour and a half the news about it had reached Manafon, even though this happened some twenty miles away, far from any house or road. This was a lonely and beautiful area; but despite its beauty, it was only a platform for seeing the hills of Merionethshire. If one stood on top of a hillock in the middle of the moorland, the green of the valleys between you and the mountains wasn't to be seen, only the brown of the moor grass and the rushes, with the curlews endlessly whistling overhead. And in May the cotton grass would wave gracefully in the breeze.

After moving to Eglwys-fach, R. S. discovered that he had moved nearer to the real mountains, such as Cadair Idris, which was only some fifteen miles to the north. In June he would climb it to see the alpine flowers growing amongst its rocks and ravines. You have to climb the rocks in order to experience the charm of these flowers as they appear red or white against the bareness of their background. And once, as he was climbing a chimney amongst the cliffs, he came close to putting his hand in a ring ouzel's nest. But the hills behind Eglwys-fach were beautiful, too, with their streams and waterfalls tumbling in a rush to the plains. And lower down in the area of Tregaron and Pont-rhydfendigaid there were similar valleys with their slopes covered in oak trees, where the kite would nest, and where the song of the pied flycatcher and the redstart would be heard, as R. S. searched for the nests of the great birds of prey. And while roaming the high ground between Tregaron and the Towy Valley, he would remember the time when he went to look for Twm Siôn Cati's cave. He was a student at the time and staying for a fortnight's holiday with his parents in Llanwrtyd, where his father fished. He set out one morning and walked in the direction of the Towy Valley. When he was in the middle of the high ground a small bearded man approached him on a pony and directed him to the cave. 'From where we are standing now,' he said, 'you can throw a stone into three counties.'

From his many visits to this tract of country between Tregaron and Abergwesyn R. S. tended to think that this was the only part of south Wales that was to be compared to the North. One doesn't have to have high mountains to create beauty. The hills in the Towy Valley were high and craggy enough to create wild and lonely prospects. Later he came to understand that this was part of the old Cantref Mawr, where the Welsh soldiers would disappear after a sudden foray against the Normans. But to anyone asking where the most beautiful part of Wales was, R. S. would answer without hesitation: the area between Tan-y-bwlch and Beddgelert, with its rocks and streams, its rowan and birch trees. And above the hills themselves, there would be the occasional glimpse of the real mountains rising to the clouds. So great was his admiration for this region that he succeeded at one time in buying a small cottage in Nanmor. But having later received the tenancy of Sarn-y-Plas in Y Rhiw, he saw no reason for hanging on to it, as he had been given the opportunity to return to his first love, the sea. The sea! What is more pleasant than sitting on the rocks in Braich y Pwll in August and seeing the porpoises and the dolphins raising a black fin above the waves, before plunging out of sight to appear, within a few seconds, somewhere else? What is more exciting than seeing the guillemots and the skuas, the terns and the gulls flowing past, and the gannet plummeting into the water after some unfortunate fish? Here is a way of life that is indescribably older than us, and it is a great privilege to be able to go to the coast in order to see such life in all its energy and merriment. And the views on a clear day are incredible. Who in his right mind would think of living anywhere else while all this wealth is available?

While speaking in this way, naming the areas of Wales as a mother names her children, there takes shape in the mind a unified picture of Wales that pleads for the heart's loyalty. The land of Wales has to be loved as well as its people. That is where the Irish beat the Welsh. Éire has stolen their heart away. In one of Yeats's plays, there is an account of an old woman coming to a young man's cottage the day before his wedding, calling on him to follow her. He does so. Later a neighbour asked someone else whether he had seen the old woman. 'No,' said the man. 'But I saw a young, beautiful girl who walked like a queen.'

People will disappoint you, but Wales will never be unfaithful. She is always there in all her unspotted virginity, despite all the atrocious things that we do to her.

As his life starts to draw to a close, does R. S. have any message, any advice to offer? Nothing. He hasn't had enough experience of human life to dare to preach to anyone. People tend to dwell in the realm of his imagination instead of being part of his personal experience. As he wasn't a novelist, there was no need to follow people closely to study them in detail in order to have them as living characters in a book. His view of people is that there are some good and some bad ones, with a large complement of the neither-bad-nor-good in the middle, following their banal daily course. It worries him that more English people than Welsh appreciate the beauty of Wales. It is very disappointing that the English are on the whole more knowledgeable regarding the birds and flowers of our country than we ourselves. They are also readier to stand up for their language than is the greater number of our fellow Welsh.

We know what Saunders Lewis said – that direct political action is not something to be looked for from a creative artist. And he spoke the truth. The creative artist will contribute in his own way. Though practical action is of course necessary, so also is the inspiration that no-one but a poet can give, as the poets kept the flame alive from the killing of Our Last Prince, Llywelyn, through to the revolt of Owain Glyndŵr. R. S. would often think of this, and at the same time would lament the fact that he had to make his own contribution through the medium of English. Each nation needs its prophets, but it is a bad thing to wash dirty clothes in public. It would have been very much better had R. S. said what he had to say in Welsh. But evening draws on. He wrote political, patriotic poetry in English, and then fell quiet. He portrayed the life of the small farmer as an act of protest against the ignorance and apathy of the rich and the well-off. But through those poems there ran a religious vein that became more visible during his last years. After all, there is nothing more important than the relationship between man and God. Nor anything more difficult than establishing that relationship. Who is it that ever saw God? Who ever heard Him speak? We have to live virtually the whole of our lives in the presence of an invisible and mute God. But that was never a bar to anyone seeking to come into contact with Him. That is what prayer is. In the Llŷn Peninsula we are reminded daily of the old saints and hermits who sought a vision of God amidst the beauty and quiet of the peninsula. But one must be careful. It is easier to pray in such circumstances. It is easier to be good while on your knees than in the middle of all the temptations and hubbub of the world of society. It is a poor religion that believes that it is only in the places set at a remove that God is to be found. R. S. tried to be liberal. Some have found God through serving and ministering in the outside world. It is not possible to confine Him in any way. And yet there is a tension. Is it as easy to find God in the noisy, technological world as it is in the quiet of nature? The Llŷn Peninsula isn't a complete paradise. The aeroplanes scream overhead; the visitors arrive in their cars. The media announce bad news from all corners of the world. How, therefore, can anyone hide his head in the sand? At the same time, R. S. had lived long enough not to be easily cast down by passing fashions. He witnessed the materialism of the last century going out of fashion amongst the intellectuals. He saw the disastrous effect of two world wars on people's faith and morals, and how licence failed to satisfy them. He has also lived long enough to know that the discoveries and theories of the scientists have given birth to a universe that even the imagination of man fails to comprehend. Space is huge. For years the astronomers have revealed the distance between us and the nearest star. And beyond that, there is star after star, galaxy after galaxy; and having come to the borders of our own galaxy, there is only another galaxy, and so on almost to eternity. And yet this cannot prevent man from dreaming of travelling out into space, despite the fact that space-time can play all sorts of tricks with man's reason, as Einstein and the physicists who came after him have shown. Aren't we back with the people who wrote the Bible, who would confess that such knowledge was too wonderful for them?

In the face of all this, in the end, the only attitude for a wise man is humility. What mortal can say how it was before the existence of the world, or how it will be after it has ceased to exist according to the second law of thermodynamics? R. S. is no-one. He leaves it to God to decide whether he will become someone in another world; whether there is work for him to do in some mysterious future, or whether he is a link between here and some other kind of existence. If a completely destructive nuclear war does not happen, the world will go on, and the kind of people who now live in laboratories will live in space stations. Good luck to them. But R. S. has not the smallest grain of interest in such an existence. As he has already said, if there is life after this one, and if it does not contain things akin to those so dear to him in Wales – the streams, the moorland, the birds, the flowers – he doesn't want to experience it. Thanks to the good health that he has enjoyed, and to the senses that he has, he can see colours, he can hear the *cynghanedd*, the harmony, of the seasons, so he has no need to experiment with the drugs that some use to stimulate their jaded senses.

But here again humility is called for. Thomas Aquinas believed that God revealed Himself according to the creature's ability to receive Him. If He did this to R. S., He chose to do so through the medium of the world of nature. But, of course, there are other ways. To some, He has appeared as the love they have experienced in dealing with people. To others, who possess a higher order of understanding than R. S., He has revealed Himself through the mysterious processes of the creation, as He did, perhaps, to Einstein and Schrödinger.

This is another way of saying that Christianity is not the only answer to the mystery of things. There is truth in the beliefs of Buddhism, Hinduism and Taoism. But each to his own. These faiths developed in their context, and they are appropriate, or they were appropriate, to those circumstances. But Christianity is the religion of Europe. It is through it, and through the Græco-Hebraic version of it, that God has revealed Himself to us in the West. Amidst all the wealth of that tradition there is therefore little purpose in anyone in Europe adopting one of the other faiths as one superior to Christianity. It is not on Christianity that blame for the evils of the West is to be laid, but on what people have made of it.

What has just been said did not prevent R. S. from trying to plumb the mysteries of the creation. Life is a pilgrimage, and if we have not succeeded in coming a little nearer to the truth, if we do not have a better comprehension of the nature of God before reaching the end of the journey, why was it that we started on the journey at all? As a priest in the Church R. S. knew that he should pray regularly. But as life went on he became increasingly conscious of its problems. One major obstacle was the existence of secondary causes; that is, God is the prime mover of things, but there are secondary causes that not even He can prevent, if life is to continue in the world of today. If a man drinks too much liquor, and then insists on driving home too quickly, it is very difficult to believe in the ability of God to protect him, despite all the prayers of his family and his vicar and others. The corollary of this is that there is a series of problems that makes it difficult to believe in the short term that God is omnipotent in the face of man's stubbornness or wilfulness. War is another example of the same problem. And although it is the meekness of a child that is best before God, one needs also to grow and mature in prayer. For R. S., as he grew older, it became obvious that many of the problems of religion arise in the wake of erroneous ideas concerning God, which cause us to ask erroneous questions. Our image of God must be transformed, as Bishop Robinson has said. The Church has up to this day produced a great number of thinkers of the quality of Paul and Augustine and Thomas Aquinas and Pascal. But somehow the alternative element in Christianity, the popular, somewhat sentimental element, has displaced the other, with unfortunate consequences to say the least. We have already heard of the problem of killing as a part of the economy of the God of love. There is also the problem of the inventing mind. People like Roger Bacon continue to be born into the world, people who possess the kind of mind that can drive them to invent deadly and ruinous things. These are the people who are responsible for discovering nuclear energy with all its problems and temptations. And yet we believe that nothing exists outside God. It is He who contains everything. Therefore this element, too, is part of Him. If everything derives from Him, this element was bound to surface at some time. It is here that we see the genius of the author of the Book of Genesis in being able to imagine the temptation of the Garden of Eden. It appeared to R. S. many times that it would have been far better had man not tasted the fruits of the tree of the knowledge of good and evil. How often he has shown how unsuited he is to use that knowledge for the glory of God and the benefit of his fellow human beings. And yet it is equally difficult to imagine the earth without the mind of man probing and searching and challenging itself to make the best use of his discoveries and devices.

This is the problem with which R. S. would wrestle increasingly in his life and in his poetry, as time went by. He could no longer consider prayer as a matter of reciting an orison, or asking for something. He became aware of the silence of God. He had no patience with the kind of man who would talk to God as if God were eavesdropping in the doorway. If you wanted to claim that you had heard the voice of God talking to you, how could you be certain that it wasn't some part of your own complexity that was talking? Take for example the atrocities committed because some people believe that they have heard God ordering them to commit them. And in the world of poetry R. S. was familiar enough with what Coleridge had said, that the opposite of poetry is not prose, but science; and yet, since science plays such an important and obvious part in contemporary life, he felt that poetry could not continue to be one of the great arts, if it could not understand

and use science. And perhaps it wasn't pure science that was to blame, but applied science, the kind that was used under financial pressure to exploit and exhaust the earth's resources in order to satisfy the needs that science herself had created. The classical word for this was *cupido*, the insatiable greed in man that gave birth to machines and aeroplanes and missiles and all the technology of the contemporary world.

Perhaps it is natural for a man getting on in years, after the lust and restlessness and thoughtlessness of his youth have subsided, to start worrying that he has not been sparing and provident enough. But certainly, for anyone who is vigilant in our time, the danger facing the earth and its tenants is clear. The population increase is drawing ahead of the means of feeding it. The greed of the developers is threatening to change the climate substantially by the end of the century. The emphasis placed by capitalism and industry on continuous progress is creating more demand for raw materials than can be met. And on top of all this, the mind of man has discovered a power that is endangering his own future; and instead of admitting this and facing it, the superpowers have been caught in an arms race that is certain to lead to a war that will destroy all the work of the centuries in addition to mankind itself.

Long ago, before the advent of the press and the media, man would be more or less ignorant regarding what was happening in other parts of the world. Therefore he had an excuse for not worrying about the rest of the population. But by now we do know. We know that two-thirds of the human race cannot get enough to eat, while the rest fill their stomachs to excess with delicacies. While some cannot make two ends meet, others own two or three cars, two homes, boats and the like. The possibility of judgement is clear on the horizon.

All this had an effect on R. S.'s poetry. The tension had existed when he was in Manafon, the contrast between the beauty of nature and the squalor of man. But there were excuses. The work on the land was so hard that there was no way or time to refine the mind. R. S. showed this in his poetry in order to make his readers conscious of the difference between their comfortable lives and the labour and sweat of the farmers. But after moving to another area, to the traditional beauty of the Llŷn Peninsula, he saw a new threat to beauty from technology. Reading how the heavy machines were busy felling the forests of Brazil and south-east Asia, and hearing the pilotless aeroplanes above practising in preparation for another war, R. S. was aware of a new tension. The machine and the nuclear bomb and references to the myth of Eden became more obvious in his poems.

Living in a four-hundred-year-old cottage, and thinking of the tenants of that cottage throughout the centuries, he would imagine seeing their faces watching him from the stones in the walls. Hearing the eternal sound of the waves breaking on the beach in Porth Neigwl, or responding delightedly to the dance of the sunlight through his room, then turning on the radio and hearing another example of man's folly or beastliness – all this causes R. S. to brood on thoughts that are, as Wordsworth put it, too deep for tears. What, any longer, is it fitting for man to do but repeat, day after day, '*Miserere me, Domine*'?

A YEAR IN LLŶN

A YEAR IN LLŶN

January

This morning I discovered the newborn year on my doorstep, begging to be welcomed into the house. I hesitated a moment for fear of what might come in its wake. But it continued to plead until I picked it up, not out of pity, but because I had to.

Last night I placed a candle in the window as a signal to whatever spirit was lost in the twilight that there was a welcome for it here. Was it this new year that saw it? The morning was pretty colourless, but the two sparrowhawks above the trees of Ty'n-y-coed played as if they were already intent on mating. Just as I had to receive the new year into my house, so they, too, were having to respond to the call of life by showing that they were suited for mating and raising chicks for the continuation of their species.

Who is Meri? She sent me a Christmas card without giving her surname. And there I was playing with the idea that some young girl had fancied me! But a small voice whispers in my ear: You silly fool, you are old. And yet on the threshold of a new year, who feels old? The mistle thrush doesn't, since he is already busy singing his love song on a bare tree. I know I will not cease from asking and questioning who this Meri is. There is a tale about Blondel, isn't there, when Richard, king of England, was a prisoner somewhere in France – how he went from prison to prison singing at the foot of the walls, until he eventually heard Richard's voice answering him with the same song. Is there such a place as heaven? If there is, perhaps we will have to search there, too, for the one we loved while we were on earth. And because 'Charity never faileth', we shall be certain of finding her in the end.

A great sea-swell came to Porth Neigwl today following a tempest in the Atlantic. Although there was not much wind here, the sea rose and hurled its tons on to the beach. The waves could be seen running white along Pen Cilan on the far side of Y Borth. It is the sea that makes the

Llŷn Peninsula what it is. Didn't I once see the foam being whipped higher than the summit of Bardsey during a storm from the west? The sea has to be respected. In the old days I used to tell Wil, Tŷ Pellaf, about the wave that would come ashore from time to time and would reach far higher than expected; and he would shake his head and wink. Didn't I hear, when I was in Ireland, of a woman who was sitting on top of a cliff in the west, to all intents and purposes sufficiently out of danger? And yet one of these waves came and snatched her away, and no-one saw her after that. In Pwllheli this afternoon, I heard a young mother speaking to her little son in English, and the next minute, on meeting some of her friends, switching to fluent Welsh. Here is a Welsh mother deciding, like Glenys Kinnock, that it is an English future that her children are to have. Tell me, do we deserve to survive as a nation? Will God spare the nation for the sake of five righteous ones? And yet who can deny that the present is an exceedingly interesting period to live in? Who would choose to be out of Wales, with the language in the balance like this?

I was on the shore of the river Menai this afternoon, with the wind strengthening near Y Foryd. It was raining as I was driving along the Clynnog road, but above my head the slopes were already beginning to whiten. The difference a few hundred feet make! For every three hundred feet you climb, the temperature drops one degree Fahrenheit. If people remembered this, there would undoubtedly be fewer accidents on the mountains. Didn't I once leave the plains on the first day of spring, with the intention of climbing Aran Fawddwy? Though the sun wasn't out, it was yet quite mild. But having climbed up to Pennant Dyfi, I found that all the country there was in the grip of a great frost, and long icicles were hanging from the cliffs, while a keen wind whistled through them.

The murderer has been round since last I visited Tŷ Mawr pool – to go by the signs, two blackheaded gulls killed by the peregrine falcon – only the wings left and the ligament linking them. Why are birds of prey so fond of the heads of their victims?

Being in Llŷn at a time like this is a strange experience. It is as if we had crawled along a branch suspended in time. Whispers reach us of a world that is almost totally different, where miracles happen in the field of technology. Art, nature and the individual himself are under great pressure. The young cannot live in the past. They instinctively welcome the newfangled things, the so-called new world. That is why they are retreating from the Welsh language, because it is England, or America, that is for them the mediator of this new world. But every large country is experimenting in this new field. If we were living next door to Russia or Japan, we would come under the influence of their language and culture. What future is there for Llŷn? The wind rose from the south-east, the sea and the sky darkened, and it was obvious that snow was near. But it was rain and some sleet that we had here, and later in the afternoon the sky cleared sufficiently for me to see the snow that had fallen on Merionethshire. It will be quite tricky tonight away from the coast, while we, thanks to the Gulf Stream from Mexico, won't have any problem at all.

I have been lucky. From Holyhead I could see Snowdonia under snow; from Eglwys-fach I could see the hills of Merionethshire, as I can now from Llŷn. It was only in Manafon that I experienced all the difficulties of heavy snow. What if I had been born an Eskimo and had to learn forty different names for snow, because there was so much of it? Talking of the Eskimo: while they lived in their natural habitat and ate enough fat, they were not affected by heart disease. But after moving to Canada and eating the white man's food, they inherited his diseases. I heard recently that *olew iau penfras* is good for curing rheumatism, but how can I ask the chemist for it in Welsh without raising a laugh? This shows the extent to which we have been anglicised. We accept 'Cod Liver Oil' as the normal name, and laugh at those who speak correct Welsh.

Out in Braich y Pwll today I saw a group of seagulls loitering in circles above the water. Soon a seal came to the surface with a large four-pound fish in its mouth. What it did was dive and return to the surface several times, simultaneously tearing pieces of the fish, and the seagulls feasted on the bits of meat that came from the body. This is nature at its work. I have many times pondered the fact that fish suffer at the hands of people and animals alike. The only hope is that they don't suffer to the same extent as the animals higher up the chain of being. But who knows? And are we much troubled about how they died when we eat them for lunch?

I saw in Uwchmynydd that there were more houses for sale. This means more English, very likely. As far as I understand, the young are moving to the towns where they work in order to save petrol money, with the result that their parents are accompanying them. How many Welsh will be left in the Llŷn Peninsula by the end of the century apart from a few farmers?

The man from the BBC was here today. He is making two programmes dealing with people's ideas about heaven and hell. 'Time,' I said, 'how can you experience heaven if you are conscious of time?'

So, too, with hell. Memory has a great deal to do with it. If we have memory in the next life, we shall be tortured by grief, because of our mistakes and our sins. But behind everything, of course, is the fact that we have no notion of how it will be, if there is such a thing as another life.

For a walk this afternoon in the area of Llaniestyn. Despite having tried many times, I cannot see any appeal in Llaniestyn; a harmless enough village, with an interesting church and a large rectory, but without a grain of character. There is no attractive feature, no trees, no river worth mentioning, and even though Garn Fadrun rises majestically to the north, I can think of many other Welsh villages of greater distinction. I wonder whether in my early days in the Church, when I was looking for a Welsh-speaking parish, I would have accepted Llaniestyn solely for the sake of the Welsh language? Places looked so different from Manafon because they lay to the west and closer to the sea.

This morning, after a night of high wind from the west, I saw for the first time the spray rising in Porth Neigwl. I recalled how I used to see it rising higher than the summit of Bardsey when I lived in Aberdaron. And Bardsey is five hundred and fifty feet high. This salt water, whipped off the surface, was the bane of the boatmen in days gone by. A sudden gust could fill and sink a boat in an instant.

From my reading I continue to see that the present is the age of relativism. It used to be believed that if one wanted to be a historian one had to have the ability to see the past through the eyes of its contemporaries; and of course, I am continually encouraged to do so here in an old cottage above Porth Neigwl. Y Borth must be seen through the eyes of the former tenants of this house. But how can I? Even though it is the same stars that are above me at night, my consciousness of them is very different from theirs. Woe to the people in days gone by who claimed that this is how things were meant to be, and that such and such was the fundamental truth. And woe to us, if we think something similar. Time has shaken our belief in eternal truth. No sooner do we accept something as unshakeable fact than something else comes to supplant it. And yet, how can I look at the stars and the sea underneath them, how can I see the human patterns in the sky, without continuing to believe that love and beauty are eternal? Is this only a yearning?

Today I was looking across the marsh on either side of the river Rhydhir in Pwllheli, and it struck me that marshland is the land safest from being developed today. Nothing can be built on marshy land, except in the manner of the native people of the past, or of people in the tropics who used to build flimsy wooden houses on stilts above the water. In the future, as the pressure increases, every tract of land will be developed, and only the marshy, foundationless land will be spared to remind people how it once used to be. And as if they wanted to emphasise the fact, three greenshanks arose as I was musing, and their primitive notes echoed through the relatively young streets of the town.

It is always a joy for me to see the tree creeper. I hear its particular shriek, and then some feathery little body flashes past me, clings to another tree, and starts hopping on its way up like clockwork. He keeps from sight as best he can, but as soon as I see his white underside, I know who's there. These are birds that stayed after the primitive forests receded to the north, and that is their appeal. Wherever there's a clump of trees, this little bird will be at work with his crooked beak, looking for his morsel in crevices in the bark, working his way up in his own funny way.

It is the wind from the north-west that brings the pleasantest nights. Tonight the moon is at half-full, and great white clouds pass across her face. Between them the blue space is full of sparkling stars. Beneath them the sea is roaring and turning to silver as the waves break on the beach. Years ago, on a night such as this in Manafon, I would look north-westwards in the direction of Anglesey and Llŷn, yearning for them. And here I am now, having arrived. So few people are allowed to realise their dreams like this, though it is late indeed in the day for me.

Part of the clayey cliff in Porth Neigwl fell last night, as it will do from time to time. In this way the sea continually gnaws at the land. Is the time imaginable when there will not be an England apart from the Lake District, and with Wales nothing but a couple of islands, where Snowdonia, Cadair Idris and the Brecon Beacons have succeeded in keeping their heads above water?

These days, it is rain, rain, rain. Weathermen love to promise storm after storm from the Atlantic, but they never say why. Looking back, they can explain how the path of the storms changed, but they cannot say why. The weather is one great mysterious machine which continues to produce periods of fair and foul weather, heat and cold; but it keeps its secret, just as the soul refuses to tell us how it becomes incarnate in the womb. We are not, and never shall be, all-knowing.

The sound of the sea, which is heard here so often, reminds me of the part that water has played in my life. After coming to live in Holyhead as a child of six I became aware of the omnipresence of the sea, and that is what I lost in moving to the church at Chirk. Thus arose the yearning within me that was to last for so long. That yearning was relieved a little by the move to Manafon where there was a river close by the rectory. That river, in all its moods, became part of my life, and I would lie in bed at night listening to it as to the blood in my veins. But it was only an imitation of the sea, and there was no satisfaction to be had until I was able to return to live beside the sea, as I did in moving to Aberdaron. And here I am towards the end of my life, listening to it once again, sometimes purring, other times snarling in Porth Neigwl.

The birds have started to sing. The song thrush is at it from time to time, and the goldcrest. Nature can't wait, even though there are rough times between us and the spring. I remember how, in the dark days of the war, a bluetit started singing one January, raising our spirits. Life is stronger than death. Even though it appears otherwise very often, life, like love itself, gives the impression that it is inextinguishable, and even if they were both to die out on earth, there are other places in the universe where they would continue to flower.

I have seen it many times like tonight – the bay white under the moon, as the waves break on the beach. But its beauty is eternally new. I never surfeit of it, and if I personally don't come back, this particular 'I' will be able to gaze on it through the eyes of others.

I awoke to a white world today, even though Pen Cilan is free from snow. Mynydd y Rhiw will attract the occasional shower. Seaside snow is something of an oddity. It is quite attractive on the trees and the grass, but, as a rule, the water takes on a kind of brown, dark look, which shows that nature's taste isn't always sound! There are people, and myself amongst them, who like to think that nature is always right; but it is well known that she will sometimes kick over the traces. But perhaps the fault is in the eye of the beholder. I remember the drollery of Oscar Wilde, who laid the blame for a misty day in October on the Impressionist painters!

In Nietzsche I read, as I have read before: it is only as an aesthetic phenomenon that eternal life can be justified. I have many times felt this truth while gazing on the impersonal, pitiless beauty of nature. Consider the beauty of the birds of prey. And yet they are killers. Today I saw a stoat in Braich y Pwll, another beautiful killer, but moving so nimbly across the earth, as light as a feather. It stopped behind a clump of heather, craning now and again to peep at me. So white were its breast and throat, and its eyes sparkled either side of its pink nose. In the distance I saw Holy Island in sunlight, and there came the same old impossible yearning for her, not as she is, but as she was. I was once a boy there. If I could choose! As I put the possibility into words, I begin to totter. I have thought many times that I am not like Yeats, willing to live it all again. And yet the voice at my side whispers: of course you're willing. And that is what justifies life. The young accept it and say Amen, by virtue of their vigour and their vivacity.

After all, Llŷn is only a part of Wales, only a platform from which to see the rest. Here's a letter today from young people in Aberystwyth, who are worried about the whole of Wales, about what is happening to her under the power of the English state and the newcomers from England. It's not only Llŷn that is suffering, but the whole of Wales; and indeed extensive parts of her are by now in their hands. Nuclear weapons have shown that the days of power are over, but how can we convince a nation that still believes in power, and which respects only those who use it, of the rightness of our cause?

They say that Villon is one of the world's great poets. Reading him today, and experiencing his savour of the Middle Ages, I saw his similarity to Siôn Cent, no lesser a poet. But how many know of the Frenchman and how few of the Welshman. This is now our fate as a small nation yoked to England.

Today my wife received a letter from a friend of hers, denouncing those people who burn holiday homes, because her cottage in Mynydd y Rhiw was set alight recently. 'It would have been better had the whole place been burned to the ground,' I said, 'that ugly old thing.' 'It was a Welshman built it, most likely,' my wife said. 'Yes, and it was an Englishman bought it,' I answered. And there you have it. How much of Llŷn's beauty is indebted to the taste of its inhabitants? The old simple smallholdings had a certain character. But they were too small for raising a family. And yet most of the suitable houses that have taken their place are ugly and lacking in taste.

As sometimes happens when the wind is from the mainland, a ship came to anchor in Porth Neigwl last night. When I see a ship that has slipped in, the same old *hiraeth* wells up in me. Where did she set out from? What is her destination? I have a memory of my father saying that that was what made him decide to go to sea – the romance surrounding a ship visiting the mainland. Didn't I once see in the docks at Liverpool a ship at the quayside, and a brown man appearing suddenly from somewhere before disappearing into one of the cabins, conveying all the romance of the east? Last night the ship in Y Borth was all light. Tomorrow, perhaps it will have vanished like a dream.

February

A prolonged wet January has gone at last, and good riddance to it, even though I am a month older. And here is the short month starting dry but cold, with six degrees of frost last night. But the days are getting longer, there are little lambs in the fields, and Brian and Linda have a little baby, all signs that the scowling winter didn't succeed in killing everything. Indeed, there were flowers to be seen through it all. I often think what a pleasant picture is created by the description, 'It was a region where there were always flowers to be seen.' And certainly this is literally true of the Llŷn Peninsula. Walk the lanes and you'll be sure to see something in bloom, however late or early in the year it is.

It is always a joy for me to see a group of tits together. And there they were this morning, the long-tailed tits, the coal tits, the great tits, and the bluetit itself amongst them, slipping through the branches and darting from hedge to hedge like children out for a lark, with the same merriment and the same agility. They congregate like this for safety, of course. As there are so many of them, one is sure to see the predator coming and give a warning in time.

This afternoon, while reading in the kitchen, I looked up and saw a ray of sunlight falling on one of the room's large stones. Oh, what a contrast! Bitterly cold outside and dark inside; but with the sun suddenly breaking through the clouds to illuminate one of the stones that have been here for centuries. 'And God said, Let there be light: and there was light.' Every time this happens I think of a prisoner in his cell and how he yearns for the moment during the day when a glimmer of sunshine comes to cheer the twilight of his prison.

It is still cold, but the wind dropped during the night, and now the goldcrest is singing, the robin is singing, and the chaffinch is displaying a desire to do the same. This is nature responding to the promise of the spring, as it has done since time immemorial. What have we done to the earth? In London last weekend I grieved for the people who were trying to create a yard or two of garden in the midst of all the concrete and macadam, in order to feel that they hadn't been completely alienated from the green earth.

Out in Braich y Pwll this afternoon I saw a phenomenon that I also saw in the hill-country of Montgomeryshire years ago. A small cloud driven by the east wind came to hide the sun for a minute, as I imagined it, because the sun was already about to break free from its shadow. But even though the wind was quite strong, what the cloud did was continue to dawdle about the sun for some five minutes or more. When you consider the distance between the sun and the cloud in relation to that between the sun and observer, it is a strange phenomenon.

There was ice up to the edge of the sea, with the icicles hanging like white fingers from the fists of the rocks, showing that there is no way of escaping the cold, even on the edge of the Gulf Stream. By the way, where are the birds? In place of the ones that have fled the snow, that today covers most of Britain, only a few lapwings and blackbirds were to be seen in the soft fields towards the point.

I was thinking today, while consulting *British Birds*, how meticulously good ornithologists observe a bird, noting every last feature. This leads naturally to the need to remember to stop and look at anything out of the ordinary that catches the eye. This is the time-honoured message of the Book of Exodus about the burning bush. 'And when the Lord saw that he turned aside to see, God called unto him . . .' The message only reaches the person who stops and pays attention. For the careless and the impatient everything is much of a muchness. All black birds are crows, and everything that swims on the surface of the lake is a duck. But as a shepherd knows his sheep, so the ornithologist differentiates between a raven and a carrion crow, or between a carrion crow and the chough.

For a walk today in the vicinity of Madrun and Ceidio. Three fieldfares reminding me again how few fugitives there are, because the weather is still so wintry. Today is Ash Wednesday, when I should repent of my sins, but, as I walked, my thoughts turned instead to the deterioration of life at the heart of the countryside. Today's way of shredding the hedgerows with machines is making the countryside quite untidy. Where did the old craft of pleaching hedgerows go to? Since people follow one another like sheep, how can we open our eyes to what's happening? The machine has displaced the farm hand, and enables the farmer to complete his work in any old way, so that he can sit and stare at television of an evening. Not having been educated in how to appreciate nature, the youngsters belt around all day and flee their cultureless homes in the evening for the snooker halls and pop and the like. The have no love of the countryside, of Wales, or of art. And now, to make things worse, this government deprives them even of the right to work, without teaching them how to make civilised use of their time. What can be done? Is the idea of Cyfeillion Llŷn, The Friends of Llŷn, likely to appeal to more than a tiny minority?

As a symbol of all this, I came across a badger by the side of the road, hit by a car, most likely. There's no room for his kind in today's world, any more than there is for a Welsh-speaking Welshman in the heart of the countryside. I also caught a glimpse of a weasel flashing into the ferns to avoid me. Wherever man appears, the beasts of the field flee for their lives.

February, and the wind still strong from the east; not February Fill-dyke, the filler of ditches, as the English say, but the flayer of the earth's carcass, drying the soil like old bones, and turning the pools dull like cataracted eyes. I found a spot between the trees at the edge of Tŷ Mawr pool where I could stand and hear the wind roaring around me, together with the sound of the sea nearby. At moments such as these, every problem concerning the purpose of life, death and morality disappears, and man feels in touch with existence, pure and simple. For a moment he is one with the creation, participating in the genius of life, as every creature in turn has done over millions of years. My name for such a rare, but not alien, experience is nature-mysticism.

Today I saw her again after months of absence. A car passed me without my recognising who was at the wheel; but memory was prompted. And soon, a hundred yards up the street, there she was, disappearing into the surgery. Woe is me – her face! – the most beautiful that I have seen since my wife was young. Who is she? I want to know, and yet, I don't. Let her keep her strangeness, and let me catch a glimpse of her now and then, like Dante his Beatrice, so that I may drink for a moment from her beauty until the next time. If I were to point her out, how many would agree with me that she is wonderfully beautiful: because she looks mournful, as if she were suffering, and how many think that a fine thing? Elsi would agree with me, because she is an artist, and neither an artist nor a poet sees as others see. I'm so glad that this woman is Welsh, with a face fit to be placed in the gallery of faces that have inspired poets over the centuries. Oh, that I were a poet in the Welsh language, so that I might make a poem to this Dyddgu or this Morfudd who has come again among us!

This was meant to be a description of a year in Llŷn, but, of course, given our contemporary mobility, it happens that, as in this month, I am at times away from Llŷn. At the beginning of the month I was in London giving a poetry reading, seeing the two extremes: the great city with all its millions, and the Llŷn Peninsula with its hundreds; the one the final word in development, and the other not very different from what it has been for centuries, a Welsh-speaking peninsula with the sea on all sides of it.

Today I was in Caernarfon listening to a representative of the government trying to convince Gwynedd County Council that it is possible to protect people from an attack with nuclear weapons. It was amusing to listen to a speaker who was trying to convince by distorting facts, being economical with the truth and refusing to answer the question directly when cross-examined. One thing was obvious: he wasn't at all happy fielding half a dozen questions in Welsh, and having to wait for them to be translated before answering. This is an aspect of the contemporary situation that most of the people of Llŷn prefer to ignore, going about their own trivial affairs. But how long will they be allowed to do this?

Here's February come to an end, the short month that became a giant; the coldest month of the century, they say, without a drop of water in the rain gauge. It was the wind that was to blame, a strong almost daily wind from the east, flaying the land and drying the skin. But Llŷn proved once again that it is much more temperate than the greater part of Britain. The temperature was very low in the glens of Scotland, while there was a great deal of snow in eastern England and in the south. I would have expected to see far more feathered fugitives here, but Llŷn was relatively empty all month.

March

Very often it isn't easy to decide whether March came in like a lion or like a little lamb. Today the sun was shining, as it had been almost throughout February, but the wind was quite tempestuous. Porth Neigwl was deceptively quiet, because the wind was from the north; but by the time I reached Pwllheli the waves were white, and on the shores of the river Menai a strong breeze was blowing from the north-east, past Abermenai towards the sea. I stopped in the hollow between Ceidio and Madrun on the way back and went for a walk through the wood where it was quiet, with enough sunshine through the bare trees to create the illusion of spring. And yet the wind roared in the branches to remind me that it wasn't yet spring by a long way. But this is the magic of Llŷn. Although the sea is on all sides of it, there are wooded spots of this kind where one can experience all the blessings of mid-Wales without the disadvantages of its rough weather.

What a difference there is between the political outside world and the heart of the countryside. In Caernarfon at a meeting of the Campaign for Nuclear Disarmament we sat for two minutes in remembrance of Olof Palme, prime minister of Sweden, an ambassador for peace, who was murdered yesterday. Evil men are able to escape because good men are not willing to kill them. But it is a different matter when an evil man has a gun in his hand. Two hours later I was in a wood in Llŷn, with nobody there to fear but myself.

To live in the country is to understand that man isn't everything. Around you nature is busy with her own concerns, not heeding man when he is not threatening her. Tonight in the mist I heard the oystercatchers flying overhead, making a worried noise. It was something unfamiliar to me that had disturbed them. As I walked down the lane in the dusk I heard the tumult of the blackbirds, a sign that somewhere there was an owl sitting on a branch, too close for their comfort. When I returned, the three cats of Treheli were sitting by the pigsty, as if holding an inquest on the dead rat at their feet. There are several cats at Treheli with a good deal of incest between them. But it is here that they come courting, as if ashamed of sinning openly over there! Don't they know that I have been a priest and that the law of the Church is against incest? The ground must have frozen a good deal more after the cold of the last five weeks, because the water stands in large pools after heavy rain last night and today.

As one grows old, time doesn't just go by, it rushes! Today the sparrowhawk was mewing in the trees of Ty'n-y-Parc. Was it yesterday I heard it last, or last year? Ah, wretched man that I am.

March – the month of my birth! It is without doubt an exciting month, one that sees the earth waking from its deep sleep. It is also a turbulent month, one that brings the turn of the wheel towards us, with its strong winds and the first migrants amongst the birds. Am I glad to have been born? There's a question! Yeats said that he would be willing to live it all again. Would I? An answer to the contrary seems abhorrent.

Compared with so many wretches who are blind and lame or sick, I have so much to be grateful for. And yet can life be praised on every occasion and in all its aspects? This is the time of year when the little lambs are frolicking in the fields. What better evidence is there of life's dominion? But would they rejoice if they knew that we, who praise them, are ready to eat them? Is life something more that a huge complex machine that has to have millions of gallons of blood daily and millions of tons of flesh to sustain it? It has been said that it is a comedy to the one who thinks, and a tragedy to the one who feels, but set against all the knowledge we possess today, life is hardly amusing for the thinker either. As T. S. Eliot said, 'After such knowledge, what forgiveness?'

Today it wasn't the view *from* Llŷn that I had, but a glimpse of Llŷn from Anglesey, which is always enchanting, especially at the close of day. This afternoon, with the sun starting to set, I stopped, as I would in the old days, to see the light colouring the clouds around the mountains of Snowdonia, with a long layer of mist embracing Yr Eifl. There came the silence that used to fall on my spirit every time I looked at them when I was younger. But alas! Though the road I was on was quite obscure, the traffic was incredible – car after car rushing past, as if there wasn't a minute to lose. Thinking of Anglesey as she used to be in centuries gone by, a platform from which to see the drama of the sunset, I felt more certain than ever that man's discovery of the machine with all its consequences was a mistake. And as if to emphasise the gap between the Anglesey of today and yesterday, two little girls went by on their bicycles, cackling the patois of the big English towns.

Today, when I was out in Pen-y-cil and Parwyd, as I was looking over the precipice, there came the old urge to leap down. Almost everyone has experienced it. There is a psychological explanation most probably, but not everyone has a steady enough head to be able to look down, let alone climb down. Mercifully no-one today has to do it, if he doesn't want to. But I remembered how it used to be on islands like the Faroes, where every young man had to face the challenge of climbing down the steep rocks to gather eggs, otherwise he wasn't eligible to marry and support a family. But despite the fact that we have quite high cliffs in Llŷn, things were never so straitened for its young men that they were forced to lower themselves over the precipice, thanks to the fertile land we have. But I also recalled the case of my father, who went to see as a young apprentice in the old days of the sailing ships. Did he foresee how it would be for him high amongst the sails on a day or night of storm?

This afternoon in Llanengan, for the first time this year, the skylarks were busy singing above the dunes. When I left the car in Llangïan, I heard the sea thundering on the beach in Porth Neigwl and thought how characteristic of the Llŷn Peninsula is the din of the sea on the beach. Oh, what a loss it is for someone who was brought up by the sea and has moved to live far away from it in his later life. As Lockley once told me, 'It isn't possible to live away from the sea.' I noticed with pleasure that they had raised a number of gravestones in the graveyard at Llanengan and placed them as two rows of slates on either side of the path leading to the church door. I also noticed, with disgust, that a warning notice had been placed on the gable-end of the community centre. The Welsh-only slate looked fine, but now someone has had the servile idea of placing a parking warning in English there as well!

The lesser celandine is already in bloom. Since when? That is the kind of flower they are: unremarkable, and yet once you've noticed them, able to glitter like quickgold. How characteristic they are of the lanes and hedgerows by the sea. They take me back to Holyhead. Certainly, they were the first wild flowers I became aware of, and there would usually be the smell of elder trees about them.

On the eighteenth I heard the first chiffchaff of the year near Tŷ Mawr lake. I have noticed it many times before, arriving in March and starting to render its monotonous song, and yet every year it affords me an opportunity to marvel at the old and new miracle of this bodikin accomplishing the task of flying thousands of miles from Africa to Wales to raise a new generation that will do the same thing when their time comes. When the weather is adverse, as it is at the moment, it isn't the song of this little bird that I hear, but its little sad note, which is, even so, contradicted by the sprightliness of the bird itself, as it flits from twig to twig in the bushes to gather its morsel.

Shouldn't one feel angry that on the first morning of spring, when the earth wakes up to live, the harbingers of death are filling the sky with their tumult, drowning the song of the birds that responds to the call of the spring? 'And who are you to challenge the power and authority of the state? These are a means of preserving peace.' 'Yes, yes.' We've heard this before over the years. I know who constitutes this state – a clique of ambitious people who have persuaded their constituencies to swallow their propaganda and who, once elected, instead of representing the interests of their constituents, represent the greed and avarice and power tied in with them. What interest do these people have in the world of nature, with its old and marvellous dispensation? But we are in authority to protect you from the enemy, they say. Friends, I do not need you to tell me who the enemy is. It is you who are the enemy, so long as you are prepared to pollute the earth and the environment for your profit. The only grain of truth in the claim is that any country that succeeded in overcoming you would become an enemy to us, since it is the same kind of man who aims for political and financial power in every country. I don't need anyone to govern me. That is the true meaning of self-government – that you are capable of disciplining yourself. The one thing necessary is a body of people to organise social and practical affairs, using the police force in the true meaning of the Welsh word *heddlu*, peace force, to ensure that no-one tries to bring down a just society, or take advantage of its weakest part.

Over to Mold today, along my favourite road from Llan Ffestiniog to Ysbyty Ifan, and then over Mynydd Hiraethog. Today, according to the BBC, is the first day of spring. They must have changed the equinox! Until now, throughout my lifetime, it has fallen on the twenty-first of March, but now it is a day earlier. Be that as it may, the sense of spring was to be felt in the moorland even though things hadn't begun to grow green yet. This is the difference between Llŷn and mid-Wales. The seasons aren't as marked near the sea, but there is a certain freshness apparent in the hills at winter's end. It is the light that causes this, bringing to mind Gwili's words:

> *Duw ieuanc ydyw Duw, Duw'r gwanwyn clir;*
> *Y Duw sy'n cyffro calon oer y tir*
> *I guro'n gyflym, ac yn galw cân*
> *Yn ôl i neuadd fawr y goedwig ir.*

> God is a young God, the God of the clear spring;
> The God who stirs the land's cold heart
> To beat quickly and who calls a song
> Back to the great hall of the verdant wood.

The idea of a young God was common to the Celtic nations. Living near the sea, conscious of geological time, there is within me a tendency to think of God as an old being, but a journey through mid-Wales at this time of the year is enough to remind me that he is also young.

To Llanengan last night to the literary circle. On the way there in my car I suddenly realised that I was in the Llŷn Peninsula, and I rejoiced on that account. Through most of my life, I would look towards the west with longing, but now, towards the end of my time, I have at least reached the place where I want to be. There is too much light in Llangïan and Llanengan. With some pleasure I looked over in the direction of Y Rhiw. Were it not for the strange desire to be fashionable, which has caused the lamps to mushroom, Mynydd y Rhiw would have been in total darkness like some giant rising threateningly on the horizon.

Stormy weather in the true sense of the word: the tempestuous wind of March roaring, and the sea and the trees responding to it; the clouds put to flight, and showers of sleet and snow galloping past, leaving the summits white. And yet, this afternoon, out in Braich y Pwll, I saw the first gannet of the year battling bravely against the wind, like a large snowflake. It had been prophesying from the sea, as the chiffchaff had done from the bushes, that spring was approaching.

Down to Carmarthen to protest against the nuclear bunker there by holding a three-hour service on Good Friday on that very spot; the guards watching us from behind the iron bars, and the big dog barking throughout. Then the big rally on the Saturday, when thousands came together and encircled the bunker itself. At one o'clock everyone fell down feigning death, as a warning of how it would be after a nuclear attack. I heard of the bravery of some of the members of the anti-nuclear movement, who still challenge the unspeakable authorities by breaking in and being bitten by dogs, or abused by the guards. Then back to the silence of Llŷn, where the sea still breaks on the beach, as it did before man was created, and as it will do after a nuclear war. From the world of man back to the world of nature, with me unworthy of the bravery of the one and of the beauty of the other.

March went out – how? As happens so often, it was somewhere between mild and rough. The sun is now strong, were it only given a chance by the clouds. Yet these continue to gather, despite the fact that the number of chiffchaffs is on the increase, proving that they succeeded in slipping into this country between the spells of bad weather. Today in the Llŷn Show I marvelled at the number of Llŷn countrymen who had come from the remote parts of the hundred, attracted by the merriment and fun that has rehearsed mankind's pageant over the centuries: the horses prancing, the dogs barking, the sheep bleating, and men and women promenading, showing themselves off and making it difficult for the person who insists on asking whether it is man who imitates history – or history, man.

April

The month that should be amongst the most exciting is in Llŷn one of the most disappointing. It is the weather, of course, that is responsible. And it is the sea that controls the weather. The days are getting longer, the sun is getting stronger, but the wind remains sharp because of the temperature of the sea, which is far lower than that of the normal air of April. Stand at the edge of the precipice in Pen Cilan or in Braich y Pwll and you will feel the wind cutting like a knife, however strong the sun.

For birds this is a month full of expectancy, but often the arrival of the migratory birds is postponed by rough weather, with a corresponding scarcity of the insects that are food for the warblers, the small brown things that slip through the willows once the wind has dropped sufficiently. Sometimes there is a barren period of some ten days during which the new arrivals, through some instinct that tells them of the scarcity of food awaiting them, keep away. And yet there are signs that spring is not far behind: the occasional blue flash when the first swallow darts past, or, at sea, black dots here and there that indicate that the Manx shearwaters have already returned to take possession of the hundreds of holes on Bardsey Island.

Sometimes a father eager to encourage his children will say to me, 'Huw's interested in birds.' But if I enquire, it is obvious that neither has any idea how to go about bird-watching. Like this, you see: get a pair of binoculars. If you're young there's no need to have a strong pair; a pair that magnifies sevenfold is enough, if your eyesight is normal. Later on is the time to see the benefit of a stronger and more expensive pair. Start in your home area. Learn to recognise the most common birds first, and learn how to describe them, every part of their bodies, starting with the head. There is a name for every inch of them. Buy a good book that gives a picture of the birds in addition to a description of their main features. And buy a book in which to make notes, so that you can describe the birds you have seen to someone else, so that he can identify them for you, if you don't know. After this, when you have familiarised yourself with the birds closest to you, you can go further afield to look for others. Having learnt to recognise as many of them as possible, you will realise from consulting your book of birds that there are some that you will never see, unless you travel to the region where they are to be sighted. For instance, if you wish to see an eagle, you won't see it without travelling to the Scottish Highlands. But that will come in its own time. I can assure you that, once the habit has taken hold of you, you will never look back. When someone in the house is ill, I always advise the family to hang a strip of fat outside the window so that the invalid can watch the capers of the tits. In this way will many an entertaining hour go by.

April is the month of listening. Secretly, I find myself waiting for the song of the blackcap or the grasshopper warbler, and of course, later on in the month, for the cuckoo's double note. Every year without fail it is heard by someone before it arrives, because people's ears are ready for it, and when you're waiting there are other sounds that are very similar to it, such as those of the collared dove, or even of mischievous children imitating it. But the cuckoo is a punctual bird, arriving here around the twenty-fourth of April, and although it is the people of the hillsides that hear it first, I am very sceptical of anyone who claims to have heard it long before then. It is by its voice that most people recognise it, although it is only the cock that sings, of course. It is a sort of whistle, like a melodious bleat, that the hen has. I don't know how many are familiar with the bird itself. It is similar to the sparrowhawk, and this was responsible for an amusing item I heard years ago when Dr Alun Roberts used to be on the panel of *Byd Natur*. An old wag from the area of Bethesda claimed that he often used to see the cuckoo in the winter. Given that he was adamant, the interviewer asked him whether he had told Dr Alun. 'Well, to what end?' the man asked scornfully, as good as rejecting the possibility that he could have made a mistake. Of course, Dr Alun's answer would have been, 'Without a doubt, it was a sparrowhawk that you saw, my friend.' As far as I know, there is no report of a cuckoo ever wintering here, although there is a growing list of birds that do so because of the mild winters that we now have.

There is a tendency to link the cuckoo with the woods of England, but for me it is a Welsh bird, that sang its sweetest-sounding song in Abercuawg:

> Yn Abercuawc yt ganant gogeu.
> In Abercuawg cuckoos sing.

And yet it also sings in Nant Gwrtheyrn. Now is the time to visit this blessed spot, as I did on the day of the opening of Tŷ'r Faner there. It was a wonderfully fine day, and as I descended towards the blue sea the shadows of the clouds were moving silently and idly over the slopes of the Nant to the bitter-melodious song of the cuckoo.

That's enough about birds for the time being. There are other experiences to be had in April, because it is in this month that Easter almost always falls: the church full of the new flowers of spring on the morning of the festival with, in Saunders's words, '*[Y] Tad yn cusanu'r Mab yn y gwlith gwyn*', 'The Father kissing the Son in the bright dew'. Then the moment of pure pleasure, when the sun strikes warm on some recess sheltered from the wind, and the willow warbler showers its silver notes on you from the arbour above your head. And if the wind turns to the north, this is the month to make for some hiding-place in the rocks in the sun's face and watch the waves breaking white over the dark blue ocean. This is the month of dreaming, when everyone, whatever his age, feels young because of the liveliness in the air, the bees and the gnats humming, the birds building their nests and the smell of the newborn earth filling the air.

I mentioned the church at Easter, but that was a memory. It pains me greatly, but ever since the Church reformed the Liturgy, I cannot partake of the Sacrament. The new order of the Church in Wales has changed the whole atmosphere of Holy Communion for me. The pinnacle of the original service was when I, as a priest, would say the words of consecration over the bread and wine, with my back to the congregation as one who had the honour of leading them to the throne of God's grace. But now it is the congregation that the priest faces, inviting them to speak, as he breaks the synthetic wafer before them. It is to God that mystery belongs, and woe to man when he tries to interfere with that mystery. As T. S. Eliot said, 'Human kind cannot bear very much reality.'

But there are two sides to existence, too, the transcendental and the subordinate, as it were. It is an abysmal rift that exists between those who seek to exalt life and those who want to reduce it to the 'bare facts', as they term them. 'Life is nothing but . . .' they say. But this won't do in April. William Blake talked of seeing the world in a grain of sand. Look at the nest of the long-tailed tit, if you can, with its three thousand feathers inside. Take out carefully one of the small eggs contained in it and think of the fragile life that is developing under this miraculous shell. Nothing but? Lift your head at night and look at the heavens with their 'thousand peacock eyes', to quote Saunders again. Nothing but? I saw the Northern Lights this month, the huge electric curtain that is to be seen from time to time in Wales, but which is one of the wonders of the far north. Years have passed since I last saw it, and this is the first time I have seen it here in Llŷn. It is in the same class as thunder and lightning and earthquakes. If it doesn't frighten you in the same way, it nevertheless sends a shiver through your being like something '*tremendum et fascinans*'. It is likely that Jacob was too far south to see it, and yet it isn't unlike a huge ladder between earth and heaven, and 'behold the angels of God ascending and descending on it'.

Therefore April is not only something beautiful, gentle, with the shoots of life to be seen everywhere, but a month that reminds us of the mysterious element in life, when everything responds to the increasing strength of the sun. A month which, in Gwili's words, 'calls a song / Back to the great hall of the verdant wood', '*yn galw cân / Yn ôl i neuaidd fawr y goedwig ir*'. In the West the month is heavily influenced by Christianity with its message of the victory over death, prompted by the return of life to the withered and barren earth. It is in this month that the swallow returns to the same spot in the byre, making us marvel at its ability to remember the way over the thousands of miles between South Africa and the Llŷn Peninsula. It is also in this month that I hear in Porth Neigwl below me the cry of different swallows – the sandwich terns – which travel every bit as far as the common swallows, only they are bigger and stronger birds.

And here we are, having wandered back to the birds again, but I forgot to mention their speed. Because so many of us today have cars, we have a way of measuring this speed. Often when we are driving, a bird or two will fly abreast of us, which gives us an opportunity to time them. In the nature of things, small objects appear to be faster than large ones, but this isn't true. There is a belief that the teal is swifter than the mallard; but it isn't. Wood pigeons appear to be very fast, and yet the other day I saw two ravens overtaking one and passing it with ease. But the next time you're driving, if you notice that there are birds going in the same direction, as a matter of interest, time them. For many centuries man yearned to fly, and at last he succeeded. But long before he appeared on earth the birds had mastered the feat with less tumult and fuss, and without taxing the resources of the environment, or using this ability to destroy their own kind. So birds are part of the wonder of April, causing us to ponder deeply their miraculous lives. But to appreciate them fully one must be very alert, because several of them only pop into Llŷn on their way northwards. I used to think there were not more than fifty different types of bird nesting in the parish of Aberdaron; and yet, while I was living there, by keeping my eyes open at the right times, I saw around a hundred and eighty species.

Llŷn is a peninsula, a branch of rock suspended between the sea and the heavens, with the clouds like flowers about it. I sometimes like to think that I have now, in my old age, crept a great distance along it to wait for the end. When I fall, my flesh and bones will go to the depths. I wonder whether my spirit will rise and go to the sphere described by Islwyn?

> *Lle mae'r awel fyth yn dyner,*
> *Lle mae'r wybren fyth yn glir.*

> Where the breeze is always gentle,
> Where the sky is always clear.

May

> *Os marw yw hon Is Conwy*
> *Ni ddyly Mai ddeilio mwy.*

> If she lies dead in Is Conwy
> No longer shall leaves appear in May.

Dafydd Nanmor's immortal couplet is a brilliant epigraph to this month, not because there are that many leaves in the Llŷn Peninsula, but because of Dafydd's connection with this headland. Every time I pass the rock on the Aberdaron promontory, Dafydd's lines to Llio's hair come to my mind:

> *Mewn moled main a melyn*
> *Mae'n un lliw â'r maen yn Llŷn.*

> In a fine kerchief of golden sheen
> It's of the same hue as the rock in Llŷn.

We know of the awesome and incredible antiquity of the rocks of Aberdaron, which were somewhat trivialised in Cynan's verses, but to be mindful of the centuries that have gone by since Dafydd Nanmor's time is enough to cause vertigo. But it is also agreeable to think that he walked these shores and then remembered about the yellow rock while searching for a comparison with the yellow-haired girl.

It fell to Dafydd to live in an age before the dissolution of the monasteries by Henry VIII, so it is likely that there were monks on Bardsey across the water from him when the poet paused to gaze at the light-coloured rocks. I am not certain as to which rock he is referring in his *cywydd*, as there are two within a mile of each other, both facing Bardsey Sound. One is near one of the paths leading to Braich y Pwll. Pared Llech Ymenyn is nearer Pen-y-cil to the south. It was here, some two and a half thousand years ago, that the people of the Bronze Age left their implements, which were found some time this century.

These are strange reflections in a month that is so new and young. Wouldn't it be better to talk of the splendour of the gorse in May? 'If they had reaped their dandelions and sold / Them fairly, they could have afforded gold,' said the poet Edward Thomas. But what about all the wealth of the gorse in Llŷn? I know that it's a plague to the farmers, but it is like gold to a poet. But as I said, you cannot live in Llŷn without calling to mind the great antiquity of the earth; the greater is the wonder, then, in May when you see that earth's ability to rejuvenate itself.

> *Pan ddêl Mai â'i lifrai las*
> *Ar irddail i roi'r urddas.*

> When, in its green livery, May arrives
> To bestow the honour on fresh leaves.

When I was in Manafon there was a girl who caught my fancy. Mai, Plas Iolyn, was her name. She is old now, like me, if she's alive at all, and I'm not sure now whether it was her name more than she herself that attracted me, as I had at the time just started to learn Welsh and was becoming entranced by a different way of life that existed to the west of English-speaking Manafon.

Strangely enough, May is the best month of the spring for seeing the rarer birds in Llŷn. After the migration has come to an end in other places, there is a good chance that a stranger will drop by us, because in this month one sometimes sees the golden oriole, which is supposed to be in France or Germany by now. It was in this month that I saw two roseate terns in Aberdaron, and now in Y Rhiw I shall expect to hear the song of the lesser whitethroat and the wood warbler, two birds that don't nest here, but sing for a day or two on their way to their usual habitat.

May is also the month when the adder appears. They awake from their sleep earlier, of course, but it is during this month that they come out into the open, with the result that several are killed. We are an ignorant people as far as the world of nature is concerned. There are three kinds of 'snake' here, the slowworm, the grass snake and the adder, but it is only the latter that is dangerous, and it won't do anything to you unless you step on it or torment it. But all three kinds are killed, without exception. How often have I heard someone trying to justify himself by saying, 'Gosh, it was a big 'un too.' Which is enough to make it indubitably a grass snake, as these can be as much as four feet long, although perfectly harmless. And then there's the slowworm; this is an exceedingly nervous creature that can sometimes lose its tail in fright – what can this one do to anyone? The adder is quite dozy in the spring, which makes it easy enough to kill, if you must. But quite apart from the good they do in killing slugs and mice, they are beautiful creatures: the male brown-black and white, and the female larger in size and multicoloured, sometimes the colour of sand, which makes it difficult to see her in the grass and the dry leaves, sometimes red or brown or ginger. And once, outside our door here, there was a lovely golden one that I had to jump over to avoid stepping on.

There is a tendency to go over the top about an adder's bite. Certainly, no-one dies from it. It depends to some degree on your age and your health. It depends also on the size of the snake and the time that has elapsed since it last bit. The only thing that is agreed upon is that it is exceedingly painful, so the best thing is to keep your eyes open, and if you're unlucky enough to be bitten, don't rush about shouting that you've had a snakebite, but stay as still as possible and have someone take you to the doctor. Adders are characterised by the same charm as all snakes: they can stay perfectly still, like a stone, or if they want to move, can do so in a strangely quick and graceful way. In the spring, being sleepy, they are quite unwilling to move, but later, as the earth gets warmer, they can flash out of your way like lightning. That is why, I assume, so few people get bitten here. In the spring, when they're sleepy, only a few visitors are around; and later on, with scores of people groping through the bracken, they sense that someone is approaching and disappear. 'Sense,' I said, because they are deaf, and monitor things with their black tongues or through their bodies.

I have written fairly extensively about the adders because they are quite common in Llŷn, and the inhabitants know this. I have heard the older children in Anelog warning their younger brothers and sisters against going into the bracken because of them. And someone in Uwchmynydd told me that he had seen a fair-sized heap of them gathered together. 'I ran like hell from them,' he said, like a naughty boy.

Yet it isn't the adders that are most characteristic of Llŷn, but the choughs. Rarely can you walk on Mynydd Mawr without hearing this bird's screech and seeing it rising and falling in its own deceptive way, which makes it so difficult for the peregrine falcon to catch it. They nest in the crevices of the rocks and in the caves, and at winter's end I have seen as many as thirty of them in the air together. To confirm that they are characteristic of Llŷn, a picture of one was used as a logo by the Heritage Coast people.

And speaking of the Heritage Coast, this is one of the changes that I have seen in my time. Sixty years ago, when I was a lad in Holyhead, the shores were virtually empty apart from the odd beach such as Tre-arddur in August. It was doubtless much the same in Llŷn across the water. Think of the paradise that awaited the first strangers to venture past Pwllheli. Porth Ceiriad, Aberdaron and Porthor would have been empty apart from the odd fisherman, with only Welsh, if any language at all, to be heard there. Isn't there a story about the lads of Bardsey, when they wanted to join a ship in Liverpool, having to have a label hung around their necks asking someone to direct them to the ship when they had reached the end of their journey? But now with the arrival of the strangers bent on visiting and settling here, there are hundreds of people everywhere, ramblers, fishermen, scuba-divers, yachtsmen, and sunbathers, with the result that there are stiles and footpaths and English-language warnings of all sorts, while the ground is worn away more and more every year by thousands of feet. It is easy to spot the difference between the people who truly appreciate the special character of Llŷn and those who are killing time while waiting for a meal and a drink and entertainment of an evening. But both kinds equally put unbearable pressure on the peninsula. It is the narrow lanes with their hedgerows and their flowers that make Llŷn what it is, but as the traffic increases, so too grows the demand to widen them, until year after year another part of the old dear Llŷn disappears. Were it not for my love of the sea, my preference in summer would be for inland Llŷn, away from the clamour of the shores. And Llŷn is so varied, she has almost everything: hills bare and high enough to merit being called mountains; woods and streams and meadows full of flowers. And the view! Merionethshire across the water, and to the north-east the old Caernarfonshire rising gradually until it reaches the peaks of Snow-donia. For me, it is a daily miracle that I can see Snowdon from my own garden, not to mention Y Moelwyn, Y Rhinogau and Cadair Idris. In order slightly to vary the journey from here to Pwllheli it is a pure pleasure to take the road between Nanhoron and Rhydyclafdy. Here, as the strong May sun falls shadowless on the beaches and the rocks, the road twists through the trees with the leaves filtering and sifting the sunlight until everywhere is turned into fairyland.

But there we are. The sea is in my blood as it was in my father's blood, and I see no point in my living in Llŷn without seeing it. For that is what happens in places like Llaniestyn and Sarn Mellteyrn. They are only a few miles from the sea, and yet without a glimpse of it. And there aren't many lakes here either to compensate for the lack of sea. If there were, they would convey something of the blueness of the sea in May. But even then, nothing makes up for losing the sea itself, the blueness and the white of the waves when, as happens in May, there is a sudden storm of wind.

I moved to Aberdaron in May 1967. As I decorated the house ready for living in, after it had been empty for over a year, I noticed the cry of the passing whimbrel. This was something new in my experience. This bird has unique notes, a series not unlike the bleat of a young goat, but wild, conveying something of the isolation of those parts in the far north where they nest. Some people are infatuated with the cry of the curlew, but I am much more taken by the wild notes of the whimbrel, and every May since then I have awaited them enthusiastically. Sometimes in a bad year you don't hear many. At other times there are plenty, and this year was one of the best. The cry is so distinctive that it is possible to hear it above the large towns in England as the birds go by at night. Imagine your *hiraeth* if you had been brought up in Llŷn and had had to move to England, and you heard this bird going by in the solitude of the night.

There is one thing that is different in Llŷn when compared with the other parts of Wales that I have lived in. Because of the nature of the peninsula there is no transhumance here, the annual movement with the flocks from the *hendre*, the winter dwelling in the valley, to the *hafod*, the upland farmstead of the summer months. Llŷn is an area where sheep from the colder regions pass the winter, because of the fine pasture here. But every May Day, I celebrate the movement from the valleys to the moorland. It was an entertaining time, with the shepherds challenging one another with extempore *englynion*. Is this romanticising by someone who never saw the actual event? I also saw the hard facts as I gazed at several upland farmsteads or crofts in the Welsh hill-country, in a location beautiful enough to draw tears: a small stone cottage on the bank of a crystal stream, with a rowan tree bending over it and, around it, the cry of the curlew and sometimes, to add to the sadness, the heartbreaking song of the golden plover, my favourite bird-song. But it was empty; the family had had to leave it under the pressure of the modern world. What is wrong with us in Wales that we have to look back continually as if to better days, even though some people, who are old enough to remember, remind us how hard those days were? What accounts for the fact that the BBC's programme *Caniadaeth y Cysegr*, is still going after forty years or more, while the churches are more or less empty? If the life of our young people today is better than the life of their grandparents, it is, even so, a world similar to the Anglo-American world, a world that has turned its back on the natural enter-tainments I have tried to describe, for an unnatural world of pop and rock, which takes so much of the youngsters' money, and which has placed a fortune in the hands of speculators.

June

The year's halfway house. Towards its own midpoint, no sooner does the light in the west disappear than another radiance emerges towards the east. And yet, despite the brevity of the night, if it is without moon or stars, I am sure to hear Manx shearwaters above my house reminding me that there are three thousand of them nesting on Bardsey, in addition to some on the mainland. I wonder whether a few are nesting in Mynydd y Rhiw? How does one know? There is enough room there and in Mynydd y Graig for you to look for weeks without finding their holes. Be that as may be, it is lovely to hear them here, the wild creatures that never come ashore except to raise and feed chicks. In the winter they are down in the southern hemisphere experiencing great waves that are never seen here.

This month is so different beside the sea from what it is in England. It is the month of thyme and thrift here, and in the *cloddiau*, hedgerows (a word for which there is no exact translation in English, according to Robyn Léwis), the dog rose. But despite the height of the sun and the length of the days, it can be a rough month. And even though I live in

Llŷn, every time it comes I remember this stanza from Matthew Arnold's 'Thyrsis':

> So, some tempestuous morn in early June,
>> When the year's primal burst of bloom is o'er,
>> Before the roses and the longest day –
> When garden-walks and all the grassy floor
>> With blossoms red and white of fallen May
>> And chestnut-flowers are strewn –
> So have I heard the cuckoo's parting cry,
>> From the wet field, through the vexed garden-trees,
>> Come with the volleying rain and tossing breeze:
> The bloom is gone, and with the bloom go I!

I remember Emrys saying how, when he was in Aberdaron, he loved to go on an excursion to Herefordshire and Worcestershire, and it is perfectly understandable. One likes a change, and after months of the wind and the sea, it is fascinating to visit even England's woods and dales. While conversing with an Irishman who had lived for years on the Aran Islands, I told him how I would like to live there. 'My good man,' he said, 'day after day, month after month, you would tire of the sound of the sea.'

And yet romanticising is forgivable when one remembers times past in the Celtic countries and the life of the inhabitants in June. This is the time to visit the Scottish isles, and see the cotton grass in its glory and smell the odour of peat in the air. This is also the month, towards its end, that my wife and I went to Norway, and the first thing that struck me was waking at three o'clock in the morning and seeing the sun already high in the sky. The situation is something similar to this in the northern isles of Shetland. No problem in the summer, but what about the winter, with night falling at about two o'clock? Do we realise how privileged we are in Llŷn? Except for the occasional wind storm, we enjoy an unusually temperate climate, without it being too cold in winter or too hot in summer. It is natural enough to dream sometimes of the Mediterannean sun, but one often goes to extremes. I remember once calling on someone in Seville in southern Spain at the end of April. 'We shan't have rain until October now,' he said. Think, you who are accustomed to Wales's crystalline streams and her green fields, how you would yearn there for even a small shower of rain. And although one cannot drink salt water, the presence of the sea on a hot day in June is enough to alleviate our thirst and dryness a little. We also know that we should not drink cold water when sweating, but how many of us know that bathing our wrists in cold water can bring great relief? There you have a safe way of temporarily quenching your thirst until you find a drink such as hot tea or beer.

Llŷn is a peninsula, but one doesn't realise this until one approaches Rhoshirwaun on the way to Aberdaron. There is a place there near Y Fantol where you can see the sea on either side as if you were on a mountain. Consider, you who are exiles, arriving here on an evening in June, when the hay has been mown and the heady smell fills your car as you go by. They mow hay in other places, certainly, but what can compare with a hayfield by the sea?

If I have anything against June, it is the lack of migratory birds. They will have passed by to nest somewhere in the far north, and the chance of your seeing one is minimal. And yet I did. Towards the end of June in Aberdaron I saw a rose-coloured starling, native to Hungary and such places. I remember the experience to this day – seeing a flock of ordinary starlings looking for food in Mynydd Mawr, and raising the binoculars without expecting to see anything; and behold, one of them was black and pink. A black head, the wing tips black and the rest pink as a rose. What luck! Then hurrying home to fetch my wife so that she, too, might see. And that is how it is where birds are concerned. You can never say with certainty, 'I shan't see anything today.' And sometimes in June, by looking into the depths of the sky, some people have been lucky enough to see the alpine swift, which is occasionally to be spotted along the shores. We are guilty of not looking up often enough. So doing, I have more than once seen the peregrine falcon like a spot in the sky.

I mentioned the hay. Friends, you know what is happening today, the change that has come to the farms, large and small, even here in the Llŷn Peninsula. Farewell to the lovely haycocks and the friendly, fragrant hayricks. Their place has been taken by bales in their ugly plastic sacks, which need another machine to handle them. Oh, I know, indeed I know, the arguments and the advantages for the farmer, but something very beautiful has disappeared from the heart of the countryside. No playing, no sleeping, no lovemaking in the hayrick, but everywhere the big black sacks without shape or fragrance lying like slugs in the corner of the field or rick-yard.

I said that there is nothing new in the world of birds this month. And yet there are chicks about the place, in the hedgerows and on the rocks. It is easy to see where they have nested by watching the parents carrying off food in their beaks. A month ago I saw a chiffchaff making its nest in the garden, but it was impossible to find it without making too much of a mess, it was so well concealed. But now, seeing the parents going to and fro, I have a pretty good idea where it is. Nature is a strange thing. The parent goes to great trouble to hide the nest. She won't go near, but waits with her beak full of food until you move away. But once the chicks leave the nest, and sometimes before that, they will make a ceaseless noise, proclaiming their presence to friend and foe alike. And yet nature has its secrets too. In some mysterious way the birds will raise enough chicks to make sure that their species survives despite the losses.

Down in Tŷ Mawr pool mallards will nest and hatch a brood. I have noticed every year how their number decreases until one or two at the most are left. What is it that is destroying them? A stoat, according to the farmers. Cats as well, I would say, because I have seen the Rhydybengan Bach cat hunting there. I once saw a flash, as a grey and white body jumped through the air and disappeared. I waited by the gate and soon there she came towards me – and it wasn't a kitten in her mouth but a mouse. Ten yards from me she stopped and stared in my direction, not sure whether I was only a part of the gate. Then the truth dawned. She let go of the mouse, turned, and away like a guilty thing. I went to the spot and found the mouse. In fact, it was a *llygoden goch*,* a bank vole, lifeless. I was glad to know that cats can sometimes kill quickly, without playing with their prey. But it could be that the farmer is also right. On visiting a nature reserve in Aberogwen, I saw a stoat swimming quickly across the water of the pool there until it reached the island in the middle. Although the island bank was quite high, the stoat had no trouble at all jumping out of the water, and away. These are masterful hunters, able to run, swim, leap and climb, and all as light as a feather.

I hesitated in naming the mouse because of the old problem of the lack of Welsh words for some creatures; and often the dictionaries aren't much help. Cymdeithas Edward Llwyd, the Edward Llwyd Society, has done well in gathering Welsh names for butterflies, fish and so on, but we are still waiting for a list of standard terms for all the mice. The English are ahead of us in this matter, being far more concerned with detail. Faced with a lack of Welsh terms, the best thing is to use the Latin name according to Linnaeus, which is an international

* Literally, 'red mouse'.

language. At least there is no room for misunderstanding if that is done. For this reason, if I can, I shall give a list of bird names in the three languages at the end of this book. So the Latin name for the mouse that was killed by the cat of Rhydybengan Bach is *Clethrionomys glareolus*.

I mentioned the butterflies, and indeed June, if sunny, is the month for some of them. Porth Meudwy at Aberdaron is one of the best places because it is sheltered, and the habitat of many flowers. But here in Y Rhiw a butterfly that I wait to see in June is the dark-green fritillary, which is large and beautiful and greatly likes the red clover. But I have been disappointed this year by the 'painted lady'. I haven't seen one as yet, despite the good weather. And yet they are numerous enough. There is a report of someone seeing them crossing the ocean a few years ago, with the ship taking three days to pass them. I am fairly familiar with the butterflies, but I have never tried to identify the moths, given that there are so many. Does Welsh have names for these, I wonder? This is the difference between us and the English again. Because of the education they have received and the resources that came their way through having their own government, as well as leisure in the past to pursue their interests, the English have created a wealth of detailed knowledge about the world of nature, along with the necessary names. If Owain Glyndŵr had succeeded and had given us two universities in the fifteenth century, the story could have been totally different here in Wales. But, apart from a few experts, we continue to call every black bird a crow and every butterfly a butterfly.

And what about the bats? There are several kinds of those as well, although it is more difficult to identify them because they fly at night. The most common one is the *Pipistrellus pipistrellus*, the small one that zigzags through the evening twilight, sometimes even in winter, on quiet nights. They are here in our house, and the occasional one will fly through the rooms from time to time, because ours isn't a conventional house, but a four-hundred-year-old cottage, with a central big-chimneyed kitchen. Therefore the bats come in that way as they have most probably done for centuries. The only sad thing is that I cannot hear them any more. It is said that few people over forty years of age can, so high-pitched is their squeak. And yet I could, until I was sixty. And I can still hear them singing like little mice in the wall above my door.

That is enough about nature for the time being. There are also people in Llŷn! Good people; not-so-good ones. Is it right to generalise? What is true of Llŷn is true of the Welsh-speaking Welsh on the whole. They are not a people who go for a walk. Is it because they are too busy? A farm wife is busy enough, of course, but what about the others? That is one striking difference between the inhabitants and the newcomers. One sees the latter everywhere by now, out for a walk with the children or their dogs. They are conventional people who love the open air. It is said that the people of the countryside know a great deal about nature and appreciate it, but take it for granted because they live so close to it. I wonder. When I was out with the scouts one time in Manafon the question of townspeople arose. 'What would they know about nature?' one of the scouts asked with contempt. 'Much more than you, my boy,' I answered, with good reason. But there we are. I promised to give the subject of nature a rest. What about other subjects, then?

Throughout the year the Llŷn and Eifionydd Campaign for Nuclear Disarmament has been meeting and having to admit that we haven't made much of an impression on anyone. Has the majority of the people of Llŷn swallowed the propaganda of the government that we are traitors of some kind? Certainly, we are not respectable to know. When we have a stall on the field people slink past without letting on that they have seen us at all. We have staged all kinds of events, but apart from a few of the faithful, nearly one hundred per cent of the people of Llŷn ignore us. And this is true to an extent of Cyfeillion Llŷn, The Friends of Llŷn, the conservation movement we have. This has two hundred members, but despite having tried to gather them together to discuss the problems of Llŷn and how to deal with them, the meetings were almost empty.

Hand in hand with this goes the crisis of the influx. It is easy for any sensible person to see the danger to Llŷn's character and Welshness if outsiders continue to flood in and settle here. The editor of the community paper, poor soul, has urged his readers to react to the crisis in the columns of the paper. But all in vain. When you know what kind of English papers they read, how few of them take *Barn* or *Y Faner*, and how few of them attend church, or, perhaps, read the Bible, uncomfortable thoughts arise. How many of them by now can discuss subjects of importance in fluent Welsh? Their unreasonable, sometimes nasty, reaction confirms the doubts. With all the pressure from the English-language faction today, I'm afraid that we are deceiving ourselves if we think we can assimilate the thousands of English who come to live amongst us without an assiduous and unceasing struggle. I have an uneasy feeling that the will isn't there any more, but that, because it is more comfortable, we go with the tide until we wake and find that it is too late. From time to time in the pulpit, aware of the atheism that is on the increase, I have asked the congregation to face the implications of lack of faith in God and eternal life. Its implication is total extinction for us and our loved ones. Try living with that idea daily in your private and family life. I am an old man. I shan't be here much longer. But what about the middle-aged and the young? Can they live with the idea that there won't be such a thing as Welsh-speaking Llŷn left after this century? Oh, you say, the country and her place-names will be here. A skeleton. Go to the parts of Wales where the language has disappeared and where the place-names have been mutilated. It is a skeleton of a country. Despite the superb views there is something missing that no-one except a true Welshman can identify.

Such depressing ideas in such a fine month. Is it I who am at fault? I know that this is the reputation I have in the Wales of today. I also know that it was through seeing the old comely things that I loved disappearing, or being disfigured by modern technology, that I turned increasingly to bird-watching. Away from the din and violence of the world, away from man's apathy and cruelty even, it is lovely sometimes to spend an hour or two out on the rocks of Braich y Pwll, watching the birds go by and comparing the waiting for a migrant bird with the waiting for a vision of God.

May I tell you about an experience I had that shows how birds, and nature for that matter, will come to accept you, if you only cultivate enough patience to prove to them that there is no harm in you? I was in a thicket of willows. As there was a light breeze, I could hear the sound of the distant sea, but it was perfectly quiet amongst the trees. Gradually, I noticed the number of goldcrests that were there. The grove was full of them, flying hither and thither after the gnats. I stood perfectly still and they started to come closer. Some of them came within an arm's length on the branches, busily seeking their food, but hesitating nervously a moment to stare at the piece of wood that was different from the rest! They were so close I could see their dark eyes, like black-berry seeds. And the air was continuously full of the rustling of their wings, as they jumped from one twig to another. I almost expected to take one of them on my arm, but gradually they moved on in search of food, and complete silence returned to the trees, with only the sun's rays to remind me of the gold of their crests. It is moments like these that remain in the memory and that repay you for the trouble of setting about knowing and understanding nature.

July

Let no-one think that Llŷn is an escape. The aeroplanes above are practising for the next war, and in summer the thousands of visitors with their cars needing petrol are enough to remind you of the twentieth century. But apart from this I read and reflect and get to hear of the latest knowledge and theories about the nature of existence. One encouraging thing that helps to bridge the superficial gap between Llŷn and the world of today is that the old materialism is in decline. That was based on the belief that life was, at best, nothing but a complex collection of atoms, and that as soon as we had broken into the atom's most secret cell there were no secrets left. God and beauty and the like went the way of every other fancy to oblivion, leaving behind them a world that was nothing but a mathematical variation on atoms. As this idea penetrated the skull of the proletariat and the common people, we saw the decline in the churches and the victory of the materialism that is so common in Wales today. The new knowledge, physics especially, has reduced matter to a state of thin vapour like a current that connects two electric charges. The physicists came to see how amazing the universe is in which we live, and the tricks that time and space can play. Behind the atoms were found smaller particles, and behind those, others still smaller. If man were to succeed in travelling faster than the speed of light, he would disappear, and the universe with him, into a huge black hole. Therefore the sense of holy dread returned. As the Book of Job puts it, 'Then a spirit passed before my face; the hair of my flesh stood up'.

Therefore when I stand at night and look towards the stars, and think of the galaxies that stretch one after the other to oblivion, while remembering that it is all within finite space that is still expanding, I am not a dreamer belonging to the old primitive lineage of Llŷn, but someone who, partaking of contemporary knowledge, can still wonder at the Being that keeps it all in balance.

*Gorffen haf** – it is true what the word communicates. Some mysterious change comes to your attention with the arrival of this month. The clearest expression to one who is familiar with it is the change in the cry of the curlew. It no longer sings, but whistles sadly, as if realising

---

* Literally, 'The end of summer', 'end' and 'summer' being the two elements of the Welsh word for July, *Gorffennaf*.

what is happening. One also sees that the clouds have a new shape and colour as if they too are conscious that things have changed. I remember being a youngster in Holyhead and discovering the marsh gentian at the side of the road to the Plas. After gazing at length on its amazing bluey-greenness, I looked up and saw Snowdonia in the distance, dressed in a not dissimilar blue-green. And thinking of Anglesey, remembering also Llanddwyn Island, a place my friends arranged several trips to, with me always unable to go, until the situation resembled that of Virginia Woolf's novel, *To the Lighthouse*. But in the end I was able to go, and it must have been July. While we were idling on the beach a small yacht arrived and presently a sailor came towards us and asked, in English, 'Can any of you gentlemen spare me a fill of tobacco?' No chance. Mercifully, none of us smoked. Such is this drug's hold that a man is compelled to go to the trouble of coming ashore in a remote place to beg for a pinch of it. I said remote, because in those days one was faced with an hour's walk over the dunes between Newborough and the island; not like today, when the whole world will make for the place because of the car park nearby, with the sea around the island teeming with scuba-divers. It was an old woman called Mrs Jones, Llanddwyn, who looked after the place for the Society for the Protection of Birds. I also went there during the war and was given a cup of tea by the dear old thing. It was the middle of winter and night descended on us soon enough. As she and I sat there I heard aeroplanes starting to cross over our heads. The door of the house was wide open. I tolerated this for about a quarter of an hour before asking, 'Do you hear the aeroplanes, Mrs Jones?' 'Germans!' she screamed, jumping to her feet and slamming the door shut. We were lucky. I heard afterwards that the Germans had attacked Béal Feirste* in their hundreds that night.

I mentioned Llanddwyn because all was part of the small circle I turned in – Holyhead, Llanddwyn, Llŷn – looking towards Llŷn when I was young and towards Anglesey now that I am old.

When I was young, I would watch the sea. Many Holyhead people used to do the same, for different reasons. A shipwreck was what they were waiting for. I don't remember what thoughts I harboured, if any. But today, when the oystercatchers make a din, I always remember hearing their tumult along the rocks in Holyhead. I came to learn that it was on account of their eggs or their chicks that they make a noise.

* Irish for Belfast.

Back then, did I realise or even care? That is one of the differences that fifty years have made.

Because of the increase in the population, it is by now quite bad for the birds that nest on the beaches, and some species have left us. It was so lovely the other day, therefore, to come across an oystercatcher's nest at the edge of Porth Wylan with three eggs in it, and the cries of those birds about me enough to hurt the ear.

In Llŷn, this month is the month of the flowers, even though many of them – the bluebells, for instance – have come to an end. This is the month of thyme and honeysuckle, the harebell and the dog rose. It is so dry this year that you would expect to see everything withered; and yet in places in the hedgerows the harebells are thriving better than ever. And this is the pure pleasure afforded by ambling along the lanes. But with the increase in the number of tourists I am afraid that there will be pressure on the County Council to widen and widen continually. How long can we keep the narrow, winding lanes that are part of the character and glory of Llŷn? That council has already newly felled the row of beech trees near Llanbedrog that gave Lôn Crugan a special character. The excuse was the same. Safety. That is to say, widening the road so that motorists can go ever faster. Arriving, not enjoying the journey, is everything today. And what is left to enjoy on the big motorways?

We used to come to the Llŷn Peninsula on our holidays before moving to live here, and, in time, we were offered Fron Deg on the slopes of Mynydd y Rhiw by the Keating sisters. But in looking ahead to the time when we, too, would be old, we foresaw how we would have to carry everything for about half a mile across the moorland. Therefore, with regret, but with thanks for the offer, I declined. And that is how we obtained the tenancy of Sarn-y-Plas which was, in the sisters' opinion, much more convenient as it was by the side of the road. The only disadvantage is that this cottage is *too* close to the road. Since we were offered it, the traffic and the tourists have increased a hundredfold, with the result that I cannot venture on the road without someone asking how to get to the beach, which is the road for Aberdaron, or where he can have a cup of tea. This year I have begun to answer, 'No English,' or to shrug and shake my head like someone who is not all there. And very likely, I have reason to as well. I was in a large store in Bangor this month, and to be fair to the girl behind the counter, she was ready enough with her Welsh, but when she called on some young man to serve me and I asked him, '*Cymro, ie?*',* 'No,' he answered, squaring

---

* 'You're a Welsh-speaker?'

his shoulders as if under siege. 'Alright,' I said to myself, 'a dose of their own medicine for the English from now on.'

If we cannot communicate to visitors the fact that Llŷn, of all places, is Welsh-speaking, what will become of us? We know from experience that other countries are not so ready with their English, France especially. Why should we help England make the Welsh language unnecessary? 'No need to learn Welsh. They'll speak English to you.'

Time was when these people used to come here in August and then go home. Some in Llŷn were glad to see them, and glad of the little money that came with them to help make ends meet. Now they are like a millstone about our necks all year round and have created more problems than they have solved. Personally I know how to avoid them. The fields and the hedgerows and the woods are still free of them. And if you are willing to weave through them on Mynydd Mawr you can still find a secluded spot in the rocks somewhere between sea and sky. Or you can get up early and go out for an hour of quiet before the campers have stirred. All this in the knowledge that it will become worse in August, when the schools have closed. But however that may be, in August the migratory birds start their passage, and if there's a storm, it is worth going out, tourists or no, to see what is happening on the sea. August did I say? The waders start on their journey south in this month. As early as the second day, I have seen the green sandpiper on the edge of Tŷ Mawr pool, and no sooner does the last whimbrel pass by on its way north, than the first one of the autumn is on its way south. Nature never loiters. The birds crave mobility the same as the motorists, but less expensively, with a more melodious cry, and less dangerously.

The beauty of Sarn Rhiw is that I can look over Porth Neigwl and see what is happening, what kind of weather there is and what is the state of the sea. This minute, when I raised my head, I was in time to see a gannet dive into the sea. They are easy to recognise, no matter how far away they are, because they are chalk white. More came in this year and I hope they continue to do so. Sometimes dolphins are to be seen rising to the surface, and seals, too, on occasion.

'Well, what a place for writing poetry,' is what my friends say when they come here. But of course the truth is that poetry is not made from fine views, but from words and ideas and the condition of man. '*Ystâd bardd, astudio byd*', 'The poet's business is to study the world'. And yet there is room here for meditating and philosophising. But, with the weather so fine this year, I did little even of that, only worrying continually for a dying nation, and tortured by the unanswerable question: is she being killed, or does she *choose* to die? A mixture of both, I'd imagine.

August

I never thought there was much to August until I became a bird-watcher. And yet it was in August that my wife was born, and my son also, and I gave her a bunch of white heather when I went to see her in hospital after my son's birth. But it was a dry and hot month in Manafon, far from the sea and too late to fish in the river. The only thing to look forward to there was the harvest, when the haycocks would create enchanting patterns in the fields, especially in the moonlight. But after moving to Eglwys-fach, with the mouth of the river Dovey nearby, I realised that this is the month when the waders are at their most numerous in the estuaries, and one night at the end of this month I counted twenty-three various types – a record for that river.

After moving to Aberdaron it dawned on me that this is the month when the sea birds, the terns mainly, start to migrate. Speaking of these, I also remember going in this month to see a bridled tern in Cemlyn, Anglesey. There was a group of other people watching it, and as I approached them a cloud of terns arose, as they tend to do. 'Oh,' said one of the English people, 'you must have come from a society for the protection of terns.' 'Oh, that's right. And you're the president, no doubt,' I said. 'Pleased to meet you.'

No, friend, that was *not* what I said. I am not one of those people who have a ready answer. Like many another person I will think of a humorous answer about half an hour too late. Such people must be taken down a notch or two, especially the English. But I had gone there to see the rare bird and not to quarrel. There are nasty people amongst bird-watchers, people who insist on showing off. The best thing is to avoid them if possible. How was it that this person and his friends reached the place without, as I did, causing the birds to rise into the sky?

But anyway, August became for me a month when I would wait for a storm of wind to drive the birds close to the shore in Braich y Pwll.

But as the birds increase in number, so too do the tourists. I pity the girls in the shops having to try to understand the language of these people, so poor is their speech. They tell me that it was a better, more cultured, type that used to come here years ago, but it is some *Dic Siôn Dafydd* that I see now, roaming the streets of Pwllheli, or sitting in his car with a newspaper between him and the views, killing time before opening-time at the pubs, or the start of evening entertainment at But-lin's. This sounds snobbish, I know, but I have little sympathy with them because these are the people who, in their millions, are busy killing off the Welsh language, with the Welsh welcoming them because they have money. When is enough enough, I wonder? I know that the holiday-makers have helped some people to make ends meet, but it is not into their pockets that most of the money goes, but to the ones who are not hard up.

We had an exceptionally dry July that has lasted through August as well. How different the appearance of Llŷn, if you look across it from one of the hills. It is mostly greyish-yellow, because the grass has been scorched. What surprises me is that there are so few fires, though Y Foel Gron in Mynytho caught fire one afternoon. Y Foel, poor thing, gets it every year in one way or another, and this affects the heather that makes the hill so striking every summer.

August, of course, is the month of the National Eisteddfod, with the result that not much goes on in the villages, with everyone away competing, or helping others to do so, or going for the week to renew acquaintance with their friends and relatives. 'Did you catch the Eis-teddfod?' And a disappointed look when I answer to the contrary. But the truth is that there is little of the competitive spirit in me. Is this a matter of upbringing? Had I been brought up in a Welsh-speaking home and mixed more with the Welsh when I was young, learning *cyngh-anedd* and so on, would I have competed for the chair and the crown the same as the others? It works both ways, does it not? Without the spur of the acclaim and the prize, the satisfaction of proving themselves *prifeirdd*, 'chief poets', how many of our poets would have given us *awdlau* and *pryddestau*? On the other hand again, how many, after winning a chair or a crown in the National Eisteddfod have become idle and turned to other things? For me, being a poet is a full-time job, and although the muse may languish as one grows older, there is a kind of duty upon you to persevere in perfecting your craft, and to secure an answer, through poetry, to some of the great questions of life. Some are still surprised that I write my poems in English, as if it were a matter of choice. I have said many times that I was thirty before I started learning Welsh in earnest. English (my mother tongue, remember) was long since deeply rooted in me, and it is from the depth of his being that a poet draws his poems. If I believed that I could satisfy myself by composing poetry in Welsh, I would do so. But I learned many years ago, with sorrow, that it was not possible. Here again I am not sure whether it is because of my lack of mastery of the Welsh language that I feel that I cannot write my kind of poetry in that language, because with the passage of years I started writing a different kind of poem. Although my love of nature and of the heart of the countryside is still as deep, I do not write about them so often any more. Faced with the great development in technology, the lack of faith in the old traditions, and the omnipresence of the aeroplanes practising above our heads in the Llŷn Peninsula, my poetry has grown (some would say deteriorated) to be more abstract. But be that as may be, Llŷn is not an escape, but a peninsula where I can be inward with all the tension of our age.

This afternoon, on the threshold of the Bank Holiday, I went to Porthorion, hoping to be at a part of the coast that was free of the presence of other people. It wasn't free of them, but without a sufficient number to disturb its peace overmuch. So different is the coastline of the North. That of the South – because it is sheltered, apparently – is much tamer. After all, Porth Neigwl is only a bay. It takes a big storm to make you realise that the ocean isn't far away. But it is far more exposed on the coastline of the North. The birds are more characteristic of the seashore: the linnet and the stonechat; and even the flowers are different, because, although they are not yet in bloom, I know that it is here that the thyme grows, and in the spring, the sea squill. I came across pigeon feathers, which showed that the peregrine falcon had killed in that place. I wonder whether it had nested there without my knowing? This is one of its traditional territories. Ireland could be seen over the sea, raising the old romantic feelings that attach to a free country, the only Celtic country that is so. But then, as usual, came disillusionment. Behind the romance of a country across the sea were the facts: that she had to all intents and purposes lost her language, because her people had turned their backs on it. In addition, there was the knowledge that it was behind the curtain of her enchanting hills that the reality lay – the fact that the majority of her young people are infatuated with the Anglo-American way of life. I had to take my eyes off her and content myself with the nearer water, where the tide was starting to surround Dinas Fawr, the small island that long ago I used to look upon as a desirable place for burying my ashes. With time, I changed my mind. Given the strange universe we live in, what difference does it make what happens to our mortal remains? And who except your children will care where you are buried? There is too much of a fairy-tale element in the idea that Christ will visit every grave in existence. And what of the dead who have no graves?

I am at the moment reading David Bellamy and Brendan Quayle's book *Turning the Tide*, which describes the mess that over-industrialisation and the over-use of chemicals have made of the earth and the environment, and how some pioneers are trying to return to more traditional methods of producing food and cultivating the land. It could be thought that there was a time when things were much better in Llŷn – for example, when there were plenty of mills, fulling-mills, shoemakers and the like. It is certain that Llŷn was far closer to self-sufficiency than she is today. To think of how we are dependent on places like Merseyside and Birmingham for so much of our food and our equipment causes considerable anxiety. Of course some people are better off financially, but much has also been lost, so that one hates to think of all the machines and artificial fertilisers that are trying to sustain agriculture in Llŷn today. '*Peiriannau lle bu'r pererinion*', 'Machines where once the pilgrims were,' as Gwenallt said. Wouldn't Llŷn, or at least the tip of Llŷn, be an ideal area for a cooperative venture designed to create jobs and attract people back to work on the land in more traditional modes? In some places it is already happening. Would it be the major farmers who would be opposed to it, or the over-indulged youngsters? Certainly, the land of Llŷn has not been destroyed and exhausted by growing one crop only, as has happened in eastern England and other parts of the world. Unfortunately, without the help and sympathy of councils and the like, it is only the major farmers who have enough land to set some of it aside for experimenting.

A great noise is coming these days from Porth Neigwl, where the sandwich terns are congregating before continuing on their journey south. Even so, the signs are very scarce that other birds are migrating. And yet this morning, immediately before lunch, some English people appeared at the door with a Manx shearwater they had picked up on the beach in Aberdaron. It was probably tired and having difficulty in swimming against the waves. As it was pretty stormy this side, I took it over to Porth Golmon, where it was quieter, with the wind coming off the mainland. Shearwaters find taking off from the ground difficult, so the best thing usually is to throw them into the air. But because I suspected that this one had not regained its strength, I placed it in the water and watched it swim strongly for the open sea. I watched until it was nothing but a small spot on the face of the ocean. These are the birds I described as screaming above the house at night. Anyone who has visited Bardsey knows of their tumult in the night, which reminds me of the Norsemen who landed on the island of Rhum in Scotland centuries ago. There are a hundred thousand of these birds there, and when night fell, such was the shrieking and the noise that the pirates fled the island, thinking probably that the night was full of fiends.

What shall we call August? The month of holidays? The month of mushrooms? The month of the rowan? It deserves all three names, except that mentioning holidays reminds one of the change that has come upon Llŷn, not only on account of the visitors, but in connection with the places that the people of Llŷn visit more often each year. In the last century, how many of the natives, apart from the seamen, had travelled further than Pwllheli? But now I tend to smile secretly to myself as I eavesdrop on the conversation of the Pwllheli people. 'Have you been on holiday?' 'Yes.' 'Where did you go, to Liverpool?' 'No, as it happens, mate, I've been to south Italy.' Or sometimes perhaps to Corfu, or the United States. Yes, the aeroplanes that thunder their way through the blue take the people of Llŷn to the four corners of the earth. As another local inhabitant told me in Rhoshirwaun, 'The people of Llŷn aren't poor, remember.' And perhaps this is true in comparison with the misery of some of the city people.

But, to be more local, what about the mushrooms and the rowan? As I say, this is their month, too. Despite the dry summer there are plenty of mushrooms, the wonderfully white vegetables that push their dewy heads through the earth, giving a thrill of pleasure to whoever comes across them. An extensive mythology pertains to them, and of course in this nuclear age they remind us of something far more unnatural and fiendish. I wouldn't say that the rowan is characteristic of Llŷn, and yet it is worth travelling along the road from Nanhoron to Saethon because they are so numerous either side of that road. Those who know claim that an excellent jelly can be made from boiling the berries.

This morning I saw a hummingbird moth feeding on the fuchsia outside the door. I hadn't seen one for ages. Here are excellent travellers which have been sighted even in the Arctic, in those parts where there are flowers. Every time someone claims to have seen a hummingbird, it is one of this family of moths. Seeing it was a happy conclusion to a month that had been at first glance somewhat unremarkable, though, for anyone who was alert, full of unexpected things. For example, towards the end of this month the birds of prey come by. Last year in August I saw a long-eared owl sitting on a branch in the lane to Ty'n Parc; and this year Menna saw one in the lane to Bodwyddog. This is also the time to keep your eyes open for the harriers, the hen harrier and the marsh harrier and even the osprey, if you're lucky. So, having been to the Eisteddfod, don't think that there isn't a crown for you, too – somewhere in the world of nature.

September

How the weather has changed! When I came to Aberdaron in 1967 the customary winds of September still persisted, and we had a terrible storm on the fourth with hundreds of sea birds to be seen near Bardsey. It was a very strong wind from the west, and that was the best direction for bringing migratory birds closer to the shore. But gradually over the years the pattern has changed and we have had a series of calm Septembers, with the result that the birds pass by unhindered and far from the shore. It is the same this year, and here I am longing for a tempest! Of course, it is of maritime weather that I am speaking. In mid-Wales it used always to be calmer, with the harvest moon ripening hand in hand with the corn. And yet this year, because of the dry, warm summer, the majority of farmers had the corn harvest in August, and some even in July. In the old days what could you expect after such a summer but a very hard winter? But these days, you cannot be sure, the weather being so different under the greenhouse effect – the environment heating up because of the smoke from the factories and the machines, and the chemicals that are increasingly used. These days, even the old weather signs fail. In the old days a partial rainbow or a mackerel sky was a sure sign of storm, but we had both signs recently without any effect at all on the weather.

The farmer of Tŷ Mawr reported that he had seen a male spar-rowhawk killing a wood pigeon the other day, proving how strong they are. The male isn't much bigger than a blackbird, and yet capable of killing a bird as large as a wood pigeon. I remember seeing three of them together pursuing a green woodpecker. The creature was fleeing, shrieking at the top of its voice. It fled into a tree, but the three went after it, and the last thing I saw was the woodpecker coming out the other side with the three in pursuit like hunting-dogs.

Of course, a completely healthy bird usually has a good chance of escaping. It is the damaged ones that the birds of prey usually go after. And that is the good work they do. But the sparrowhawk relies on catching its prey without warning, flying low along hedges and darting suddenly to the other side.

When I entered my bedroom the other night there was a bat there flying ceaselessly hither and thither. In a confined space they appear larger than they are, but this one was a *Pipistrellus*, because every now and then it clutched the beams with its claws, and hung upside down to look at me. The expression is 'as blind as a bat', but this one acted as if it could see me, because every time I approached, it started flying round the room again. But since its ears were moving quickly, perhaps it was relying on its sonic system to gauge how close I was. It was very reluctant to leave, but at last I succeeded in getting it into the bathroom, opened the small window, closed the door, and within seconds it returned into the darkness from which it had come.

An old friend from Eglwys-fach came to see me the other day. I was picking blackberries in the lane, and when his car came by and stopped I didn't turn towards him, because I anticipated the same old stupid question in English. But when I heard a greeting in Welsh and turned round, who should be there but Gwydol Owen, the former postmaster of the village. He came into the house and we talked about the old parish. What was sad was hearing about the deterioration in Cardiganshire, and how English people had taken possession of it to the extent that villages that used to be completely Welsh-speaking had, to the same degree, become completely English-speaking, their children filling the primary schools. Though there is a considerable influx into Llŷn, thank goodness the English haven't yet taken possession of the place. Long may the situation continue whereby schools such as Crud-y-werin, Pont-y-gof and Tudweiliog are still quite Welsh. I thought of how I have succeeded all my life in stealing a march on difficulties. The rectory in Manafon was in the middle of the fields, so that it was possible to sit at the table and look out on unblemished nature, as it were. Now it is caravans that occupy the place. I foresaw that there was no future for the Welsh language in Eglwys-fach – and left. There were only a few street lamps in Aberdaron when I retired, but now at night the place is a sea of light. Here in Sarn Rhiw, because we have no neighbours, we can still enjoy the night's darkness and see the stars above our heads in their old splendour.

In this connection I have recently been rereading Samuel Beckett. I can see the intricate skill and originality of the man, and realise that he is expressing the contemporary condition of mankind in the large towns of the West, but how on earth can I cherish the same ideas in Llŷn, of all places? Although there are problems here, and the Welsh language and culture are under pressure, how, surrounded by the beauty of Llŷn, can one lose hope and consider life meaningless? That would be blasphemy. Beckett must be true to his vision as a creative writer, but that does not impair my right to my own vision either. The Irish Sea has been polluted, the aeroplanes roar above our heads, preparing for the next war; but this is the work of man. Seeing the dew in the morning and the beauty of the sea at sunset; listening to the silence after the aeroplanes have ceased their tumult, I have just as good a right to my faith as he has to his atheism.

Last night on the wireless I heard the Labour Party spokesman asking why the government couldn't give money to organic farming instead of to specialisation. I applauded. Wouldn't Llŷn be an excellent place with which to start, especially as her young people are happy here, with no desire to leave as is the case with young people in other areas?

Last night there was a meeting of the Committee of the Campaign for Nuclear Disarmament. Faced with another winter when we should campaign and hold events, everybody was somewhat disheartened. Thinking of all our efforts over the last ten years, and of how the people of Llŷn have almost completely ignored us, it hurts deeply to admit that the English government has to some extent beaten us. From its position in the centre, that government has continued to produce nuclear weapons and to build nuclear power stations, with the compliance of the majority of the English, as the Labour Party recently showed by abandoning its policy of unilateral disarmament, in order to improve its chances at the next election. And even though Wales is supposed to be a nuclear-free country, we know that this is not true. There *is* nuclear activity here and there. And by reading the English press and watching English television programmes, the majority of the people of Llŷn have swallowed the propaganda that nuclear power is essential and that we must hang on to nuclear weapons in order to 'protect ourselves' and so on, *ad nauseam*. Most of the people lack imagination. I would like to think that, if the government were to announce that it intended to bury nuclear waste in Llŷn, the great majority would wake from their deep sleep and resist fiercely, admitting that we have been right all along. But because it is elsewhere that the developments are happening, there isn't much interest here. I suggested in the meeting that it would be a good thing if we broadened our 'horizons' to include other threats such as the one to the environment, but on the other hand I don't want to interfere with the work of Cyfeillion Llŷn, The Friends of Llŷn, as that is their field of operation. The important thing as far as the Campaign for Disarmament is concerned is not to give the impression that we are giving up.

On the way home from Caernarfon I got lost looking for a friend's house in the area between Tai Lôn and Bwlchderwin. Here you have a network of lanes that tend to bring you back to where you started. I have viewed this area from the main road to Porthmadog past Pant-glas and Bryncir. It is a bare region between two mountains, which reminds one of Ireland. In the old days the railway line would pass through it from Caernarfon to Afon-wen, and I remember R. Gerallt Jones talking of coming home from his boarding school in England along that line. Imagine the excitement as you travelled on the little line at night, with the black mountains on either side of you, the stars above your head and the sea wind singing you a welcome home. It is an exceptional area. I usually think of Eifionydd as a fairly flat area and a gentler one than Llŷn. But this part is quite bare and rugged, with the mountains on either side making a tunnel for the whirlwinds to blow through. From talking to some of its inhabitants I have been led to believe that the Welsh language is still fairly healthy there. It should be. The region is not like any part of England, even the mountainous areas of England.

It was a glorious day today, typical of mid-September, the breeze light and balmy, the blackberries sparkling like girls' eyes, and the choir of gnats singing in their own *eisteddfod*, soprano, alto, tenor and bass, and everywhere the silky strands of gossamer. I haven't seen this for ages, and it took me back to Holyhead, when I used to wonder child-ishly at these strands without knowing what they were. I know now, of course, that they are a small spider's means of getting about; spinning a thin thread and letting the breeze do the rest. But to man they bring undoubtedly sweet memories of the leisurely, carefree days of his youth. And so it was in Porth Meudwy today – with me forgetting that I am old, forgetting that the world is still troubled, basking in the tranquillity of the September sun, with butterflies still flitting here and there and the occasional dragonfly chirping past like an old bicycle.

Because my wife is in hospital I was invited to supper by kind friends.

So many are the welcomes I have experienced at the hands of gentle Welsh friends in my lifetime. I returned to a house without a fire, without a candle. Shades of what is to come? My wife is older than I am. If it turns out that way, it will be difficult getting used to returning to a house where there is no light in the window. Tonight, instead of delighting in the sound of the sea below me, I heard it for once as something quite rough and comfortless.

Today, before visiting my wife in hospital, I went to Malltraeth on Anglesey to see the birds. That region is a favourite with birds, and there is almost always something of interest there. There wasn't much today, and yet I heard the particular note of the grey plover, a bird I never see in Llŷn. I looked towards Tunnicliffe's former cottage, recalling the times I used to call round, and him answering my ring, filling the doorway like a mountain. 'Come in. Come in.' He used to draw incessantly, so that you felt every time that you were disturbing him. But he was too much of a gentleman to make you seriously feel that way. I noticed that there were two telescopes in the large window; whoever has inherited the place after him, at least they are fond of birds. While I was looking at the lake at the cob, a motorbike stopped near me, and after removing all the armour that he was wearing, a young man came into view. He wanted to know where to find the grey phalarope. He had come from Liverpool. Oh, that a Welsh youngster were willing to travel even a mile to see a migratory bird!

By now Anglesey is for me only a memory. It can instill a yearning for days gone by, but I know today that it has been taken over by a throng of English people, that it is full of cars incessantly speeding here and there, and that aeroplanes from Valley fill the sky every minute with their unbearable tumult. From the point of view of the birds, worse than the aeroplanes are the helicopters, because the birds rise into the air every time a helicopter comes by. Under the circumstances it was good to come back to Llŷn because, despite the complaints I have about her, I would venture to say that more remains of the Llŷn of the past than of the Anglesey of old.

An English friend called by today, one who specialises in botany. She has been studying the flowers of Llŷn for over thirty years, and probably knows more about them than any native of Llŷn, except that her language and her names for them are English, unlike those of Vaughan Jones in former times. When we talk, with me trying to say that there are flowers in Anglesey that are not to be found in Llŷn, the answer almost every time is, 'Oh, yes, they're here,' naming some place like Pen

Cilan, or Anelog, or Mynydd Mawr. She makes me ashamed that I have myself frequented this place for over twenty years without coming across some of the flowers that she talks about. But there you have it. A bird-watcher's vision, more often than not, is skyward, and, like Keats, he cannot see what flowers are at his feet!

October

'*Oes gogr gynnoch chi*?'* The shopkeeper looked at me rather astonished and asked, quite bashfully, 'What's that?' 'A sieve,' I said. 'Why, of course,' she answered, handing me one.

And there you have it. English is the language that opens every door. It will be the same in heaven. After reaching the gates and asking Saint Peter in Welsh, 'May I come in?', the answer will be, 'Speak English, man.' It starts here so that we can get used to it! So wise is a town like Pwllheli in realising which way the wind is blowing. Out in the Llŷn Peninsula the old bad habit of using words like '*gogr*' persists, but in Pwllheli one must use a word like 'sieve', which everybody understands, especially as Llŷn is being taken over by English people.

Last night I dreamed the same old dream that returns so often: I was back in Manafon, having had to leave Llŷn to resume duties as rector of Manafon. There was the sadness at the thought that I had turned my back on the Welsh language and all my friends, and a kind of dull acquiescence in the things replacing them; no sea, none of Llŷn's beauty, no cottage where Welsh people have lived and worked over the centuries, no migratory birds going past in the spring and the autumn. Only the heartbreaking feeling that I had burned a bridge and taken an irreversible step. And then the joy on waking and slowly realising that I was in Llŷn after all, in the place where I want to be. Mysterious the ways of the man within me, but so terrifyingly real!

I was in Cardiff over the weekend at a poetry reading with Somhairle Macgill-Eain. It is twelve years or more since we last met. He is the greatest living Gaelic poet, but with a very small audience, of course.

* 'Have you got a sieve?'

Yet the impression you derive from listening to him read is that he really is a great poet. The question asked by people who don't think of course, is, 'Is there any purpose in writing poetry in a language spoken by so few?' It is a question asked even about Welsh. Oh, if Gwenallt or Saunders had written in English! But, in truth, I don't see it as a relevant question. Let a poet write in his mother tongue and forget about the size of his audience. After the overpopulated condition of Cardiff and the hundreds of characterless houses proliferating all around it, it was good to return to the north-west. There is quite pleasant countryside along the Marches, but one is very aware by now of the foreign language that reigns supreme throughout the area. It is true that Welsh can be seen in the station in Cardiff, and by now even in Shrewsbury; the trouble is the reality behind it. Although there is Welsh in the enquiry booth in Cardiff, the answer you invariably get to the question, 'Do you speak Welsh?', is a curt 'No.'

I was vexed to the point of surfeit on the train from Machynlleth to Pwllheli by a Welsh voice announcing in English before our arrival at every single station, 'Ladies and gentlemen, we are now approaching . . .', making even the Welsh place names sound English. I'm afraid that this is typical of too many of those Welsh people who earn their living by working for the big English companies. But that is the welcome received by any Welshman who returns to Pwllheli along this line.

'*Mis Hydref*', October, is a good name because it is in this month that one realises that '*yr hydref*', autumn, has arrived. But to recognise this completely one has to go to mid-Wales. Apart from the bracken, there aren't many signs of the change in Llŷn. But on the train to Cardiff, once I had left the coast and reached Powys, I started noticing the colours and recalling how I used to be infatuated with them when I lived there: the cherry, the horse chestnut and the birch all on fire, with the occasional ash tree glittering like gold in their midst. Like Holyhead, Llŷn remains more or less the same all year round because of the lack of trees. And even where there are trees, they don't change colour, but turn into scarecrows immediately after shedding their leaves in the first storm of autumn. Something that is particularly obvious in summer on the coast of Llŷn is the smell of the seaweed. It is as though there were a garden in the sea, and as the summer comes to visit it the garden starts to smell like flowers. In the stillness of summer the water becomes pellucid, and on looking down into Porth Neigwl I can see the seaweed like purple shadows under the water. For me on such occasions they are the gardens of the sea. It is lovely therefore to realise that they also have smells.

Today I had to be in Llanfairfechan, and after the meeting I went on to Glanconwy to try to see the Wilson's phalarope that I had heard was still in the vicinity. I went to the lookout station as directed, and after looking for about a quarter of an hour I saw the bird out on the sand. I wanted to see it in order to compare it with the one I saw here in 1984. I didn't secure enough details regarding that one because it took flight too quickly, and, of course, the Migratory Birds Committee of *British Birds* did not feel able to accept it. But this time I had the telescope with me and I saw the features that I had missed previously: the thin black bill and the white tail base. It was exactly the same kind of bird, and I was therefore able to confirm the accuracy of my identification on the previous occasion. It is one of the family of waders, a native of America that appears here occasionally in the autumn.

Today, after last night's force ten gale, I went out to Pen Cilan to see whether there were birds moving back to the open sea, driven by the wind towards Porthmadog. Cilan is the area in Wales most like the west of Ireland – the same bareness, the same untidiness, with a glorious prospect of the mountains rising eastwards; and mercifully it is Welsh-speaking Welshmen who are holding their ground there.

On looking over to Y Rhiw I remembered last night how she came out to escort me into the lane – so young and so pretty that it was difficult to refrain from giving her a kiss. And today, glad that I did not yield to the temptation. I remember Manafon, how I used to climb the hill behind the rectory and, by looking down and seeing the village so small, get things into perspective. How many people understand the occasional sadness of an old man? The inconsiderate words, 'the silly old fool' or 'the dirty old man', come too easily to the tongue. As long as I live I shall continue to feel the attraction of pretty young girls. I remember my father on his deathbed in hospital entreating the girls with his eyes to give him a smile as they went heedlessly past him. But one mustn't boast. There will be other times. Paul was very wise: 'Wherefore let him that thinketh he standeth take heed lest he fall.' Not that giving a girl a kiss is a great sin! But it isn't always easy for an old man to remember his age, and it would be a pity to embarrass a girl who was trying to be kind. But there are worse things. Doesn't Amos tell of a man fleeing from a lion and meeting a bear; and going to his house and putting his hand on a snake?

I have been reading *After Babel* by George Steiner, noticing how he emphasises the unique function of language in forming a nation. Why, oh why, doesn't the ordinary Welshman realise that the nation is fighting for its life? Does the anglicised Welshman, who claims that he is as much of a Welshman as we, realise that he cannot even feel Welsh without falling back on the Welsh-language past? But the fight for the language today is a fight for a future for the nation.

I was in a meeting of the Arfon District Council last night, listening to them discussing the proposed development in Glynrhonwy. The same old story: holding up to the public the promise of jobs, and succeeding by one vote. Three members of Plaid Cymru, who should have been there to tip the balance, absent – designedly? It is so sad to see Snowdonia, so valiantly defended by the princes, being offered to the developers to be plundered for a few jobs, while the capitalist developers stand to make millions from the venture. When will it dawn on the Welsh of Gwynedd that so many similar promises have been made in the past, that the Welsh have swallowed the bait and that they have subsequently been worse off in many ways, because it is not only work for a few of the Welsh that is tied in with the developments, but a new flood of foreigners who are helping to bury the remains of Wales's identity?

On returning to Llŷn after being away, it is good to see road signs such as *Perygl Llifogydd*, 'Danger of Floods', along the Penrhos road. And yet it makes one think. One of the most marked characteristics of the world of today is the number of routine things that have to be done. Faced with a hundred and one such things, what difference does it make in what language you do them? And if you have lost the habit of reading Welsh, or following some subject like bird-watching through the medium of Welsh, what function is left to the language? And in a world that is rapidly abandoning the habit of reading poetry and prose of any quality, Welsh will become totally devoid of purpose. We must face this challenge seriously and stop deluding ourselves.

And speaking of poetry, here is an example of how a poem is born. As is commonly known, the Bardsey lighthouse now works automatically day and night. Looking at it the other day I recalled the nun who, for years now, has lived a hermetic life there. The light flashing and the equally bright example of the nun were what made me play with the idea until a poem, a fairly long poem, started to take shape in my mind. A rich background is essential in the making of a poem of substance, and therefore I proceeded to gather around these two things other details such as prayers, the strain that faith is under in the modern world, the sky that was of the same colour as those painted by the Italian Old Masters, with the light scribbling over everything to turn it into a surrealist picture.

The other night in the evening twilight I was standing in the lane, looking over the hedge opposite our cottage. Suddenly what seemed like a ray of light came from the right and something went past. It was as if the pollen was being blown from off the grass. The next minute the same thing happened, but I was ready that time and I saw a grey-backed bird disappearing into the trees straight after the other one. It was the size of a tawny owl and I concluded that that was what it was. But I couldn't be sure. Man is so helpless in the dark. Yet a thrill went through me to think of the secret life of nature that starts to stir at twilight.

Tonight is Hallowe'en, the end of autumn and, in the old days, the beginning of winter. With turning the clock back and the start of the heavy rain it is quite like winter, apart from the temperature, which is remarkably mild. Are we in for a temperate winter like last year? It has been a disappointing month as far as bird-watching is concerned. The wind did not blow from the right quarter to bring sea birds in our direction; and nothing of interest happened on land either, until late in the month. Then came talk of a barred warbler, two yellow-browed warblers and two firecrests in Porth Meudwy, and the ornithologists started flocking there. This was a trivial matter, of course, compared to the pickle the English government and its chancellor are in. But that is the beauty of Llŷn. She can make you forget the fuss and troubles of politicians by offering you other things to get interested in. And how thankful I am to her for being so beautiful, for even when there aren't many birds around, it is lovely being out of doors with the sea on either hand and the sky above your head, thankful for the ability to move and see and hear, abilities that too many of the world's unfortunates do not possess.

November

Mis arch y byd, mis erch y bedd.
The month that is the world's coffin, the dire month of the grave.

That is what November is, according to the old saying. Perhaps it derived this bad name from how it is in England, in south Wales, or even in the Marches, where it can be quite cold, foggy and dismal. But here in Llŷn, there is nothing to fear. There are often sunny and mild days, despite the danger of interminable periods of rain, as we had at the beginning of the 1980s. But this year it has been glorious. Just as I was expecting heavy rain as penalty for the dry summer, there came again a series of fine, sunny days, without much wind, until Porth Neigwl appeared at times like a mirror. And how lovely it is. Although I am not overfond of the streetlamps in Cilan, of all places, yet they do have a certain charm when the bay is still at night and the beams stretch over the water almost as far as this side.

But despite the fine weather, the state of Wales is not improving at all. From every corner of the world comes report of how other countries are dying to learn English. It is said that it is difficult for an Englishman to choose his second language, but that there is no question as to which language other countries want to learn. That is the language that we have had to fight against for centuries. I have been reading George Steiner's book *After Babel*. Totally impartial, by virtue of the fact that he can speak at least five languages fluently, he shows how we are having to face the possibility that every country will one day be using English, because of how responsive a language it is in the contemporary world. But he admits that there is also a danger in this. He compares the situation to that of water: the further it spreads over the face of the earth, the shallower it becomes. So too with a world language. There is a possibility that it might lose contact with its roots and as a consequence be unable to express the depths of man's soul. To that end the native language is better. It is a lesson that Wales will have to learn, if the mother tongue is to survive.

The goldcrest continues to go past, and this since the end of July. Thousands on thousands must have gone by. I dote on them, the pretty agile little things, not much bigger than a pullet's egg. Even when there is nothing else around, some of these are to be found. Of course, in the autumn I look for its more beautiful cousin, the firecrest, but they were scarce enough here this year; indeed, the month was drawing to its close before I saw one, and not here but in Porth Meudwy. Considering how much easterly wind there has been this month I am surprised that there aren't more birds here from the Continent.

I saw half a dozen wild geese high above my head this morning. After asking someone whether he too had seen them, 'No,' he said, adding, 'they come from Ireland.' How the devil did he know? The tendency is the opposite in the autumn. It is to Ireland that they go, to take advantage of the mild weather there. How do these old wives' tales arise, I wonder? There was a belief in Manafon that Snowdon could be seen from the hill-sides nearby. This was topographically impossible, but it was no use trying to say so. They were totally convinced.

I went over to Cambridge to St John's College, Bishop William Morgan's college, to address a Welsh society there. I travelled in the car of a friend whose daughter is at the college. How lovely it was to go to her room and see, framed on the wall, the words: '*Gwinllan a roddwyd i'm gofal*', 'A vineyard entrusted to my care'. The famous choirmaster, George Guest, was at the meeting, and the next day we went to hear the boys practising. Dr Guest is someone who has learned Welsh, and he directed the boys to sing two Welsh hymns in our honour. It was lovely hearing Welsh in the heart of England like this. Then we visited the library to see William Morgan's own copy of his Bible. We were delayed by a tailback on the way home, so that night was upon us going through Welshpool and Newtown. I saw the turning for Manafon and remembered how often I used to take it at one time. No *hiraeth* at all!

In the middle of the month I went to Mold past Llanfihangel Glyn Myfyr. Every time I am in the vicinity I remember how I almost moved there as vicar. It is such a pretty parish, and the parsonage greatly appealed to me. Every 'if', of course, is futile, after things have turned in another direction. But hardly anyone can refrain from guessing how it would have been, *had* it been. Again, no *hiraeth*, oh, no. Too far from the sea for one thing.

Speaking of the sea, it is difficult to beat a cloudy day, with the sea dark but calm, and suddenly some sunray penetrating the cloud to form a pool of golden light far from the shore. Then every kind of fancy will arise, so great is the magic. Added to this, when I was out in Mynydd Mawr recently a peregrine falcon went past, flying strongly and purposefully towards the pool of light, as if being lured by it. It is good to see them around fairly often when I go out, despite the stealing that there has been from their nests.

It was a perfect morning today. After breakfast as usual, I went down the Ty'n Parc lane and saw the dew hanging from the branches, and heard the redpoll and the siskin going past. And without warning and without effort a little poem formed in my mind. It is so lovely when they come of their own accord like this, instead of your having to battle and strain to produce them. God has to do with this subject, too. In talking about how a poem will come easily and effortlessly, one must remember the possibility of being mistaken, of deceiving oneself. Not every poem that comes like this is good. Some believe that this is how they should come, and that if you have to labour, it indicates a lack of inspiration. But there are too many examples to the contrary. And similarly with God. It is lovely to think of inspiration, that '*Pan y myn y daw,* / *Fel yr enfys a'r glaw*', 'It comes when it wills, / Like the rainbow and the rain'. And certainly, as with a poem, it is thus that He sometimes chooses to come. But also, just as a poem sometimes comes after a very long period of thinking and searching, doesn't God come in the same way after a long period on your knees, or of reading and studying? And yet it cannot be proved and demonstrated. It isn't the result of long and refined reasoning, but communication that is at once mysterious and direct. As Wittgenstein said, 'There are things that cannot be expressed. And yet they show themselves.' So with God. If He wills it, He visits some people. Llŷn is not the only place where this happens, and yet, is it not a commendable place?

While these things were happening here, there was great tumult in Europe, with the countries that had been under the thumb of the Communists taking advantage of Gorbachev's new policy in order to demand more freedom for themselves. East Germany and Czechoslovakia rebelled and the Berlin Wall, which had stood for so long between East and West, came down. And instead of shooting the protesters, the armed forces and the police held back. All this is good, but it made me ashamed of my own nation. Even granting that the nations of Europe have suffered more, or more conspicuously, isn't the Welsh nation actually dying under oppression? On hearing of fifty million turning out to protest in Prague, isn't it shameful to think of the number that would turn out in Wales to demand even equality with the English and their language? England has been far more cunning than the Communists. Instead of crushing us with an iron fist, what she has done is erode our identity inch by inch, sugaring the pill at the same time. And yet one cannot ignore the fact that the countries of Europe have wise and sophisticated leaders who are nevertheless profound patriots. So it has been to some extent a dire month in Llŷn, given that we are a part of Wales and, for some, the stronghold of the language.

December

What difference is there between November and December? Not much, near the sea. As I have said before, there isn't much difference between summer and winter by the sea, except for the weather. It is the weather and the sea that make Llŷn what it is. After the dryness of the summer this year, and even a dry November, we have had heavy rain this month: water everywhere, and the streams turned into rivers overnight. And as usual in Llŷn, along with the rain, strong winds raising the highest wave I have seen in Cilan since we came here. If one includes the spray accompanying it, it was as high as Cilan itself. But after this, something I am so fond of, there came a spell of calm, the wind having abated, but the sea stirring like a giant in his sleep. What is lovelier in a peninsula of this kind than a silence so perfect that you can hear the thunder of the waves even from afar? An after the noise has died down somewhat, the full moon rises to silver the waves as they break in long rows along the beach. Pure magic!

I went down to Aberystwyth to stay overnight with a friend, and on the train back to Pwllheli I noticed as we approached the station that something was afoot. I then heard a band and a drum. Ha, I said, Pwllheli has turned out at last to give a real welcome to a poet! Nothing of the kind. Father Christmas was on the train to be welcomed by hundreds of the town's children and their parents. Fair enough, I thought, I can't compete with Father Christmas. The thing was arranged by the Round Table, with a great deal of English tied in with it. I couldn't help asking myself how many would have turned out like this to a Welsh rally, or to something arranged by the Campaign for Nuclear Disarmament.

As a result of the unnaturally mild weather a chiffchaff has been around the house. There was something sad in its voice among the bare twigs. But the weather got colder, and it disappeared. No-one knows what happens to late migrants such as these. The difficulty with the warblers is that you cannot give them crumbs to sustain them because they don't eat crumbs, but insects. They can hardly be moving south for warmer countries so late in the year.

Some literature regarding the Poll Tax came again. Dwyfor District Council is pressing ahead. Is it in order to show how obedient it is to the commands of a government responsible for such an unjust tax? It is worth mentioning because of the burden that will be placed on many unlucky individuals in Llŷn. We are getting to be more and more under the thumb of a foreign government. The other bogey on the horizon, of course, is privatisation. One feature came to light quickly enough with the arrival of the latest Telecom bills. The Welsh had disappeared. One cannot expect a company whose main objective is making a profit to go to the expense of publishing details in Welsh, when everyone understands English! Things such as water, electricity and the telephone are part of essential services, and the owners are canny enough to realise that we are in their hands. What is easier for an Englishman, or for someone who does not wish to speak Welsh, than putting the receiver down in order to bring the customer to his senses? The Friends of Llŷn have been at it for years trying to draw attention to this injustice, but in the meantime the situation gets worse.

Two rare birds that I have seen more often this month are the merlin and the barn owl; I hope that this is a sign that they are on the increase. I used to see the merlin fairly often in the old days, especially in the autumn and when I first came to Aberdaron. And the barn owl nested in the chimney of the cowshed in Aberdaron. But because they have become scarce in recent years, I have only seen a few. The barn owl is a very mysterious creature, like a ghost in the dusk. As I was coming home one evening recently, one alighted on a post a few yards from me. I saw its white shape in the twilight, but it was perfectly silent. I thought of the millions of years that its type has taken to evolve feathers that wouldn't make the slightest noise. And, in turn, their hearing is so fine that they can descend without fail on their prey in the dark. When I was in Aberdaron I gathered a few of their pellets and sent them to be analysed. That's a special skill for you, the ability to say, from a few small bones, exactly what the bird's main food was.

I was on my way home from Bryncroes after a fairly dark afternoon. As I was climbing Mynydd y Rhiw I noticed that the sun was setting and that there was an amazing light around me. I stopped at the top of the hill, came out of the car and started to marvel at the views. Despite the black clouds that cast the land into shadow, the crests of those clouds were all gold. They were like a long row of high mountains with snow on their summits. I have never seen a sight quite like it. Under my feet the land of Llŷn stretched towards the north-east, and to the south was Porth Neigwl with the rustle of the waves at its feet. In this spot there is a ruin at the side of the lane and I could hardly help thinking of the people who once lived there. Welsh-speaking Welshmen without a doubt, but who exactly, I wonder? Perhaps they saw sights like this, with the sun rising summer and winter over the distant hills. Did they notice? Did they appreciate and marvel at the miracle of the creation? They perished. I do not know even the name of the house. It is a symbol of what is happening to Wales. The houses either become ruins, or are taken over and restored by English people. Some Welsh people think it a good thing to see them being restored. I would prefer to see them decay, if the Welsh have left them for ever.

I am not half thankful enough for still having my senses and my faculties. And yet I am, too. On the mountain yesterday evening I heard the 'yik-yak' of the snipe as it went past above me, and I am thankful that I can still hear the dear sounds of the birds and the creatures, and see the delightful sights of this earth. The saints long ago would try to turn away from loving the visible world too much. I confess that I am guilty of this. And yet I tend to vindicate myself by saying that I have not loved it for its own sake, but as part of God's creation. There is another side to the argument, I know; but sometimes, and in Llŷn especially, it is not difficult to forget about it!

What no-one here foresaw were the events in Europe. Suddenly and, to us at least, without warning, there was a revolution in the Communist world. The people who had for so long been under the thumb of the Communists rebelled, and behold, countries such as East Germany, Czechoslovakia, Hungary and latterly Romania, breaking free from their fetters and demanding that democratic elections be held. All credit to them indeed. But their actions showed how helpless and, for that matter, how heedless we in Wales are. It is true that these Communist countries have suffered a great deal more under their oppressors, but one must admire their bravery, their perseverance and the acumen of the leaders who saw that the time was right for them to rise and re-establish their identity.

England has been cunning. After nearly five centuries of rule she knows exactly how to handle us. Not pressing too tightly, not letting things be too hard on us, lest we become restless to the point of rebelling – those are the tactics that have brought us to our present situation. And in addition to this many Welsh people are too well off to complain or care very much if the Welsh language and the culture of Wales are languishing. By virtue of their bilingualism they can turn to English without any difficulty at all. That is the achievement of England, which has infiltrated Wales and her language to the point where we are ready to accept the situation without realising that we have adopted a tiger cub. It was one main language that these countries in Europe had – their national language – even though they were being oppressed in other ways. Therefore they did not lose their national self-consciousness. On top of this they had leaders who were politically mature and wise. Our own unmentionable leaders are politically naïve or dishonest if they think that we can keep our identity while speaking English as our main language and making bosom friends of the English.

I have been out on Mynydd Mawr today seeing the raven, the male, showing himself off to his mate. These are amongst the first to nest, so it was no surprise to see them performing even in December. The male is a funny one. He rolls in the air exactly as if turning a somersault, although it is only a trick. It is a half-turn that he executes, as if flying upside down, and in an instant he rights himself. But equally strange are his notes. Everybody is familiar with his croaking, but how many, I wonder, have heard him quavering melodiously like bells, and then calling 'clop, clop' like a horse trotting?

Today, on the last day of the year, I heard the sparrowhawk mewing in the wood at Ty'n Parc, as if it were sharpening its beak for the feast that will come its way in the new year. This is how it was before man appeared here. That is nature. Is that God's economy? Life depends on the ability to obtain sufficient sustenance. The weak go to oblivion. In some ways, and at times, it is quite terrifying. Couldn't God have done better than to make the earth some giant mouth which devours, devours unceasingly in order to sustain itself? But before placing the blame on God, let us ask ourselves whether we could have done better, or even half as well? Sometimes the creation frightens us, and yet, on reflection, it is amazingly intricate and complex. And on the whole it isn't nature but man that kicks over the traces. For millions of years, despite the killing and the devouring, the earth has kept the balance, and it is only in our period of history, and specifically towards the close of the present century, that we have started to see how man in his blindness and greed is endangering the earth's future. Some consider it already too late. Only time will tell. In the meantime others are dreaming and planning to establish stations in space. They are more than welcome to do so. It is easy to imagine some people, who never learned how to appreciate this earth, being content with an artificial life in space. In me, the idea raises claustrophobia of the most terrible kind.

I have tried to describe an ordinary man's year in Llŷn. I have not succeeded all that well, I know. How shall one describe one's sweetheart? Instead of enumerating her virtues, one after the other, like one of the Poets of the Gentry using *dyfalu*, one cannot say much more than, 'Oh, she is the most beautiful of all maidens.'

> *Blodau'r flwyddyn yw f'anwylyd,*
> *Ebrill, Mai, Mehefin hefyd;*
> *Llewyrch haul yn t'wynnu ar gysgod,*
> *A gwenithen y genethod.*

> My love is the year's flowers in bloom,
> The months of April, May and June;
> A shadow lit by the sun's ray,
> Amongst the girls, the *nonpareil*.

During the course of this year I have seen Llŷn in all her moods, joyful and sad, quiescent and turbulent. I have seen the winter retreating and the spring bringing the birds and the flowers back to me. I have smelt the scent of the seaweed rising from the beach in the summer, as if it were an orchard. I have seen the cliffs red under thyme and thrift, and heard the oystercatcher complaining because I was too near her eggs. The seal came to stare at me with its gentle, sad eyes, and I have watched as the leaves of a few scarce bushes withered under the salt storms of September and October.

And now the year is drawing to its end. The shortest day has already passed, and the child I picked up from the threshold on the first of January has turned into a lame old woman, directing her steps towards oblivion; not a symbol of Wales, I hope. God forbid! Even the oldest amongst us will bid farewell without a tear in his eye, and yet we do not have cause to rejoice as do some of the small countries of Europe. Even so, tonight on New Year's Eve, as a symbol of hope and expectation, I placed a candle in the window to welcome the newborn to our humble but hate-free home, thankful at least for having a roof over our heads, and that in Welsh-speaking Wales.

Glossary of Birds' Names

Hebog tramor
Falco peregrinus
Peregrine

Dringwr bach
Certhia familiaris
Tree creeper

Dryw eurben
Regulus regulus
Goldcrest

Titw penddu
Parus ater
Coal tit

Titw mawr
Parus major
Great tit

Ji-binc
Fringilla coelebs
Chaffinch

Cornchwiglen
Vanellus vanellus
Lapwing

Cigfran
Corvus corax
Raven

Brân dyddyn
Corvus corone
Carrion crow

Brân goesgoch
Pyrrhocorax
pyrrhocorax
Chough

Socan eira
Turdus pilaris
Fieldfare

Saer
Haematopus ostralegus
Oystercatcher

Gwalch glas
Accipiter nisus
Sparrowhawk

Siff-saff
Phylloscopus collybita
Chiffchaff

Hugan
Sula bassana
Gannet

Aderyn drycin Manaw
Puffinus puffinus
Manx shearwater

Troellwr bach
Locustella naevia
Grasshopper warbler

Turtur torchog
Streptopelia decaocto
Collared dove

Môr-wennol bigddu
Sterna Sandvicensis
Sandwich tern

Corhwyaden
Anas crecca
Teal

Ysguthan
  Columba palumbus
  Wood pigeon

Siedyn
  Trochila
  Hummingbird

Euryn
  Oriolus oriolus
  Golden oriole

Tylluan gorniog
  Asio otus
  Long-eared owl

Môr-wennol ruddgoch
  Sterna dougallii
  Roseate tern

Bod tinwen
  Circus cyaneus
  Hen harrier

Llwydfron fach
  Sylvia corrucca
  Lesser whitethroat

Bod y wern
  Circus aeruginosus
  Marsh harrier

Telor y coed
  Phylloscopus sibilatrix
  Wood warbler

Gwalch y pysgod
  Pandion haliaetus
  Osprey

Coegylfinir
  Numenius phaeopus
  Whimbrel

Cnocell werdd
  Picus viridis
  Green woodpecker

Drudwen wridog
  Sturnus roseus
  Rose-coloured starling

Cwtiad llwyd
  Pluvialis squatarola
  Grey plover

Gwennol ddu'r Alpau
  Apus melba
  Alpine swift

Llyndandroed Wilson
  Phalaropus tricolor
  Wilson's phalarope

Rhydydd
  Wader

Dryw benfflamgoch
  Regulus ignicapillus
  Firecrest

Pibydd gwyrdd
  Tringa ochropus
  Green sandpiper

Llinos bengoch
  Acanthus flammea
  Redpoll

Môr-wennol ffrwynog
  Sterna anaethetus
  Bridled tern

Clochdar y cerrig
  Saxicola torquata
  Stonechat

Pila gwyrdd
  Carduelis spinus
  Siskin

NOTES AND REFERENCES

References to R. S. Thomas's poems are to the original editions; but most of them are also available in his *Collected Poems 1945–1990* (Dent, 1993)

Former Paths

p. 4 *Ar noswaith ddrycinog:* an old folk-verse usually referred to under the title *'Nos a Bore'* ('Night and Morning'). The translation is R. S. Thomas's own celebrated poem 'Night and Morning', from *The Stones of the Field*, 1946.

p. 5 like **Williams Parry's fox:** the reference is to *Y Llwynog* ('The Fox'), a sonnet by R. Williams Parry (1884–1956), one of the greatest Welsh lyric poets of the twentieth century.

p. 10 **reminding one of the battles of the past:** cf. 'Welsh Landscape', *An Acre of Land*, 1952:

> To live in Wales is to be conscious
> At dusk of the spilled blood
> That went to the making of the wild sky.

p. 10 **Maelor Saesneg:** 'English Maelor', became a detached part of the county of Flint under the Statute of Rhuddlan in 1284. Along with 'Welsh Maelor', it now belongs to the district known as Wrexham-Maelor in Clwyd.

p. 15 **like a golden fountain:** cf. 'The Bush' in *Later Poems*, 1983:

> I have thought often
> of the fountain of my people
> that played beautifully here
> once in the sun's light
> like a tree undressing.

and 'The Prayer' in *Laboratories of the Spirit*, 1975:

> Let leaves
> from the deciduous Cross
> fall on us, washing
> us clean, turning our autumn
> to gold by the affluence of their fountain.

p. 15 *eisteddfod:* originally, 'an assembly of poets', from the Welsh word *'eistedd'* ('to sit'). From its beginnings in the twelfth century, the event has developed into its modern form of a Welsh-language festival of literature, music and the other arts, on a competitive basis – the major one being the annual National Eisteddfod.

p. 16 *penillion telyn:* anonymous folk-verses (*'penillion'*) sung to the accompaniment of the harp (*'telyn'*).

p. 16 Gwallter Mechain and Penfro and Ieuan Brydydd Hir: the bardic names of celebrated poet-priests who were each at some stage either rector or curate of Manafon – respectively, Walter Davies (1761–1849), William John Morgan (1846–1918), and Evan Evans (1731–88). R. S. Thomas could also have mentioned many other writers associated with the immediate parish and surrounding areas of Manafon, for example, Lewys Dwnn (*fl.* 1568–1616) and John Edwards (?1692–1774). See, further, Enid Roberts, *Braslun o Hanes Llên Powys*, ('An Outline of the Literary History of Powys'), Denbigh: Gwasg Gee, 1965.

p. 16 *eisteddfodwr:* anyone involved in competing or adjudicating in an *eisteddfod* (see note above).

p. 16 *englyn:* dating from at least the ninth century, the *englyn* as a form is the oldest recorded in Welsh poetry. The intricate effects that it achieves through *cynghanedd*, the strict pattern of sound-chiming and rhyme that characterises traditional Welsh verse, are enhanced by the tight brevity of its restriction, in its most common modern form, to four lines. It can, however, also function as a verse in a longer poem such as an *awdl*. For example, the *englyn* by Gwallter Mechain quoted here is from his *'Awdl ar Gwymp Llywelyn'* ('Ode on the Fall of Llywelyn', 1821).

The Creative Writer's Suicide

p. 19 Kierkegaard: Søren Kierkegaard (1813–55), the Danish religious philosopher, often regarded as the founder of Existentialist philosophy, has long had a profound influence on R. S. Thomas's thinking. Kierkegaard's 1848 essay on the question as to whether a person has the right to allow himself or herself to be killed in the cause of the truth was published in Britain in Alexander Dru and Walter Lowrie, trans., *The Present Age, and Two Minor Ethico-Religious Treatises*, 1940. R. S. Thomas reveals his interest in Kierkegaard in an interview with J. B. Lethbridge in the *Anglo-Welsh Review* 74 (1983). Cf. the poems 'Kierkegaard' in *Pietà*, 1966, and 'S. K.' in *No Truce with the Furies*, 1995.

p. 19 Pontius Pilate's contemptuous question: John 18:38. The question was 'What is truth?' – and of course, famously, Pilate did not wait for an answer. (All biblical references are to the King James Version. It should be noted that it was from the corresponding Welsh translation by Bishop William Morgan that R. S. Thomas's original quotations were taken).

p. 19 *petitio principii*: in logic, a fallacious argument in which part or all of the conclusion is assumed in one or more of the premises; a circular argument of the kind that can be described as 'begging the question'.

p. 20 *cywyddwyr*: literally, the writers of poems in the form of the *cywydd*, one of the major metrical forms of traditional Welsh strict-metre prosody. It is comprised of couplets with alternating masculine / feminine rhymes, each line consisting of seven syllables and full *cynghanedd*, an intricate system of alliteration and internal rhyme. It was the favourite form of the *cywyddwyr*, also known as the Poets of the Gentry, who came under the patronage of the landed families when the fall of Llywelyn ap Gruffudd in 1282 brought an end to the possibility of patronage by the princes. It is a form that has flourished from the fourteenth century to the present day.

p. 20 petitionary *cywyddau*: a characteristic 'occasion' of the *cywydd* as composed by the Poets of the Gentry (see previous note) was when the poet was petitioning for a gift or a favour, which often led to a further poem in thanks for the same.

p. 21 *englynion*: the plural of *englyn* (see note above).

p. 22 Saunders Lewis: (1893–1985), poet, dramatist and critic, was arguably the greatest Welsh-language literary figure of the twentieth century, and one who had a major impact on the political-nationalist identity of modern Wales. As the artist most centrally recognised as representing and speaking out for the conscience and identity of Welsh-speaking Wales, Thomas has inherited the mantle of Saunders Lewis and has written several tributes in poetry to this major figure. See 'The Patriot' in *The Bread of Truth*, 1963, and 'Saunders

Lewis' in *Welsh Airs*, 1987. The most recent tribute is in a poem called 'The Gallery' (*Planet* 116, April/May 1996) in which R. S. Thomas records Saunders Lewis's comment to him about a problem crucial to his concerns in 'The Creative Writer's Suicide':

> And finally he,
> the small man with the big
> heart, whom I met once
> in our pretending capital,
> taking my hand in both
> his and soothing my quarrel
> with my English muse with:
> 'But all art is born out of tension'.

p. 22   David Jones: (1895–1974), poet and artist, whose work is highly allusive, especially to the various myths and literatures relevant to Wales.

p. 22   Who is wounded ... For I bear in my body: R. S. Thomas is in fact quoting two separate biblical verses: 'Who is weak, and I am not weak?' (2 Corinthians 11:29) and 'From henceforth let no man trouble me: for I bear in my body the marks of the Lord Jesus' (Galatians 6:17).

p. 23   the old language: a common term for the Welsh language is '*yr heniaith*', literally 'the old language'. Cf. the poem 'The Old Language' in *An Acre of Land*, 1952.

No-one

p. 27   *Et de ce néant indestructible qui est moi*: from 'Magnificat', the third ode in '*Cinq Grandes Odes*', *Paul Claudel: Oeuvre Poétique*, 1957, p. 255. Paul Claudel (1868–1955), French poet, dramatist and diplomat, was a major force in French literature of the first half of the twentieth century. The relevant passage translates as follows, with the epigraph here italicised: 'What is this death that you have taken from me compared to the truth of your presence / *And to this indestructible nothingness that is I* / With which I have to suffer you?'

p. 28   Cilgwri: the Wirrall. Cilgwri had one particular association which the poet employed more than once in his poetry: one of the animals in the Welsh versions of the international folk tale 'The Oldest Animals' is the ousel (blackbird) of Cilgwri. Cf. 'Wales' in *An Acre of Land*, 1952:

> Listen, listen! Where the river fastens
> The trees together with a blue thread,
> I hear the ousel of Cilgwri telling
> The mournful story of the long dead.

Cf. also 'The Ancients of the World' in the same volume.

p. 34   God calling Samuel: 1 Samuel 3.

p. 35   Charles Tunnicliffe: (1901–79), English bird artist.

p. 35   *hiraeth*: a Welsh word traditionally felt to be not susceptible to adequate translation. Its general meaning is 'longing' – especially longing for a native place and culture left behind, or felt to be irretrievable. A poem entitled '*Hiraeth*', registering his longing for his native Anglesey, appeared in the poet's first volume, *The Stones of the Field*, 1946.

p. 37   '*Hen Wlad Fy Nhadau*': literally, 'The Ancient Land of My Fathers' – Wales's national anthem. The words are by Evan James (1809–78) and the music by his son James James (1833–1902). Its adoption as the national anthem probably dates from the 1870s.

p. 38   Maeterlinck: Maurice Maeterlinck (1862–1949), Belgian dramatist, poet and prose writer, who wrote in French. His rhythmic prose dramas represent the finest achievement of the Symbolist theatre. Awarded the Nobel Prize for Literature in 1911.

p. 38   Glyn Simon: (1903–72), Warden of the church hostel in Bangor and lecturer at the university 1931–40. He was later Warden of St Michael's College, Llandaff 1940–8, and Archbishop of Wales 1968–71.

p. 39   Emrys Edwards: (1913–96), a college friend at Bangor, he was to precede R. S. Thomas as vicar of Aberdaron (1945–52). He was himself a poet and a winner of the Chair at the National Eisteddfod of 1961. His *cywydd* in praise of R. S. Thomas, and recalling their student days together, was included in the special number of the periodical *Poetry Wales* devoted to R. S. Thomas's work in 1972 (vol. 7, no. 4).

p. 42   Kreisler: Fritz Kreisler (1875–1962), born in Vienna, composer and one of the outstanding violin virtuosos of his time. R. S. Thomas's experience of sitting close to him at this particular performance is beautifully caught in 'The Musician' in *Tares*, 1961:

> So near that I could see the toil
> Of his face muscles, a pulse like a moth

> Fluttering under the fine skin,
> And the indelible veins of his smooth brow...
>
> Making such music as lives still.
> And no one daring to interrupt
> Because it was himself that he played
> And closer than all of them the God listened.

p. 44 **Toc H:** an association pledged to Christian fellowship and service, founded in 1919 by P. T. B. Clayton. The name was the army signaller's version of the initials of Talbot House which, during 1915–18, provided rest and recreation for British troops serving in the trenches at Ypres during the First World War.

p. 44 **Hewlett Johnson:** (1874–1966), English prelate, often called the 'Red Dean' because of his unflinching championing of Soviet Communism. His book, *The Socialist Sixth of the World* (1939), had a huge sale in many languages.

p. 45 **Austin Clarke:** (1896–1974), Irish poet, dramatist and novelist, born in Dublin.

p. 45 **Fiona Macleod:** William Sharp (1855–1905), Scottish novelist, poet and critic, born in Paisley. The works that influenced R. S. Thomas were the Celtic romantic tales that Sharp wrote under the pseudonym Fiona Macleod, such as *Pharais* (1893), *The Mountain Lovers* (1895), *Green Fire* (1896) and *The Winged Destiny* (1904).

p. 49 **Euros:** Euros Bowen (1904–88), poet and Anglican priest. As a fellow poet-priest within the Church in Wales, he clearly had an easy and influential relationship with R. S. Thomas. For the greater part of his career he was rector of Llangywair and Llanuwchllyn, near Y Bala in Merionethshire. He is recognised as the Welsh-language poet most in tune with the aims of the French Symbolists. As the editor of the magazine *Y Fflam* ('The Flame'), he published R. S. Thomas's early Welsh-language poetry and prose.

p. 49 **Owain Glyndŵr:** Owen Glendower (*c.*1354–*c.*1416), leader of a revolt (1400–13) against the English crown to 'free the Welsh people from the slavery of their English enemies'. Along with Llywelyn ap Gruffudd (*c.*1225–82), the leader generally regarded as Wales's national hero.

p. 50 *eisteddfodau:* the plural of *eisteddfod* (see note above).

p. 53 **Wales:** a periodical founded and edited by Keidrych Rhys (see note below) in three series, 1937–40, 1943–9 and 1958–60, a span that made it influential in presenting the work of different waves of Anglo-Welsh writers from the generation of Dylan Thomas through to that of Alun Richards.

p. 53 Keidrych Rhys: (1915–87), editor and poet, born William Ronald Rees Jones. From 1939 to 1948 he was married to the writer Lynette Roberts. As editor of various anthologies and of the periodical *Wales* throughout its existence, he was a major influence in the publication of Anglo-Welsh writing. He was one of the first to recognise R. S. Thomas's quality: his Druid Press at Carmarthen published R. S.'s first volume, *The Stones of the Field*, in 1946.

p. 53 Come to the spreading birch tree: from an anonymous fifteenth-century *cywydd*, 'To the Nun'.

p. 53 The hall of Cynddylan is dark tonight: the opening line of the central poem in a ninth-century *englyn* cycle lamenting the devastation inflicted on the kingdom of Powys and the ruin of a whole culture. Cynddylan was a seventh-century king of that kingdom.

p. 54 The sound of the little heart breaking: from a Welsh folk-verse. The poet used the line as epigraph to his radio poem *The Minister*, published in 1953, republished in *Song at the Year's Turning*, 1955.

p. 54 Y Faner: originally a newspaper, *Baner ac Amserau Cymru* ('The Banner and Times of Wales'), also known as *Y Faner*. Launched in 1859, it was contributed to by some of Wales's leading cultural figures, including Thomas Gee, Prosser Rhys, Kate Roberts and Saunders Lewis. In 1977 it changed in format and content into a weekly periodical that combined news coverage and polemic features in the Radical tradition of the original newspaper. It ceased publication in 1992.

p. 54 Douglas Young: (1913–73), poet, Greek scholar and nationalist politician.

p. 54 his review in Wales: R. S. Thomas's essay, 'A Welsh View of the Scottish Renaissance' appeared in *Wales* 8 (1948).

p. 54 Islwyn Ffowc Elis: (1924–   ), a distinguished Welsh novelist and prose writer. Formerly a Calvinistic Methodist minister (at Llanfair Caereinion, his ministry was not far from R. S. Thomas's at Manafon), he subsequently became a college and university lecturer. The works he wrote in the early 1950s, especially the first collection of essays *Cyn Oeri'r Gwaed* and the first novel *Cysgod y Cryman* (respectively, 'Before the Blood Grows Cold' and 'The

Shadow of the Sickle'), proved major influences on Welsh prose writing into our own time.

p. 54   Llwyd o'r Bryn: the affectionate common name for Robert Lloyd (1888–1961), a major figure in the world of the *eisteddfod* in Wales, and one of the great advocates of traditional Welsh-language culture.

p. 54   Gwenallt: the bardic name of David James Jones (1899–1968), one of the most striking Welsh-language poets of the twentieth century, concerned especially with the relationship between social justice and the Christian faith, and who drew equally on knowledge of rural and industrial Wales. For the major part of his career, he was a Lecturer in the Welsh Department of the University of Wales, Aberystwyth.

p. 54   Aneirin Talfan: Aneirin Talfan Davies (1909–80), critic, poet and broadcaster. His broadcasting career led to his appointment in 1966 as Head of Programmes for BBC Wales. He had already developed a friendly broadcasting relationship with the poet Dylan Thomas, a critical study of whose work he published in 1964.

p. 54   Waldo: Waldo Williams (1904–71), one of the finest and most popular Welsh-language poets of the twentieth century, very much associated with his home county of Pembrokeshire, although some of his best short poems of Welsh nationhood were written during a period as a schoolteacher in England between 1944 and 1950. He decided, in response to the Korean War, to make direct action as well as poetry a means of protest, and he was twice imprisoned. His influential volume of poetry, *Dail Pren* ('The Leaves of a Tree'), was published in 1956.

p. 55   D. J. Williams: (1885–1970), a prose writer who, apart from his fine autobiographical works, also became a national figure through his role, along with Saunders Lewis and Lewis Valentine, in a token act of arson in protest at the building of a bombing school at Penyberth in Llŷn in 1936, for which he spent nine months in Wormwood Scrubs. His *Hen Dŷ Ffarm* ('An Old Farmhouse', 1953) and other related works are recognised as classics of autobiographical writing, celebrating an instinctive sharp-eyed love for his native ground and its particular culture.

p. 55   Gwynfor: Gwynfor Evans (1912–   ), politician and historian, President of Plaid Cymru, the Welsh Nationalist Party, from 1945 to 1981, and that party's first Member of Parliament (for Carmarthen, 1966).

p. 56   Gwydion: the name of the poet's son is that of one of the main characters in 'Math Son of Mathonwy', one of the medieval Welsh tales known collectively as *The Mabinogion*.

p. 56 **'what stuff his roots were made of':** the quotation is from a poem by Tudur Aled (*c*.1465–*c*.1525): '*Hysbys y dengys y dyn / O ba radd y bo'i wreiddyn*' ('Every man shows clearly / What stuff his roots are made of').

p. 57 **Carneddog:** Richard Griffith (1861–1947), a sheep farmer renowned also as an author, local historian and journalist. He was a collector of books and manuscripts, and the editor of several editions of Welsh poetry, one of which must have been the 'anthology' he presented to R. S. Thomas on this occasion. The visit took place towards the end of Carneddog's long life. Soon afterwards Geoff Charles's famous photograph (National Library of Wales) was taken of Carneddog and his wife looking out over the landscape on the eve of leaving the farm where Carneddog's ancestors had lived for generations and where he had spent his whole life. It is a cultural image as powerful as Robert Howlett's celebrated photograph of Isambard Kingdom Brunel (National Portrait Gallery) standing under the chains of industry in a different, English, industrial culture.

p. 58 **Cynan:** the bardic name of Albert Evans-Jones (1895–1970), poet and playwright, and a major figure in the history of the National Eisteddfod in the twentieth century, as Archdruid (1950–54, 1963–6) and President of the Eisteddfod Court (1963–5).

p. 60 **William Condry:** (1918–), one of Wales's leading naturalists.

p. 60 **the Keating family:** the three Keating sisters referred to worked closely with the National Trust over many years. They were staunch guardians of the natural-life interests of the Llŷn Peninsula, and were successful in buying back for the Trust the remainder of the Plas-yn-Rhiw estate sold off in 1874. See M. Honora Keating, *Plas-yn-Rhiw*, The National Trust, 1982. Cf. the poem 'Plas-yn-Rhiw' in *Mass for Hard Times*, 1992.

p. 62 **William Havard:** (1889–1956), bishop of St Asaph and subsequently of St David's.

p. 63 **Kate Roberts:** (1891–1985), novelist and short-story writer, one of the outstanding Welsh-language prose writers of the twentieth century.

p. 64 **the Birds of Rhiannon:** Rhiannon is one of the main characters in the tales 'Pwyll Prince of Dyfed' and 'Manawydan Son of Llŷr' in *The Mabinogion*. In another tale, 'Branwen Daughter of Llŷr', the birds of Rhiannon, three in number, are described as singing over the sea at Harlech, and in the story of

'Culhwch and Olwen', are said to wake the dead and send the living to sleep.

p. 65   James Hanley: (1901–85). After a period as a freelance journalist, the novelist James Hanley arrived in Wales in 1930, settling first in Merionethshire and afterwards in Montgomeryshire, where he lived from 1940 until his move to London in 1964. *Song at the Year's Turning* (1955), which made R. S. Thomas's name beyond Wales, was dedicated 'For James Hanley'.

p. 65   small presses in Wales: the poet's first volume, *The Stones of the Field* (1946), was published by Keidrych Rhys's Druid Press at Carmarthen, and his second, *An Acre of Land* (1952), by the Montgomery Printing Company, Newtown.

p. 65   a preface ... by John Betjeman: John Betjeman was the 'name' that the publisher, Rupert Hart-Davis, chose in 1955 to introduce *Song at the Year's Turning*. Betjeman concluded his perceptive 'Introduction' with characteristic generosity: 'The "name" which has the honour to introduce this fine poet to a wider public will be forgotten long before that of R. S. Thomas.'

p. 66   Hubert Mappin: (1891–1966), landowner.

p. 67   Emyr Llywelyn: (1941–   ), schoolteacher, and one of the leading young activists in the cause of the Welsh language from the 1960s onwards; the son of the distinguished poet and children's novelist, T. Llew Jones.

p. 68   to find his grave: for Kierkegaard, see note above. For the point about failing to visit Kierkegaard's grave, see 'A Grave Unvisited' in *Not That He Brought Flowers*, 1968.

p. 68   Coto Doñana: a National Park of some 190 square miles on the south-western coast of Spain. As a common crossing-point migrating between Africa and Europe, it is famous as an area in which nearly half the bird species of Europe can be seen. Cf. also, for other reflections of this visit to Spain, poems in the volume *Not That He Brought Flowers* (1968): 'No, Señor', 'Coto Doñana', and 'Burgos'.

p. 72   chandelier: the maker of the circular wrought-iron chandelier was Alan Knight FWCB, of Hanbury in Worcestershire. A photograph showing the impressive effect of the chandelier in the south nave of the church at Aberdaron can be seen in W. J. Elliss, *The Church of Saint Hywyn, Aberdaron*, reprinted from vol. 2 of the *Transactions of the Caernarvonshire Historical Society*.

p. 72   Y Fflam: literally, 'The Flame', the title of a Welsh-language literary magazine, edited by Euros Bowen (see note above), of which eleven numbers were published between 1946 and 1952. It sought to provide a new forum for young, progressive Welsh-language writers of the day. It was the main medium for R. S. Thomas's early publications in Welsh, including one of only two poems that he ever published in that language ('Y Gwladwr', Y Fflam, August 1950).

p. 72   Soar-y-mynydd and Maesyronnen: the poet's essay 'Dau Gapel' ('Two Chapels') appeared in Y Fflam (see note above), no. 5 (1948). Soar-y-mynydd is some seven miles from Tregaron in Cardiganshire, and Maesyronnen some three miles from Hay-on-Wye on the Wales–England border. Cf. the poem 'Maes-yr-Onnen' in An Acre of Land, 1952.

p. 72   Christmas ... near the sea: cf. the poem 'Sea Christmas', Christmas Dragoncards, Mandeville Press, 1979 (collected in The Echoes Return Slow, 1988):

> This is the wrong Christmas
> in the right place: mistletoe
> water there is no kissing
> under; the soused holly
>
> of the wrack, and birds coming
> to the bird-table with
> no red on their breast...

p. 73   his new book: this was H'm, published by Macmillan in 1972.

p. 74   Ellis Wynne of Y Lasynys: Ellis Wynne (1671–1734), devotional writer born in a farmhouse called Y Lasynys near Harlech; ordained an Anglican priest in 1704. His major achievement was Gweledigaetheu y Bardd Cwsc ('The Visions of the Sleeping Bard', 1703). In 1710 he also produced an edition of the Welsh Book of Common Prayer.

p. 76   'Almost thou persuadest me': Acts 26: 28.

p. 76   'Woe unto you': Luke 6: 26.

p. 76   St Mary's Well and Y Gegin Fawr: both final stages on the pilgrimage to Bardsey Island. The former was where the pilgrims offered final prayers, and the latter ('The Great Kitchen') where they were able to rest and eat, before the crossing. Cf. the poem 'Ffynnon Fair (St Mary's Well)' in Laboratories of the Spirit, 1975.

p. 78   pre-Cambrian rocks: the great age of the rocks in the Llŷn Peninsula is a recurrent image in the later poetry and prose, as in this 'prose' piece from *The Echoes Return Slow* (1988):

> There is a rock on the headland mentioned by Dafydd Nanmor in a *cywydd*. But it was already immemorially old in his day, five hundred years ago. The mind spun, vertigo not at the cliff's edge, but from the abyss of time. In the strong sun and the sea wind sometimes his shadow seemed more substantial than himself. But this also was part of the spilled dream.

p. 78   Pindar: the quotation is from the end of the eighth *Pythian* Ode, one of the last, and most celebrated, works by the poet Pindar (*c.*518–*c.*438 BC), the greatest of the Greek choral lyricists. The Greek text translates, 'Man is but a dream of a shadow; but, when a gleam of sunshine comes as a gift of heaven, a radiant light rests on men, yes and a gentle life.'

p. 78   *In Memoriam*: in Tennyson's poem see, for example, section LVI.

p. 79   'Night and Morning': see the first note above.

p. 81   calling on Charles Tunnicliffe: The artist's home on Anglesey was Shorelands, a house on the Cefni estuary at Malltraeth.

p. 84   television programme: 'R. S. Thomas: Priest and Poet', John Ormond's film for BBC Television, broadcast 2 April 1972.

p. 90   Sarn Rhiw: cf. the poem 'Sarn Rhiw' in *Destinations*, 1985.

p. 92   Cymdeithas yr Iaith Gymraeg: literally, 'The Society of the Welsh Language', founded in 1962 in response to Saunders Lewis's 1962 radio lecture, *Tynged yr Iaith* ('The Fate of the Language'). The Society continues to be active and influential in furthering the cause and status of the Welsh language.

p. 93   Parry-Williams: T. H. Parry-Williams (1887–1975), poet, essayist and scholar, and the poet most influential in modernising the idiom of Welsh poetry in the twentieth century. The quotation is from his sonnet '*Cyngor*' ('Advice').

p. 95   The Referendum of 1979: called by the Labour Party to decide on the question of devolved government for Scotland and Wales.

p. 95   Isaiah's vision: Isaiah 11:6.

p. 96   Gregynog: a country house near Tregynon in Montgomeryshire, donated to the University of Wales as a conference centre in 1964. It continues also as the home of the prestigious Gregynog Press, which in 1975 published a special edition of R. S. Thomas's *Laboratories of the Spirit*.

p. 98   the Act of Union of 1536: together with a second Act of Union in 1543, the legislation that resulted in the political annexation of Wales to England.

p. 100   looking over the sea: for the comparison with praying, see the poem 'Sea-watching' in *Laboratories of the Spirit*, 1975.

p. 102   Twm Siôn Cati: the popular name for Thomas Jones or Johns (*c.*1530–1609), antiquary and herald, about whom several apocryphal tales survive. Commonly remembered as the Welsh Robin Hood.

p. 103   Cantref Mawr: 'The Great Hundred', formerly an area lying to the north of the River Towy.

p. 104   Our Last Prince, Llywelyn: Llywelyn ap Gruffudd (*c.*1225–82), also known as '*Y Llyw Olaf*' ('The Last Prince'), military leader and national hero, whose death at the hands of the English brought to an end hopes for an independent Welsh state.

p. 106   *cynghanedd*: see note on *cywyddwyr* above.

p. 106   Schrödinger: Erwin Schrödinger (1887–1961), Austrian theoretical physicist and discoverer of the basic equation of quantum mechanics.

p. 107   Bishop Robinson: J. A. T. Robinson (1919–83), biblical scholar and theologian. He is probably best remembered for his book *Honest to God* (1963), a statement of the non-miraculous New Theology, and an international bestseller.

p. 107   Augustine: Saint Augustine of Hippo (354–430), whose doctrines are a development on those of Saint Paul, and one of the major influences on the theology of the West.

p. 107   Pascal: Blaise Pascal (1623–62), French physicist, mathematician and religious writer.

p. 107   Roger Bacon: (*c.*1220–92), English experimental scientist and philosopher.

p. 107   Coleridge: Samuel Taylor Coleridge, *Biographia Literaria*, ch. 4, George Watson, ed., Everyman Library, 1975, p. 172.

p. 109   too deep for tears: from the last line of William Wordsworth's 'Ode: Intimations of Immortality from Recollections of Early Childhood'.

p. 109   *'Miserere mei, Domine'*: 'Have mercy on me, O Lord'.

A Year in Llŷn

p. 113   'Charity never faileth': 1 Corinthians 13:8.

p. 114   five righteous ones: see Genesis 18.

p. 119   Yeats: the poem referred to is Yeats's 'A Dialogue of Self and Soul' from *The Winding Stair and Other Poems*, 1933:

> I am content to live it all again
> And yet again...

> I am content to follow to its source
> Every event in action or in thought;
> Measure the lot; forgive myself the lot!

p. 119   Villon: François Villon, pseudonym of François de Montcorbier, or des Loges (1431–after 1463), one of the greatest French lyric poets.

p. 119   Siôn Cent: (*c.*1400–30/45), a Welsh religious poet famous for his treatment of the theme of transience. One of R. S. Thomas's favourite poets.

p. 121   the burning bush: see particularly Exodus 3:4.

p. 121   as a shepherd knows his sheep: John 10:14.

p. 121   The machine has displaced the farm hand: cf. 'Cynddylan on a Tractor' in *An Acre of Land*, 1952.

p. 122   Elsi: Mildred E. Eldridge (1909–91), a celebrated artist, the poet's first wife.

p. 122   Dyddgu ... Morfudd: the names of two women in the poetry of Dafydd ap Gwilym (*fl.* 1330–70), Wales's greatest medieval poet. Dyddgu, a dark-haired aristocratic lady, was the unattainable object of the poet's amatory attentions; Morfudd was her opposite – the blonde girl who was, according to the poems, Dafydd ap Gwilym's main love.

p. 124   Olof Palme: (1927–86), succeeded Tage Erlander as prime minister of Sweden in 1968, and was renowned for his opposition to American involvement in Vietnam.

p. 124   Yeats: see the note on Yeats above.

p. 125   'After such knowledge, what forgiveness?': T. S. Eliot's line is from the poem 'Gerontion'.

p. 126   Lockley: R. M. Lockley (1903–   ), author and naturalist, best known for his pioneering work on the wildlife of the Pembrokeshire coastal islands.

p. 127   Gwili's words: the lines by Gwili (John Jenkins, theologian and poet, 1872–1936, and from 1897 a friend of the poet Edward Thomas) come from '*Natur a Duw*' ('Nature and God'). It is not surprising that R. S. Thomas should like this particular poem, given lines such as '*Mewn byd heb swyn, gan dwrf peiriannau croes*' ('In a world without magic because of the tumult of cross machines').

p. 130   In Abercuawg cuckoos sing: Abercuawg, a place mentioned in a ninth-century *englyn* cycle, was used by R. S. Thomas as a symbol for a timeless Welsh-speaking Wales of the imagination. His 1976 National Eisteddfod lecture, *Abercuawg*, in which he emphasises the importance of not abandoning that ideal, unattainable vision, is amongst the most powerful of his prose works.

p. 130   Nant Gwrtheyrn: a Welsh-language centre on the north coast of the Llŷn Peninsula. It occupies the abandoned village of Glan y Nant, formerly a small port for exporting stones from Llithfaen quarry. Cf. the poem 'Nant Gwrtheyrn' in R. S. Thomas's latest volume, *No Truce with the Furies*, 1995:

> I listen to the echoes
> of John Jones crying: 'God
> is not good,' and of his wife
> correcting him: 'Hush, John.'
>
> The cuckoo returns
> to Gwrtheyrn, contradicting
> John Jones, within its voice
> bluebells tolling over
>
> the blue sea. There is work
> here still, quarrying
> for an ancient language...

p. 131   Saunders's words: the line is from Saunders Lewis's poem '*Difiau Dyrchafael*' ('Ascension Thursday').

p. 131   'Human kind cannot bear very much reality': the words are from T. S. Eliot's 'Burnt Norton', the first of the *Four Quartets*.

p. 131   the world in a grain of sand: from the opening line of William Blake's poem 'Auguries of Innocence'.

p. 131 'thousand peacock eyes': the quotation is from Saunders Lewis's poem '*Caer Arianrhod*' ('The Milky Way').

p. 132 a huge ladder between earth and heaven: Jacob's ladder in Genesis 28:12.

p. 132 'calls a song / Back': see the note on Gwili above.

p. 133 Islwyn: William Thomas (1832–78), the finest Welsh poet of the nineteenth century. The quotation is from '*Hapus Dyrfa*' ('Joyous Crowd').

p. 133 If she lies dead in Is Conwy and In a fine kerchief of golden sheen: both couplets are by Dafydd Nanmor (*fl.*1450–80), one of the greatest of the Poets of the Gentry, often quoted by R. S. Thomas. The first quotation here is from '*Marwnad Bun*' ('Elegy for a Girl') and the second from '*I Wallt Llio*' ('To Llio's Hair'). The latter ties in with R. S. Thomas's own poetic use of, and sense of amazement at, the sheer age of the pre-Cambrian rocks in Llŷn.

p. 133 Cynan's verses: for Cynan, see the note above. The reference here is to Cynan's lyric, '*Aberdaron*', which R. S. Thomas claims romanticises the location in too slight a way.

p. 134 'If they had reaped their dandelions': the couplet is from Edward Thomas's poem 'Lob'.

p. 134 When, in its green livery: from an anonymous fifteenth-century poem, '*I'r Llwyn Banadl*' ('To the Bush of Broom').

p. 134 Mai: the girl's name, Mai, is the Welsh word for the month of May.

p. 138 *Caniadaeth y Cysegr*: a radio programme of chapel hymn-singing.

p. 139 Emrys: Emrys Edwards. See the note above.

p. 141 Edward Llwyd Society: a society, founded in 1978, for the study of natural history through the medium of the Welsh language, named after Edward Llwyd (or Lhuyd, ?1660–1709), scientist and philologist.

p. 143 *Barn or Y Faner*: for *Y Faner*, see above. *Barn* (literally, 'Opinion') is a monthly magazine founded in 1962 which has had (particularly under the editorship of Alwyn D. Rees between 1966 and 1974) a decisive impact on the political and general cultural climate in Wales.

p. 144 I was in a thicket of willows: cf. 'A Thicket in Lleyn' in *Experimenting with an Amen*, 1986.

p. 145 'Then a spirit passed before my face': Job 4:15.

p. 148 'The poet's business is to study the world': from the poem '*I'r Wyth Dial*' ('To the Eight Vengeances') by Siôn Cent (*c.*1400–30/45).

p. 150 *Dic Siôn Dafydd*: a name usually applied to a person who has stifled his Welshness and parades an 'English' identity.

p. 150 the chair and the crown ... *awdlau* and *pryddestau*: in the National Eisteddfod, the winning poem in the strict metres (*awdl*) *is recognised with the award of the Chair, and that in the free metres (pryddest)* with the award of the Crown.

p. 152 'Machines where once the pilgrims were': for Gwenallt, see the note above. These lines by Gwenallt are from his poem '*Cymru a'r Rhyfel*' ('Wales and the War').

p. 157 R. Gerallt Jones: (1934–   ), poet, novelist and critic, and a native of Llŷn.

p. 159 Keats: the allusion is to the line 'I cannot see what flowers are at my feet' in Keats's 'Ode to a Nightingale'.

p. 159 Somhairle Macgill-Eain: Sorley Maclean, 1911–96, one of the most important and influential Gaelic writers of the twentieth-century Scottish Renaissance.

p. 161 Paul was very wise: 1 Corinthians 10:12.

p. 161 Doesn't Amos tell?: Amos 5:19.

p. 162 Plaid Cymru: see note on Gwynfor (Evans) above.

p. 165 Bishop William Morgan: (1545–1604), the translator of the Bible into Welsh. He entered St John's College in the University of Cambridge in 1565. The translation was magnificently achieved, against tremendous practical odds, during his period as priest at Llanrhaeadr-ym-Mochnant, Denbighshire, an achievement celebrated by R. S. Thomas in his poem 'Llanrhaeadr ym Mochnant' in *Not That He Brought Flowers*, 1968.

p. 165 'A vineyard entrusted to my care': from a famous speech in Saunders Lewis's play, *Buchedd Garmon* ('The Life of Garmon'), 1937.

p. 166 'It comes when it wills': from the poem '*Y Dylanwad*' ('The Influence') by Islwyn, for whom see note above.

p. 166 Wittgenstein: Proposition 4.1212, *Tractatus Logico-Philosophicus* (1922).

p. 171   *dyfalu*: the technique of accumulating fanciful comparisons, a device much used in medieval Welsh poetry.

p. 171   My love is the year's flowers: the first stanza of a pair of anonymous folk-verses.

ACKNOWLEDGEMENTS

The main thanks, of course, go to R. S. Thomas himself, for the wisdom and keenness of the prose, for his kindness in sanctioning the translations, and for permission to quote from the poetry. Warm thanks also go to Betty Thomas for, as always, her stimulating interest and enthusiasm.

This is also to record my gratitude to Hilary Laurie, Pamela Norris and Andrea Henry for their patient guidance at Dent; to Gerallt Lloyd Owen and Professor Gwyn Thomas for their encouragement in the work; and to the University of Wales, Bangor, for an award from its Research Centre Wales fund.

For help in preparing the manuscript for the press, I am indebted to Christine White and Marian Weston.

The texts here translated appeared in their original Welsh-language form as follows: *Y Llwybrau Gynt* (*Former Paths*) in Alun Oldfield-Davies, ed., *Y Llwybrau Gynt*, Gwasg Gomer, 1972; '*Hunanladdiad y Llenor*' ('The Creative Writer's Suicide') in *Taliesin* 35, December 1977; *Neb* (*No-one*), Gwenno Hywyn, ed., Gwasg Gwynedd, 1985; and *Blwyddyn yn Llŷn* (*A Year in Llŷn*), Gwasg Gwynedd, 1990.